The Stephen King Movie Quiz Book

by Andrew J. Rausch
and R.D. Riley

Foreword by George Beahm

Published in the USA by:
BearManor Media
P O Box 71426
Albany, Georgia 31708
www.bearmanormedia.com

ISBN 978-1-59393-631-0

Printed in the United States of America.

Book design by Darlene Swanson of Van-garde Imagery, Inc.
Cover design by R.D. Riley.

"I love the movies and when I go to see a movie that's been made from one of my books, I know it isn't going to be exactly like my novel because a lot of other people have interpreted it. But I also know it has an idea that I'll like because that idea occurred to me, and I spent a year, or a year-and-a-half of my life working on it."
—Stephen King

"Why do they keep making these fucking Children of the Corn *movies?"*
—Tom Savini

"Who writes this crap?"
—from *Cat's Eye*

This book is dedicated
to the memory of
Riley Rosenstiel

CONTENTS

FOREWORD: THE KING OF POP: THE POP OF KING

by George Beahm

When Stephen Spignesi published *The Stephen King Quiz Book*, I picked it up with trepidation. Knowing that Spignesi is indisputably one of the world's foremost experts on all things King, I knew he would tax my knowledge to the max: He'd serve up one hell of a set of quizzes.

He sent me a copy and challenged me to answer as many as I could.

I gave it my best shot and fell short. Far short. Clearly, Steve's encyclopedic knowledge of all things King exceeded mine, but I wasn't surprised. Steve, after all, was the guy who published the telephone book-sized *The Shape Under the Sheet: The Complete Stephen King Encyclopedia*.

The second time around, when Steve published *The Second Stephen King Quiz Book*, I mentally crossed my fingers, dipped into its pages, and hoped to do better. After all, I was known as someone who knew a thing or two about Stephen King and his work.

Unfortunately, I fared no better on the second go-around. I had to admit that either I was not as careful a King reader as I had thought, or more likely, I simply got caught up in King's storytelling and saw only the big picture. The fine details—the people, places, and things that populate his novels—obviously require a slower, more contemplative pace that is only possible on a second reading. As Steve explained to me, that was his goal. "I didn't want fans to be able to answer the questions off the top of their heads. I wanted them to go back to the source and reread the work because I feel King's work is worth revisiting. The intricacies, the ins and outs, and the minutiae are interesting and compelling."

What one discovers on a careful rereading is that King's work is festooned with all manner of trivia and brand names. In part, that's what gives his fiction verisimilitude: "the appearance or semblance of truth" (*Random House Dictionary*). This appearance of truthfulness is one of the elements that make King's books such compulsive reading. It was true in 1974 when *Carrie* was published, and true in 2010 when *Under the Dome* held us captive, along with the unlucky citizens of Chester's Mill, who found themselves prisoners of a force beyond their reckoning—the beings who created the Dome that sealed off their small Maine town from the rest of the world.

All of which explains why Stephen Spignesi and the others who followed in his footsteps have compiled trivia quizzes based on King's fiction: We love the books, we love to test our knowledge as well as our friends who claim to be experts, and most of all, we welcome any opportunity to go back to reread King's fiction.

What makes Rausch and Riley's *The Stephen King Movie Quiz Book* unique is that they have focused strictly on the films, which run the gamut from execrable (*Children of the Corn*) to the extraordinary (Reiner's *Stand by Me* and anything by Frank Darabont).

I waded into this quiz book and found myself comfortably putting my toes in shallow water (the "Easy" questions), testing the slightly deeper water ("Medium Difficulty"), and purposely avoiding the sudden drop-off when the water became deep and very cold ("Hard as Hell").

I think I'll leave the "Hard as Hell" questions to King's movie fans who have obsessively studied every frame and memorized every trivial detail because, again, as with the stories and novels on which they are based, I'm more likely to be swept up in the visual narrative than I am to stop and smell the roses.

Or, as Clint Eastwood as Inspector Harry Callahan reminds us, "A man's got to know his limitations."

I know my limitations, insofar as *The Stephen King Movie Quiz Book* is concerned. I'll dip into it and rejoice that the "Easy" questions are within grasp, that the "Medium Difficulty" questions are like hanging grapes just *slightly* beyond my grasp, and that my getting any of the "Hard as Hell" questions would be on par with Glenn Beck and Sarah Palin having an epiphany conversion and becoming Democrats, which is to say: not a snowball's chance in hell.

I tip my hat to the iron-butted Rausch and Riley, who have sat through the entire canon of King films—the good, the bad, and the ugly—based on his fiction, to derive the questions that will tantalize, tease, or torment you. Just think of the countless hours they spent in darkened cinemas obsessively watching *Maximum Overdrive* or *Children of the Corn IV: The Gathering*, just to bring you this quiz book. (Okay, they probably sat comfortably on their couches and freeze-framed stills with their VCR or disc player, but you get the idea.)

They *suffered* the viewing of even the groaners so that you, the reader, could enjoy the fruits of their labor—the brain-teasing, head-scratching, and memory-searching trivia questions like "What is the name of the book penned by Max Freedom Long that Carrie checks out from the school library?" (A "Hard as Hell" question from *Carrie*.)

After spending a half hour going through and selectively attempting to answer some of these questions, I need to go pop a couple of Advil. You may fare better—in fact, you will almost *certainly* fare better than me!—and if you want to make it competitive and fun, may I suggest a friendly wager? Bet your friend who reads King to a competition using this movie quiz book: The loser has to cough up a hardback copy of King's forthcoming novella collection, *Full Dark, No Stars*, which will set you back $27.97 (or $16.77 on Amazon). But if you don't want to step out on *that* ledge (ha ha, bet you can't guess *that* King reference!), stay inside, grab a Silver Bullet and a bag of chips, and dip into the pages of *The Stephen King Movie Quiz Book* to find out what you *really* know, and don't know, about King's visual adaptations. It may be for you, as it was for me, a humbling experience.

And if you don't fare any better than me, just remember Clint's admonition: A man's got to know his limitations...

George Beahm is the author of numerous books on Stephen King and his work, including *The Stephen King Companion*, *Stephen King from A to Z*, and the biography *Stephen King: America's Best-Loved Boogeyman*..

QUIZ #1: CARRIE (1976)

Screenplay by: Lawrence D. Cohen
Directed by: Brian De Palma
Starring: Sissy Spacek, Piper Laurie, and Amy Irving
United Artists

Brian De Palma's *Carrie* was the first Stephen King work adapted to screen, and it remains, some 60 adaptations later, one of the finest films crafted from a King novel. While *Carrie* doesn't aspire to the artistic levels of such films as *The Shawshank Redemption* (1994) or *Stand by Me* (1986), it's a solid adaptation packed with memorable scenes.

[*Carrie* is] a great film," King would later tell *Entertainment Weekly*. "Even I thought it was really scary. I wanted Brian De Palma to direct it from the beginning, and I liked the way he used the split screen. I was very impressed by how lush the photography was. Best of all, it didn't look like a horror movie, and that's one of the reasons I thought it succeeded."

Since its release in 1976, *Carrie* has become a staple in American popular culture—seemingly everyone knows about the pig blood, whether they've seen the film or not—and has spawned a remake, a Broadway musical (the biggest failure in history), and an unnecessary sequel, *The Rage: Carrie 2* (1999).

EASY

1. What does Margaret White refer to as "dirty pillows"?

2. What does Carrie liken to "being on Mars"?

3. The year after *Carrie* was released, actress Betty Buckley began a five-year stint on a popular TV series. What is this series?

4. What, according to Margaret White, never dies?

5. Fourteen years after his screenplay for *Carrie* was produced, Lawrence Cohen adapted a second King novel. Can you name this film?

6. What is the punishment for skipping detention?

7. In the final scene of the film, what is scrawled on the "For Sale" sign where the White house once stood?

8. What is Miss Collins' nickname for Principal Morton?

9. Sue asks "something special" of Tommy. What is this?

10. What does Carrie say she can do if she concentrates hard enough?

11. What sport are the schoolgirls playing in the film's opening scene?

12. Someone scrawls graffiti regarding Carrie on the wall of the school gymnasium. What does this say?

13. What does Tommy say under his breath as Mr. Fromm chides Carrie about her criticism of Tommy's poem?

14. Who co-wrote the first draft of the *Carrie* screenplay with Lawrence Cohen?

15. Actress Sissy Spacek had previously worked on director Brian De Palma's *The Phantom of the Paradise* (1974). In what capacity?

MEDIUM DIFFICULTY

1. Principal Morton addresses Carrie by the wrong name. What does he mistakenly call her?

2. What was the first name of Carrie's father?

3. What does the tapestry hanging beside the dinner table in the White home depict?

4. In 1981, actors John Travolta and Nancy Allen reunited with director Brian De Palma. On what film was this?

5. What Kansas City, Missouri-born actress went on to appear in films such as *Ferris Bueller's Day Off* (1986), *Planes, Trains & Automobiles* (1987), and *Natural Born Killers* (1994) after making her film debut in *Carrie*?

6. What does Miss Collins suggest Tommy might "look a little ridiculous" doing?

7. Who notices the bucket of blood hanging over Tommy and Carrie just before Chris releases it?

8. Actress Betty Buckley would later appear in the ill-fated musical version of *Carrie*. What character did she play?

9. Sue Snell and her mother were played by real-life mother and daughter Amy Irving and Priscilla Pointer. Through 2010, the two have appeared together in seven more films. What are these?

10. Three years after *Carrie*, producer Paul Monash served as screenwriter on another King adaptation. What is this film?

11. What is the name of Carrie White's sadistic female classmate who always wears a baseball cap?

12. In 1978, a *Carrie* rip-off directed by Brice Mack and starring Lisa Pelikan was released. Coincidentally, this film shares its title with a 1964 film directed by Brian De Palma. What is this film?

13.   Actress Sissy Spacek was initially hired to appear in a different role. What was this role?

14.   Who appears in the film as the boy riding on the bicycle who teases Carrie?

15.   What was used as pig's blood during filming?

HARD AS HELL

1.   What is the title of the tract Margaret White offers Mrs. Snell?

2.   What was the height of Miss Collins' Senior Prom date?

3.   What is the theme of the Prom?

4.   Dale Norbert and his date are nominated for Prom king and queen. Who is his date?

5.   The name of the high school Carrie attends is a nod to Alfred Hitchcock's *Psycho* (1960). What is this?

6.   What are Tommy's last words before he's struck by the falling bucket?

7.   Director Brian De Palma's follow up to *Carrie* was criticized as being too similar. The film even features actress Amy Irving. What is the title of this John Farris adaptation?

8.   What is the name of the drug store where Carrie purchases her make-up?

9.   Two different characters slap Chris Hargenson. Who are they?

10.   *Carrie* is the first of four films directed by Brian De Palma which feature actress Nancy Allen. What are the other three films?

11. What is the name of the student Freddy asks about collecting the ballots?

12. What is the name of the book penned by Max Freedom Long that Carrie checks out from the school library?

13. In 1977, *Carrie* was nominated for two Academy Awards, losing both. In what categories were these nominations?

14. Through the scene in which Tommy and his friends try on clothes in a department store, director Brian De Palma pays homage to one of his own films. What is this film?

15. As Sue does her homework, Tommy watches a Western television series. What is this series?

QUIZ #2: SALEM'S LOT (1979)

Screenplay by: Paul Monash
Directed by: Tobe Hooper
Starring: David Soul, James Mason, and Lance Kerwin
Warner Bros.

Based on Stephen King's novel of the same title, Tobe Hooper's telefilm *Salem's Lot* is the story of novelist Ben Mears' (David Soul) homecoming to the small town of Jerusalem's Lot, Maine, to pen a new opus. The arrival of a mysterious newcomer (James Mason) corresponds with Ben's. After a number of townsfolk disappear, Ben uncovers the horrible truth: Straker is the caretaker of a vampire named Barlow.

"Most of what television touches within the horror genre turns out to be absolute drivel," King would later comment. "I think (producer) Richard Kobritz and Tobe Hooper made *Salem's Lot* rise well above that. It certainly wasn't typical of horror movies made for television."

In another testimonial, *Phantasm* (1979) helmer Don Coscarelli raves, "When I watched the television movie for the first time, my television stopped working halfway through. I had this small, battery-powered TV and I placed it on my lap and continued watching. When the master vampire jumped out of his coffin unexpectedly, I was so startled that I dropped the TV and broke it!"

EASY

1. What real-life town served as Jerusalem's Lot for the film?

2. Where does Straker tell Larry Crockett to have his men leave the four padlock keys?

3. Susan Norton mentions the movie theater in a nearby city. What is the name of the city?

4. Actor George Dzundza appears in the film as Cully Sawyer. He also appears prominently in the film which won Best Picture the year *Salem's Lot* was released. Can you name this film?

5. What is Ned Tebbets' occupation?

6. What is Ben's religious denomination?

7. What is the name of the book written by Ben Mears that Susan is reading when they meet?

8. Who does Bill Norton remember "sashaying down the street"?

9. Reggie Nalder received no credit for his performance in *Salem's Lot*. What character does he play?

10. What does Ben say he believes would attract evil men?

11. As homage to a film directed by Stanley Kubrick, Marie Windsor and Elisha Cook Jr. were reteamed as former lovers. What is this film?

12. Sixteen years after directing *Salem's Lot*, Tobe Hooper helmed another King adaptation. What is this film?

13. Richard Kobritz produced another King adaptation in 1983. What is this film?

14. Ben says he would never have written his books if not for whom?

15. What is Bill Norton's occupation?

MEDIUM DIFFICULTY

1. The filmmakers opted to make Barlow resemble the character Count Orlock from the classic German film *Nosferatu* (1922). *Nosferatu* was remade the same year *Salem's Lot* was made. Who directed this second version?

2. When Ben arrives in town, there is a sign in the window of Straker's shop. What does it read?

3. Actor Reggie Nalder appeared as Dr. Van Helsing in another film about vampirism the same year *Salem's Lot* was released. What is this film?

4. On what street is Eva Miller's boarding house located?

5. *Salem's Lot* director Tobe Hooper appears in a brief cameo as "Forensic Tech" in a film written by Stephen King. What is this film?

6. Although it's spelled differently, Barlow shares his first name with a character from Stephen King's novel *The Dark Tower*. What is Barlow's name?

7. What is Bonnie Sawyer's nickname?

8. A year before *Salem's Lot* aired, producer Richard Kobritz worked on a successful telefilm directed by John Carpenter. What is this film?

9. What four doors does Straker request that Larry Crockett's men lock up with the padlocks?

10. What screenwriter did Stephen King say he wanted to adapt *Salem's Lot*?

11. What awards nominated *Salem's Lot* for Best Television Feature or Miniseries?

12. Another film featuring James Mason was nominated for nine Academy Awards the year *Salem's Lot* first aired. What is this film?

13. Actress Bonnie Bedelia appears in the film as Susan Norton. Four-teen years later she appeared as Polly Chalmers in another King adaptation. What is this film?

14. What is the name of the cemetery where Danny Glick's grave is located?

15. Which cast member also appears in *The Maltese Falcon* (1941), *The Big Sleep* (1946), *Shane* (1953), and *Rosemary's Baby* (1968)?

HARD AS HELL

1. Two major made-for-television films written by Paul Monash were produced in 1979. One of these is *Salem's Lot*. The other is a Golden Globe-winning remake of a classic film which features Lew Ayres, who also appears in *Salem's Lot*. What is this film?

2. Before Paul Monash was hired to write the screenplay, four different scribes tried their hand at adapting the novel. One of these was Stephen King. Can you name the other three writers?

3. Actress Clarissa Kaye appears as Marjorie Glick. While filming *Salem's Lot*, the actress was married to someone involved with the film. Who was this?

4. What is the alternate title of *Salem's Lot*?

5. What is Constable Gillespie's first name?

6. What is Ted Petrie's occupation?

7. One year after playing Straker in *Salem's Lot*, actor James Mason appeared in a Stephen King-related documentary which aired on TV. What is the title of this documentary?

8. What is the population of Jerusalem's Lot?

9.   How much did it cost the film's producers to construct the exteriors of the Marsten House?

10. At what school does Susan teach art?

11. *Salem's Lot* scribe Paul Monash served as a producer on two other Stephen King films. Can you name them?

12. As Mike explains what happened at the cemetery, Ben orders him a drink. What beverage does he order?

13. What is Ben's room number at Eva Miller's boarding house?

14. Actor James Mason was nominated for three Oscars, but never won. What were the three films for which he was nominated?

15. When *Salem's Lot* originally aired as a miniseries in 1979, it was 210 minutes long. It was then cut, repackaged, and released theatrically in Europe. How long was this heavily-trimmed version of the film?

QUIZ #3: THE SHINING (1980)

Screenplay by: Stanley Kubrick and Diane Johnson
Directed by: Stanley Kubrick
Starring: Jack Nicholson, Shelley Duvall, and Danny Lloyd
Warner Bros.

When legendary auteur Stanley Kubrick announced his plans to direct *The Shining*, he predicted that the result would be the most terrifying horror film ever produced. By any standard, this was a hefty claim, but few cineastes doubted Kubrick's abilities. However, when the slick film was released in 1980, audiences were divided. Kubrick fans touted it a masterpiece, but many of King's fans (and King himself) were displeased with the liberties Kubrick and co-writer Diane Johnson had taken with the novel.

Noted director (and *Christine* lead) Keith Gordon believes Kubrick had no intentions of truly making the most horrific film ever produced. "With *The Shining*, he went around saying he was making the scariest movie ever made," Gordon recalls. "So when he made a movie that was essentially a dark comedy about the American nuclear family and writer's block, a lot of people jumped on that and said, 'This isn't the scariest movie ever made!' And they're right. At times Kubrick was a victim of his own success as a salesman because he wasn't always selling what he was making. He would sell it like a Hollywood showman and then make these films that were really art movies."

Despite initial negative criticism, *The Shining* has become a bonafide classic and is considered one of the finest horror films ever made. In his essay "The Movies and Mr. King," writer Bill Warren suggests one possible explanation for King's disdain for the film: "Stephen King's novels are cinematic partially because the author himself is so fond of movies. Perhaps King's disappointment with *The Shining* lies in that it was not the film he would have made, the movie he saw in his head while writing. Perhaps in time he can readjust his opinion and regard it as another man's variation on his theme. It is the best movie yet made from a Stephen King book, and one of the best horror movies ever made."

EASY

1. Who informs Jack of Danny's "very great talent"?

2. Two paintings hang in Dick Hallorann's bedroom. What do these paintings depict?

3. In the novel upon which the film is based, Jack discovers Clark Gable's name in the registry from 1930. With whom did Gable stay?

4. What is Danny's nickname?

5. Who does Jack suggest left the bruises on Danny's neck?

6. In Stephen King's novel, the woman in the bathroom is discovered in room 217. Why was this number changed in the film?

7. What is Danny's favorite food?

8. Who wrote the famous line, "Here's Johnny"?

9. Who does Jack say he would do "any fuckin' thing" for?

10. Where did the Torrances reside before relocating to Boulder, Colorado?

11. The phrase "all work and no play makes Jack a dull boy" was changed in foreign versions of the film. What phrase was used in the Italian version?

12. How many United States Presidents does Ullman claim have stayed at the Overlook?

13. What is the name of Mr. Ullman's secretary?

14. What is the name of the Overlook's phantom bartender?

15. Stephen King originally planned a novel entitled *Darkshine*. Where was this story to have taken place?

MEDIUM DIFFICULTY

1. The first time Dick Hallorann speaks telepathically to Danny, what does he say?

2. In what room is Wendy when Danny ventures into the room Dick Hallorann advised him never to enter?

3. Stephen King began writing *The Shining* (then titled *The Shine*) in a large hotel. What is the name of this hotel and where is it located?

4. Stephen King has said he initially considered employing a hedge maze rather than topiary animals in the original novel, but decided against it when he realized that this had already been done in the 1953 William Cameron Menzies film *The Maze*. Interestingly, the screenwriter of *The Maze* shares his surname with the Overlook Hotel's general manager. Who is this?

5. Danny wears a sweater with a National Aeronautics and Space Administration spacecraft depicted on the front of it. What is this spacecraft?

6. Mr. Ullman explains that a decorator recently refurbished the hotel. Where was this decorator from?

7. In Stephen King's original novel, what is "The Monkey Is Here, Paul DeLong"?

8.   When Jack has "the most horrible dream (he) ever had," what does he dream?

9.   How many people can be comfortably entertained in The Gold Room?

10.   Which cast member was the first person ever to play James Bond?

11.   How high are the walls of the hedge maze at the Overlook Hotel?

12.   When Danny goes upstairs to retrieve a toy, his mother warns him not to wake his father. What is the toy Danny goes after?

13.   When Wendy and Danny race outside the Overlook Hotel, what does Wendy say the loser must do?

14.   Just after the film's release, Stanley Kubrick cut four minutes from it. What did this four minutes entail?

15.   At Jack's interview, how long does he say it took him to travel to the Overlook from Boulder?

HARD AS HELL

1.   What is the name of the man who loans Dick Hallorann a Snow Cat?

2.   What is the ham radio handle for the Overlook Hotel?

3.   A 24-year-old Aspen woman is reported missing. What is her name?

4.   Dick Hallorann's past as a cook in the army is discussed in another novel written by Stephen King. What is this book?

5.   *The Shining* was the fourth film to feature both Jack Nicholson and Scatman Crothers. What are the other three films?

6.   From what dates does the season run at the Overlook?

7.   What room does Dick Hallorann advise Danny to steer clear of?

8.   The Timberline Lodge was used for the exterior shots of the Overlook Hotel. Where is the Timberline Lodge located?

9.   How many legs of lamb are in the freezer of the Overlook Hotel?

10.   On what airline does Dick Hallorann fly when returning to Colorado?

11.   In what year did Delbert Grady slaughter his family?

12.   On September 29, 1969, director Stanley Kubrick completed the screenplay for a film which was to have starred Jack Nicholson in the lead role. However, the film would eventually be aborted due to budget problems. What is this unproduced film?

13.   What is Jack's drink of preference?

14.   In what year was the Overlook built?

15.   The baseball bat Wendy uses to hit Jack is a signature model. Whose signature appears on the bat?

QUIZ #4: CREEPSHOW (1982)

Screenplay by: Stephen King
Directed by: George Romero
Starring: Hal Holbrook, Adrienne Barbeau, and Fritz Weaver
Warner Bros.

After their collaborative efforts fell apart in the early stages of *Salem's Lot* (1979), Stephen King and director George Romero remained friends and vowed to work together on something else. This decision led to *Creepshow*, an anthology of five E.C. Comics-inspired vignettes penned by King and directed by Romero. In addition, Romero enlisted the talents of special makeup effects wizard Tom Savini, an artist/actor he had worked with previously on *Martin* (1978) and *Dawn of the Dead* (1979). During production of the film, King commented that he and Romero were attempting to craft a film which would terrify audiences so "continuously that they'd have to crawl out of the theater."

The result? Well, *Creepshow* is hardly so terrifying a film that audiences found themselves under their seats, but it is immensely entertaining and effectively retained the essence of the pulp comics which inspired it; like those classic comics such as *Tales from the Crypt*, King and Romero's baddies revel in their own misdeeds but receive their just desserts in the end.

The editors of *Cult Flicks and Trash Pics* observe, "[The] best vignette deals with a phobia-ridden millionaire recluse besieged by swarms of cursed cockroaches. The feature is less than the sum of its parts, with the novelist's dialogue especially flat, but Romero's direction cleverly mimics narrative style of comic books."

EASY

1. Ed Harris and Stephen King appear in three films together. These are *Knightriders* (1981), *Creepshow*, and *The Stand* (1994). In addition, the two also appear in a 1994 documentary directed by Ken Burns. What is this documentary?

2. Where does Billy say his father keeps his "sex books"?

3. What is the title of the short story "The Lonesome Death of Jordy Verrill" is based upon?

4. What is the name of the body of water where Henry dumps the crate?

5. *Creepshow* was one of two films released in 1982 starring Adrienne Barbeau. The other film was directed by Wes Craven. What is this film?

6. Jordy Verrill imagines a doctor amputating his hand. What instrument does the doctor use for this?

7. Richard Vickers has a rule he says he never makes exceptions to. What is this?

8. Two of the vignettes are based upon King short stories. One of these is "The Lonesome Death of Jordy Verrill." What is the other one?

9. The scene in which Nathan Grantham's hand shoots up from the ground is very reminiscent of the closing scene in another King adaptation. What is this?

10. A former E.C. Comics artist was hired to create splash pages for the film. Who was this?

11. In "They're Creeping Up On You," what city does George Gundron say he has just returned from?

12. The crate belonged to someone with the surname Carpenter who was a member of an Arctic expedition. This is a reference to another film released in early 1982. What is this?

13. What does Henry suggest Billie tell the creature just before her death?

14. Who appears in a cameo as Garbageman #2?

15. Five years after the release of *Creepshow*, cinematographer Michael Gornick would make his directorial debut on another King adaptation. What is this film?

MEDIUM DIFFICULTY

1. What is the name of the businessman who commits suicide just before his corporation is taken over in "They're Creeping Up On You"?

2. What does Billie say makes her "wanna ralph"?

3. How many cockroaches were used to film *Creepshow*?

4. The Italian version of Creepshow features only four vignettes. Which segment does not appear in this version?

5. Two years before their turn in *Creepshow* as husband and wife, Hal Holbrook and Adrienne Barbeau appeared in another film together. What is this film?

6. Where does Carl Reynolds telephone Upson Pratt from?

7. When Jordy imagines taking the fallen meteor to the university, what department does he take it to?

8.   What is the name of the building where the mysterious crate is discovered?

9.   In "The Lonesome Death of Jordy Verrill," what do Jordy's father, the doctor, and the professor all have in common?

10.   What does Stephen King say he would have written into the script had he known he would be the actor playing Jordy Verrill?

11.   How many days did it take Stephen King to complete the script for *Creepshow*?

12.   Who is the young boy who appears as Billy in the wraparound story?

13.   The university where Henry Northrup teaches is also referenced in King's novel *Christine* and his short story "The Raft." What is the name of this university?

14.   What is the name stenciled on the side of the crate?

15.   How many miles from Castle Rock does Jordy reside?

HARD AS HELL

1.   What two species of cockroaches were used in making "They're Creeping Up On You"?

2.   Who appears in an uncredited role as Billy's father?

3.   Stephen King reportedly carried a *Star Wars* (1977) action figure to the set each day for luck. What was the character of the action figure?

4.   How much is the monthly rent for Upson Pratt's "germ-free" apartment?

5.   What is the name of the janitor who discovers the crate?

6. What are the Granthams having for dinner?

7. What is the name of Richard Vickers' beach house?

8. From what did special-effects makeup wiz Tom Savini form the maggots on Nathan Grantham's corpse?

9. What is the year stenciled on the side of the crate?

10. Where was *Creepshow* first screened publicly?

11. Another professor is on leave in England, temporarily making Dexter Stanley the boss. What is the name of this professor?

12. The local farm report appears on Jordy's television just before he shoots himself. Who is the sponsor of this report?

13. What is the name of the Granthams' ill-fated cook?

14. The wrestling match Jordy watches features the World Wrestling Federation champion of the time. Who is this?

15. What was the original length of the film before the distributor requested that it be cut?

QUIZ #5: CUJO (1983)

Screenplay by: Don Carlos Dunaway and Lauren Currier
Directed by: Lewis Teague
Starring: Dee Wallace-Stone, Danny Pintauro, and Daniel Hugh Kelly
Warner Bros.

While *Cujo* may not be *Citizen Kane* (1941), director Lewis Teague's film—a sort of *Jaws* (1975) on land—receives points with fans for its faithfulness to the original Stephen King novel. Teague also pulled some strong performances from his cast. In fact, King has since commented that he believes Dee Wallace-Stone should have won an Oscar for her turn as mother-on-the-run Donna Trenton.

Of the film, King said, "It keeps the spirit and flavor of the work; it's this big dumb slugger of a movie. It stands there and keeps on punching. It has no finesse; it has no pretensions." King has also dubbed filmmaker Teague the "most unsung film director in America." BBC Online critic Almar Haflidason agrees: "Essentially, this should not be exciting for any more than five minutes. The setting is confined, and options are few. But Teague wrings out a surprising amount of suspense."

Stephen King was so taken by Teague's work on *Cujo* that he suggested the director for *Cat's Eye* (1984) the following year.

EASY

1. The year *Cujo* was released, actor Daniel Hugh Kelly began a four-year stint on a popular television series. What is this series?

2. The film's cinematographer later became a successful filmmaker. His directorial credits include *Speed* (1994), *Twister* (1996), and *The Haunting* (1999). Who is this?

3. In 1985, "Cujo" made a cameo appearance in another Stephen King adaptation. What is this film?

4. The year after *Cujo* was released, screenwriter Don Carlos Dunaway saw another of his screenplays produced. This film starred Tim Matheson, Meg Tilly, and Hume Cronyn. Can you name this film?

5. Who wrote the first draft of the screenplay?

6. *Cujo* was nominated for an International Fantasy Film Award at Fantasporto in the category of Best Film, but ultimately lost. However, it did pick up one award there. What was this?

7. What is the name of Vic's partner?

8. Whose home did the Trentons move into in the novel?

9. Lauren Currier is credited as one of the film's screenwriters. However, this is a pseudonym. What is the real name of "Lauren Currier"?

10. Danny Pintauro began an eight-year stint on a popular sitcom the year after his turn in *Cujo*. What is this sitcom?

11. Who was the first director hired to make *Cujo*?

12. What is the significant difference in the storyline of the film compared to the book regarding the character Tad Trenton?

13. Dee Wallace-Stone was married to another member of the cast. Who was this?

14.   How did Tad hurt his head at summer camp?

15.   Tad believes there's a monster in his closet. (This is investigated much more in King's novel.) Two years after the release of *Cujo* another King work was adapted into a film about a monster who lives in childrens' closets. What is this film?

MEDIUM DIFFICULTY

1.   In 1983, Danny Pintauro was nominated for Best Young Supporting Actor in a Motion Picture by the Young Artist Awards. However, he lost. Who defeated him?

2.   What is Steve Kemp's nickname for Tad?

3.   A product Vic helped market creates a scare because of the red dye used in manufacturing it. What is the name of this product?

4.   A 1984 documentary on horror cinema, which was directed by Andrew J. Kuehn, features footage from *Carrie* (1976), *The Shining* (1980), and *Cujo*. What is this film?

5.   Who is Cujo's first victim?

6.   Mrs. Camber wins the lotto. How much does she win?

7.   As Cujo ravages Donna inside the car, what does she use to fight him off?

8.   In 1991, editor Neil Travis won the Academy Award for Best Film Editing. For what film did Travis win this honor?

9.   What is the name of Joe Camber's son?

10.   Which cast member revealed that they were homosexual in 1997?

11.   What is the name of the company Vic and his partner created the Professor for?

12.   How many St. Bernards were used in the filming of *Cujo*?

13.   Actress Dee Wallace-Stone began her career playing a maid in a 1975 film. What is this film?

14.   What is the name of Joe Camber's wife?

15.   Three years prior to *Cujo*, Lewis Teague directed another film about a man-eating animal on the loose. This film was written by John Sayles. What is this film?

HARD AS HELL

1.   What is the name of the auto mechanic Vic takes his car to before going to see Joe Camber?

2.   Actor Ed Lauter appears alongside *Firestarter* (1984) actors Martin Sheen and George C. Scott in a 1972 film with the same title as a 1977 novel by Stephen King. What is this film?

3.   What road do the Cambers live on?

4.   Who appears in a cameo as Dr. Merkatz?

5.   When Donna and Tad enter the Camber's house, what brand of cereal is sitting on the table?

6.   What is the number on Bannerman's police cruiser?

7.   The year *Cujo* was released, actress Dee Wallace-Stone appeared in a play which ran at the Starlight Theater in Kansas City, Missouri. What is this play?

8.   The character Sheriff Bannerman plays a much greater role in another King adaptation released the same year as *Cujo*. What actor appears as Bannerman in this other film?

9.   *Cujo* producer Daniel H. Blatt served as producer on a film co-written by *A Return to Salem's Lot* (1987) helmer Larry Cohen in 1979. What is this film?

10. How many miles outside Castle Rock is the Camber's farm located?

11. In 1974, "B" movie impresario Roger Corman hired *Cujo* director Lewis Teague to recut a film directed by Monte Hellman. The film was then released under a different title. What is this film?

12. In what state does Mrs. Camber's sister reside?

13. What popular culture character appears on Tad's lunch box?

14. Lewis Teague made his directorial debut in 1974 with a film written and co-directed by Howard Freen. This film stars Pat Anderson, Tommy J. Huff, and Sam Laws. What is this film?

15. Which cast member has siblings named Scott, Bobby, Susan, and Laura, who are all actors?

QUIZ #6: THE DEAD ZONE (1983)

Screenplay by: Jeffrey Boam
Directed by: David Cronenberg
Starring: Christopher Walken, Brooke Adams, and Tom Skerritt
Lorimar Film Entertainment

Director David Cronenberg's masterful film, *The Dead Zone*, remains one of the finer Stephen King adaptations to date. Cronenberg retains the moody essence of King's novel, while leaving his own imprint on the film. *The Dead Zone* should also be commended for the stark visuals provided by cinematographer Mark Irwin and a superb performance from lead actor Christopher Walken, who gives one of the finest performances of his career.

Although King has expressed reservations regarding Cronenberg's decision to have Greg Stillson use Sarah's child as a shield ("...of all the babies in New Hampshire, it turns out to be Sarah's own baby..."), the author was pleased with the overall effectiveness of the film. "[Cronenberg] added a dimension to the visions which hadn't even occurred to me—that of putting Johnny Smith in his own visions," King said. "I thought it was wonderful." King reportedly called other decisions made by Cronenberg, such as making Johnny's pupil an innocent 12-year-old rather than a spoiled teen as he appears in the novel, better than his own original ideas.

In *Roger Ebert's Home Movie Companion*, film critic Ebert raves further, "*The Dead Zone* does what only a good supernatural thriller can do: it makes us forget that it is supernatural. Like *Rosemary's Baby* and *The Ex-*

orcist, it tells its story so strongly through the lives of sympathetic, believable people that we not only forgive the gimmicks, we accept them. No other King novel has been better filmed...and Cronenberg, who knows how to handle terror, also knows how to create three-dimensional, fascinating characters."

EASY

1. Martin Sheen's character, Greg Stillson, says he's had a vision that he will be the President of the United States. Sixteen years after the release of *The Dead Zone*, Sheen played the president on a popular television series. What is this series?

2. What is the name of the clinic where Johnny Smith lies in a coma?

3. Roger Stewart says he hired Johnny because of his abilities as a teacher. What does he say he did not hire Johnny for?

4. Greg Stillson tells Roger Stewart he needs his support and expertise. What does he then say he needs "most of all"?

5. Who informs Johnny that Sarah is now married?

6. Christopher Walken's character, Johnny, assigns *The Legend of Sleepy Hollow* to his class, describing it as being "about a schoolteacher who gets chased by a headless demon." Walken would later play this "headless demon" in another film. What is this film?

7. In 1981, Sydney Pollack was hired to work on *The Dead Zone*. In what capacity was Pollack to have worked?

8. What is Sheriff Bannerman's first name?

9. What does Johnny's father boast about having made the day Johnny was born?

10. What is Dr. Weizak's reasoning for not speaking with his mother?

11.   Who does Dr. Weizak say he would have no choice but to kill if given the opportunity?

12.   Just before Johnny's attempted assassination of Greg Stillson, he accidentally drops something from the balcony. What?

13.   Just before traveling to kill Greg Stillson, Johnny writes a letter. To whom does he write it?

14.   What diet does Johnny jokingly say allows you to "lose weight while you sleep"?

15.   What is the name of Johnny's father?

MEDIUM DIFFICULTY

1.   What is the name of Sarah's son?

2.   What is the name of the journalist blackmailed by Stillson?

3.   Stephen King's first choice for the role of Johnny Smith was a comedian. Who is this?

4.   In screenwriter Jeffrey Boam's first draft, Johnny sees Sarah killed when he kisses her in the hospital. Who kills her?

5.   The only clue the Castle Rock serial killer leaves behind is an empty cigarette pack. What brand is it?

6.   What is the name of Stillson's goon, played by Geza Kovacs?

7.   Who was director David Cronenberg's first choice for the role of Sheriff Bannerman?

8.   The Castle Rock Killer opens his jacket to show something to his victim at the gazebo. What?

9.   At the time of her death, how old is Debbie Linderman?

10. Who does Chris Stewart say "lives in a shell"?

11. How many years is Johnny in a coma?

12. A film directed by David Cronenberg is mentioned in Stephen King's 1987 novel *Misery*. What is this film?

13. Although Jeffrey Boam is the only screenwriter credited on *The Dead Zone*, Boam's final draft was actually co-written with two other people. Who are they?

14. At one point, director Michael Cimino considered directing the project. According to Stephen King, Cimino wanted to make Johnny Smith "show his sensitivity" by talking with animals. What type of animals?

15. A Russian screenwriter was hired by Dino De Laurentiis to adapt *The Dead Zone*. This proved to be a headache as the screenplay then had to be translated into English (and Italian for De Laurentiis). Who was this scribe?

HARD AS HELL

1. What is the name of the woman Johnny's father begins "carrying on with" after the death of his wife?

2. What is the name of the waitress murdered in the gazebo?

3. What does Johnny learn when he touches Henrietta Dodd's hand?

4. When Stillson shoots himself, we see a close-up of a *Newsweek* magazine. What does the cover say?

5. Director David Cronenberg reshot the scenes in which Johnny sees the little girl's bedroom on fire. Why?

6. What director was first hired by Lorimar to helm *The Dead Zone* in 1981?

7.   In 1983, the character Sheriff Bannerman appeared in both *The Dead Zone* and *Cujo*. In this film, Bannerman is played by Tom Skerritt. Who appears as the sheriff in *Cujo*?

8.   What did director David Cronenberg do to make Christopher Walken's flinches look more natural?

9.   What is the name of Roger Stewart's butler?

10.   What is the name of Sarah's husband?

11.   Who plays the young man who photographs Stillson using a baby as a shield?

12.   Who does Johnny say has been a "real sport" to him?

13.   What is the company name printed on the side of the 18-wheeler that hits Johnny?

14.   What is the name of Dr. Weizak's mother?

15.   What is the name of the nurse's daughter Johnny sees enveloped in flames?

QUIZ #7: CHRISTINE (1983)

Screenplay by: Bill Phillips
Directed by: John Carpenter
Starring: Keith Gordon, Dean Stockwell, and Alexandra Paul
Columbia Pictures

Director John Carpenter's adaptation *Christine* hit theaters a mere nine months after King's book landed in book stores. While *Christine* has a number of flaws—many of which could have been avoided had Carpenter explored the evilness of the car's former owner, Roland LeBay, who plays a more significant role in the novel—it is an entertaining film. The film features a superb performance by actor Keith Gordon, a tremendous soundtrack of great '50s tunes, a less-memorable-but-no-less-effective Carpenter score which echoes *Halloween* (1978) and *The Fog* (1980), and the beautiful '58 Plymouth Fury herself, Christine.

So why was the film so poorly received? Although some of this was likely an aftereffect of Carpenter's then recent flop, *The Thing* (1982) (which has since become a cult classic), *Christine* also had problems in its pacing, character development, and was constructed around a mediocre script. However, the biggest problem with *Christine* might have been the success of the novel. As author Stephen J. Spignesi explains in *The Shape Under the Sheet*, "Much of the problem with filming King is that Stephen King has already created the 'movie of the book' in the Skull Cinema: his writing is so overwhelmingly cinematic that we literally 'see' the book as we read. When attempts are made to transfer his stories to film, the end result is often an abbreviated 'mutation'; it's the same thing that happens when food manufacturers try to produce a perfect four course frozen meal: the final product is certainly edible, but it sure as hell ain't the same as fresh."

EASY

1. In what year was Christine built?

2. What word does Arnie use when referring to someone he doesn't like?

3. Which cast member made their directorial debut five years after the release of *Christine* with *The Chocolate War* (1988)?

4. The man who served as Stephen King's literary agent from 1977 to 1988 received an executive producer credit on *Christine*. Who is this?

5. What does Arnie threaten to do unless his parents register the car?

6. Screenwriter Bill Phillips had worked on another King adaptation before *Christine*, but his contributions were uncredited. What is this film?

7. How much does Arnie pay for Christine?

8. Arnie brings Dennis a book in the hospital. What is the title of this book?

9. When Arnie discovers that Christine has been vandalized, what does he find on the dash of the car?

10. What does Arnie describe as having a "voracious appetite"?

11. What is the message Dennis scratches on Christine's hood?

12. Another film about a murderous automobile was produced six years before *Christine*. This film was directed by Elliot Silverstein. What is this film?

13. Dennis pulls a book off the shelf in the library just before he asks Leigh out. What is this book?

14. What is the name of the bully who steals Arnie's lunch and later vandalizes Christine?

15. Sixteen years after his turn in *Christine*, actor Harry Dean Stanton would appear in a second Stephen King adaptation. What is this film?

MEDIUM DIFFICULTY

1. In what city does *Christine* take place?

2. What does Dennis call Christine, causing Arnie to warn that "she's sensitive"?

3. Which cast member also appears in *Cool Hand Luke* (1967), *The Godfather Part II* (1974), and *Alien* (1979)?

4. What is Dennis' last name?

5. *Christine* was one of the three King adaptations released in 1983. What are the other two films?

6. Who is the first of the vandals killed by Christine?

7. As Dennis attempts to get inside Christine, the radio comes to life blaring a Little Richard tune. What is this song?

8. What is the name of the do-it-yourself garage where Arnie restores Christine?

9. Whom does Detective Junkins call "heroes"?

10. What does Arnie enter the garage to retrieve when he finds that Christine has been vandalized?

11. Actors Harry Dean Stanton and Roberts Blossom would later reunite in a film directed by Martin Scorsese. What is this film?

12.   Which then-unknown cast member went on to appear in films such as *From Dusk Till Dawn* (1996), *Jerry Maguire* (1996), and *For Love of the Game* (1999)?

13.   *Christine* was one of two horror films featuring actress Alexandra Paul in 1983. The other film was directed by Don McBrearty. What is this film?

14.   Arnie's parents wanted him in a club rather than in the school band. What was this club?

15.   Arnie says during Scrabble he had a "triple word score" which his mother refused to count. What is this word?

HARD AS HELL

1.   Which cast member has received four Obies for his work in theatre and is also an accomplished poet?

2.   Prior to his appearance in *Christine*, Keith Gordon had made two films with *Carrie* (1976) director Brian De Palma. What are these films?

3.   Of the 17 Plymouth Furys used to film *Christine*, how many survived untouched?

4.   What Rolling Stones song is playing inside Buddy Repperton's car when Christine pulls up behind him?

5.   How many red 1958 Plymouth Furys were produced in real life?

6.   *Christine* was the second collaboration between producer Richard Kobritz and director John Carpenter. What film had the two made together previously?

7.   How many miles were on the speedometer when George LeBay's "asshole brother" purchased Christine?

8. How many miles are on the speedometer when Arnie purchases Christine?

9. At what auto parts store does Arnie say he purchased the touch-up paint he used on the door?

10. What does the sign hanging on the side of Will Darnell's desk read?

11. What is Dennis' football jersey number?

12. What is the name of the sophomore girl Dennis refers to as a "sperm bank"?

13. The year after *Christine* was released, actor Robert Prosky landed a role on the popular television series *Hill Street Blues*. What character did Prosky play on the series?

14. What does Arnie observe as being "part of being a parent"?

15. What is Christine's license plate number?

QUIZ #8: FIRESTARTER (1984)

Screenplay by: Stanley Mann
Directed by: Mark L. Lester
Starring: David Keith, Drew Barrymore, and Freddie Jones
Universal Pictures

When Universal Pictures announced the cast of their forthcoming film *Firestarter*, the film seemed promising indeed: George C. Scott, Martin Sheen, Louise Fletcher, and David Keith, still hot from his turn in *An Officer and a Gentleman* (1981). The film also boasted an Oscar-nominated screenwriter in Stanley Mann. Yet, interestingly, not a single thing in this film seems to work. The acting is wooden, there is little chemistry between the performers, and each time Drew Barrymore's character, Charlie, uses her powers, her hair blows as if she's standing in a wind tunnel. Because of these flaws (and many more), the film was dismissed by critics. In his essay "Why The Children Don't Look Like Their Parents," Harlan Ellison referred to Mann's screenwriting as "creative typing" and called filmmaker Mark L. Lester's direction "lugubrious."

King himself has taken a few pot-shots at *Firestarter*, as well: "There were $3 million worth of special effects and another $3 million worth of Academy Award-winning talent up there on the screen, and none of it was working. Watching that happen was an incredible, unreal, and painful experience." King and director Lester would later engage in a battle of words. In an interview with this author, Lester commented: "It was strange that (King) turned on the movie in the press after having said all these wonderful things after seeing it. In fact, he even did a premiere in his own home town for charity. He invited everyone to come see this film in his home town of Bangor, Maine. That's where the premiere was that he set up. So why later he decides to attack all these movies, I don't know. I think he has an evil side to him from writing too many horror books."

EASY

1. The film's producer is the son of a legendary filmmaker. Who is this?

2. An Egyptian producer first purchased the rights to *Firestarter* for $1 million. In 1997, this producer would become a household name, but not because of his work. Who is this?

3. What is the name of the lake where the McGees' summer cottage is located?

4. Who predicts of Charlie, "she'll trust me like a brother"?

5. *Firestarter* was actor Martin Sheen's second King adaptation in as many years. What was the Stephen King adaptation in which Sheen had appeared in 1983?

6. A well-known filmmaker was first attached to *Firestarter* before being removed by Universal. This filmmaker then helmed another Stephen King adaptation released the year before *Firestarter*. Who is this director?

7. Actress Heather Locklear was appearing as a regular on two popular television series when this film was released. What are these two series?

8. Dino De Laurentiis was so taken by Drew Barrymore that he signed her to appear in another King adaptation the following year. What is this film?

9. What is the name of the drug given to Andy and Vicky McGee which gave them telekinetic powers?

10. Director Mark L. Lester and Stephen King later squared off in dueling interviews in a popular science fiction magazine. What is this magazine?

11. When Andy McGee hands a one dollar bill to a cabbie, he "pushes" the cabbie, making him believe it is more money than reality. How much does the cabbie believe he's holding?

12. Throughout the film, Charlie expresses regret over an incident involving her mother. What was this?

13. What veteran actor appears in the film as Dr. Pynchot?

14. Someone closely involved with the production of *Firestarter* makes a cameo in the film as a motel owner. Who is this?

15. *Firestarter* was the third film to feature both Art Carney and George C. Scott. What are the other two films?

MEDIUM DIFFICULTY

1. What is Dr. Pynchot's first name?

2. What does Andy McGee describe as having the appearance of "copper set on fire"?

3. In 1966, screenwriter Stanley Mann was nominated by the Academy Awards in the category of Best-Adapted Screenplay. For what film was Mann nominated?

4. Andy McGee believes the letters he's mailed to various newspapers will change things for him. However, they don't. Why?

5. Actor Martin Sheen's sons, Emilio and Ramon Estevez, each appear in separate Stephen King adaptations. What are these?

6. In a flashback, what does Andy find on a foldout ironing board?

7. When Andy catches the agents who murdered his wife and kidnapped his daughter, what does he do to them?

8. *Firestarter* is one of two screenplays Stanley Mann saw produced theatrically in 1984. The other film features *The Running Man* (1987) actor Arnold Schwarzenegger. What is this film?

9. Fifteen years after the release of *Firestarter*, Martin Sheen would appear alongside *The Dark Half* (1993) actor Tim Matheson and Rob Lowe of *The Stand* (1994) on a popular television series. What is this series?

10. Where does Andy tell Irv Manders that he and Charlie are going?

11. Why does Rainbird tell Charlie he cannot use his key card?

12. In the note Andy has delivered to Charlie, he instructs her to destroy the letter. How?

13. *Firestarter* was the second film to feature both Art Carney and David Keith. Can you name the first?

14. What is the name of the horse Charlie rides at the compound?

15. What false name does Andy give Irv Manders when they first meet?

HARD AS HELL

1. Editor David Rawlins served as second unit director on a film featuring *Christine* (1983) actor Keith Gordon in 1986. What is this film?

2. *Firestarter* was director Mark L. Lester's first big league production. What independent film had Lester directed which caught the eye of executive producer Dino De Laurentiis?

3.   Of the ten volunteers tested in the experiment which altered Andy and Vicky McGee, how many of them had died or committed suicide prior to Vicky's death?

4.   Where is the headquarters for The Shop located?

5.   What was Vicky McGee's maiden name?

6.   Before Stanley Mann came on board, two screenwriters had penned a number of rejected drafts of *Firestarter*. Who are these writers?

7.   What is the name of Irv Manders' wife?

8.   After Charlie is kidnapped from the scene of her mother's murder, Andy telephones a neighbor looking for her. What is the name of this neighbor?

9.   What does D.S.I. stand for?

10.   *Firestarter* was the third film featuring actors Moses Gunn and Antonio Fargas. What are the two films in which they had already appeared together?

11.   What is the name of the agent Hollister orders to take Charlie to the stables at night?

12.   What is Dr. Wallace's first name?

13.   What is the false name Charlie gives Irv Manders?

14.   Hollister says The Shop has a small compound located on a Hawaiian island. On which island is this compound located?

15.   John Rainbird's genealogical lineage is one half Native American. What is his tribe?

QUIZ #9: CHILDREN OF THE CORN (1984)

Screenplay by: George Goldsmith
Directed by: Fritz Kiersch
Starring: Peter Horton, Linda Hamilton, and R.G. Armstrong
New World Pictures

The fact that *Children of the Corn* is widely regarded as the worst direct film adaptation of a Stephen King work after so many adaptations is truly a testament to this film's overall shoddiness and lack of effectiveness. The acting is bad, the script is weak, the direction is poor, and none of the story holds up to any sort of analysis. How has the disappearance of an entire town's adult population gone unnoticed by the rest of the world? How can there still be working electricity in Gatlin? How can an already dead child wander out into the road? And, humorously, some of the children are wearing the same clothes in scenes which take place several years apart. As *The Films of Stephen King* author Ann Lloyd observes, the film is a "treasure trove" for those given the unlimited ability to suspend disbelief.

In a *Fangoria* interview King remarked, "You really have to work to bring out a clunker like *Children of the Corn*. One of my favorite memories is when this kid stands in the middle of a deserted town and says, 'Outlander, we have your woman!' That's when you feel like you're going to crawl under your seat and get jujubes in your hair and popcorn on your knees 'cause you never want to see another frame." King has also likened this adaptation of his short story to having one's daughter raped at a fraternity party.

EASY

1. Who wrote the first draft screenplay for *Children of the Corn*?

2. What is Job's "usual" at Hanson's Cafe?

3. Who does Isaac promise that "the god of Hell will punish"?

4. Which cast member also appeared in *White Lightning* (1973), *Heaven Can Wait* (1978), and *The Man in the Iron Mask* (1998)?

5. During the Monopoly game, who owns a hotel on Boardwalk?

6. What was the occupation of the ill-fated "blue man"?

7. The final draft of the *Children of the Corn* screenplay was written by George Goldsmith. However, New World first submitted the name of another scribe as having been the sole writer on the project. Who was this?

8. Who uses a knife hidden beneath the pinball machine in the massacre at Hanson's Cafe?

9. Actor John Franklin, who appears as Isaac, would later cowrite the screenplay for one of the *Children of the Corn* sequels. Which one?

10. What book is sitting on the dash of Burt's car?

11. Where does Sarah tell Vicky "all the grownups are"?

12. Malachai says He Who Walks Behind the Rows is "the god of blood and sacrifice." What does he insist that He Who Walks Behind the Rows is not the god of?

13. What does Vicky suggest might be using the telephone inside Hanson's Cafe?

14. What beverage do the children poison in Hanson's Cafe just before the massacre?

15. The story begins 13 years after the adults are murdered in Stephen King's original short story. In the film, how many years pass between the massacre of the adults and Vicky and Burt's arrival in Gatlin?

MEDIUM DIFFICULTY

1. What is Burt's birthday wish?

2. At one point *Children of the Corn* was slated to be a $2.75 million film made by Home Box Office. At this point, an actor from *Salem's Lot* (1979) was to have appeared in the film. Who was this?

3. In 1981, actor Peter Horton married an actress. The two were divorced in 1988. Who was this?

4. In 1997, actress Linda Hamilton married a director. The two were divorced in 1999. Who was this?

5. What do Burt and Vicky discover in the dead boy's suitcase that Vicky calls "repulsive"?

6. What song is Sarah listening to when Burt and Vicky find her?

7. When Vicky asks Sarah to draw a picture for her, what does she draw?

8. What is Burt's surname?

9. In the September 1985 issue of *Castle Rock*, Stephen King listed what he felt were the 10 worst films ever made. What number was *Children of the Corn* on this list?

10. Who does Isaac say has the "gift of sight"?

11. What is Vicky's surname?

12. How long does Burt say he has been working toward his internship?

13. Who is producer Donald Borchers' brother?

14. Who does Burt run over in his car just outside Gatlin?

15. What is the name of Chester Diehl's dog?

HARD AS HELL

1. Burt grabs two things from his trunk after running over the child in the road. What are these?

2. What is the name of the town located 19 miles away that Chester Diehl suggests Burt and Vicky go to instead of Gatlin?

3. How many days did the *Children of the Corn* shoot last?

4. What production company first held the rights to the short story "Children of the Corn"?

5. Which Monopoly piece does Job say represents Isaac?

6. Whose blood is being "shared" when Burt interrupts the ceremony in the church?

7. Vicky lip-syncs to the song "School is Out." Stephen King quotes this song in a short story that is collected in *Skeleton Crew*. Which story is this?

8. Who does Burt jokingly assure Job they won't have to worry about?

9. In 1979, documentary filmmakers Harry Wiland and Joseph Masefield purchased the rights to Stephen King's short story "Children of the Corn." How much did they pay for these rights?

10. What is the price for a corn fritter at Hanson's Cafe?

11.   How many minutes does Burt say it takes for blood to begin coagulating?

12.   What brand of ice cream is advertised prominently inside Hanson's Cafe?

13.   What does Malachai say that he and the others want to give Vicky?

14.   Filmmakers Harry Wiland and Joseph Masefield, who had first owned the rights to "Children of the Corn," insisted that a metaphor be incorporated into their would-be film. What was this?

15.   What is the name of the bank which is located beside the Gatlin Town Hall?

QUIZ #10: CAT'S EYE (1985)

Screenplay by: Stephen King
Directed by: Lewis Teague
Starring: Drew Barrymore, James Woods, and Alan King
Metro-Goldwyn-Mayer

Executive producer Dino De Laurentiis tapped Stephen King to pen the script for *Cat's Eye*, an anthology containing two adaptations of the author's short stories and one new tale, "The General." Each of the three vignettes is connected by a wraparound story about a stray cat traveling across the country to help a young girl. The resulting film is engaging—especially "Quitters, Inc."—but the film was not a commercial success and drew mixed criticism.

King himself blamed the film's failure on Metro-Goldwyn-Mayer. "There are reasons for (the failure) which don't have anything to do with the movie," King explained. "They have to do with the production end of it. At MGM, the whole top echelon of executives fell, and all the pictures that had been produced under those people became orphans... There were no trailers, no publicity, and no promotion—that sort of thing."

As for the film itself, King raved, "*Cat's Eye* is a great movie! It was truncated by MGM, who made a bad mistake by taking the prologue off, which was hilarious, and clarifies the picture a lot....I mean, the picture is there, it's literate, it's funny, it's sort of sophisticated in a different kind of way. It just happened to be a picture nobody wanted."

EASY

1. The cat is nearly hit by a '58 Plymouth Fury. What does the bumper sticker on the car read?

2. *Cat's Eye* was the second Stephen King adaptation featuring Drew Barrymore. What was the first?

3. In what city does "Quitters, Inc." take place?

4. In one scene Dick Morrison asks, "Who writes this crap?" while watching a Stephen King adaptation. What film is Morrison watching?

5. Actor Kenneth McMillan had already appeared in one King adaptation. In this film, he played a character named Parkins Gillespie. What is this film?

6. How much does Junk bet Donatti that Dick Morrison's wife will slap him?

7. *Cat's Eye* was one of two films directed by Lewis Teague in 1985. The other project he directed that year was a hit film written by *Sometimes They Come Back* (1991) scribes Lawrence Konner and Mark Rosenthal. What is this film?

8. What make of automobile does Johnny Norris drive?

9. What is the "old wives' tale" Sally Ann believes regarding General?

10. *Cat's Eye* was the second Stephen King adaptation directed by Lewis Teague. What was the first?

11. In what film written by *A Return to Salem's Lot* scribe Larry Cohen does James Woods play a character named Cleve?

12. What song plays as Donatti shocks Cindy Morrison?

13. In 2001, James Woods and Drew Barrymore appeared together in a second film. What is this film?

14. Sally Ann is shown reading a book written by Stephen King. What is this book?

15. In 1986, actor Kenneth McMillan appeared in a film directed by *Firestarter* (1984) helmer Mark L. Lester. In this film, McMillan played father to Meg Ryan. What is this film?

MEDIUM DIFFICULTY

1. How old is Dick Morrison's daughter, Alesha?

2. In 1990, producer Martha Schumacher married someone else involved with the production of *Cat's Eye*. Whom did she marry?

3. In the film, counselor Donatti's first name is Vinnie. What was it in King's original short story?

4. The character Drew Barrymore plays in the film is quite different from the character King first envisioned. In what way?

5. What is the name of the school Alesha Morrison attends?

6. The filmmakers' most glaring mistake takes place during Johnny Norris' trip around the building on the ledge. What is this?

7. When General knocks the troll onto the phonograph player, what song comes roaring to life?

8. What is Mrs. Cressner's name?

9. In the original short story, "Quitters, Inc.," Dick and Cindy Morrison had a mentally handicapped son. What was his name?

10. In a scene cut from the final film, Sally Ann chases someone with a machine gun. Whom does she chase?

11.   What song composed by Phil Medley and Bert Russell plays as Donatti demonstrates electric shock therapy on the cat?

12.   What is the name of Our Girl's pet parakeet?

13.   When filling out the enrollment form at Quitters, Inc., Dick Morrison leaves one space blank. What question does he refuse to answer?

14.   One of Cressner's goons, played by journeyman actor Mike Starr, wears a Donald Duck T-shirt. What is this character's name in the film?

15.   What name does Cressner give the cat?

HARD AS HELL

1.   What is the name of Alesha Morrison's Cabbage Patch doll?

2.   How many cats were used in making this film?

3.   Several scenes were cut from the film. One of these scenes—originally intended as the film's opening—takes place at a funeral. Whose funeral was this?

4.   Cressner wagers that the cat can cross the busy street without getting hit. How much does he bet?

5.   The troll in the film was designed by the special effects expert who created E.T. Who is this?

6.   In one scene, Dick dreams about a box of cigarettes, dancing. What brand are the cigarettes?

7.   According to Donatti, what percentage of Quitters, Inc. clients develop a weight problem after they stop smoking?

8.   A prop constructed for the film was later listed in *The Guinness Book of World Records*. What was this?

9. *Cat's Eye* was one of two films Oscar-winning cinematographer Jack Cardiff filmed which was released in 1985. The other is an actioner which grossed more than $300 million worldwide. What is this film?

10. In one scene, Cressner promises that if Johnny walks the ledge, he will get "the girl, the gold watch... everything." What film does this line reference?

11. *Cat's Eye* reunited producer Martha Schumacher, production designer Giorgio Postiglione, stunt coordinator Glenn Randall, and special effects coordinator Jeff Jarvis, who had all collaborated previously on another Stephen King adaptation. What was this film?

12. What was the real height of the ledge actor Robert Hays walked?

13. When Junk catches Dick Morrison smoking on the interstate, the goon is wearing a baseball cap. What team is represented on the cap?

14. What does Donatti dub "unfashionable, but useful"?

15. The cat is chased by a Saint Bernard at the beginning of the film. What city serves as the setting for this scene?

QUIZ #11: SILVER BULLET (1985)

Screenplay by: Stephen King
Directed by: Daniel Attias
Starring: Gary Busey, Everett McGill, and Corey Haim
Paramount Pictures

When it was announced that Paramount would be producing *Silver Bullet* (under the working title *Cycle of the Werewolf*), expectations were high. When it was later announced that Stephen King himself would be writing the screenplay, expectations soared even higher. Many fans predicted this would be the definitive werewolf picture. However, when *Silver Bullet* was released, the film failed to meet these expectations. Rookie director Daniel Attias seemed unsure of himself and was unable to pull off even the most routine scares, and many of King's best scenes were left on the cutting room floor.

Phantasm (1979) helmer Don Coscarelli, initially hired as a producer and screenwriter on *Silver Bullet*, explains the atmosphere on the set and how producer Dino De Laurentiis inadvertently sabotaged the film. "This could have been a great movie, but the producer didn't have a clue," Coscarelli recalls. "I had the great pleasure of meeting Stephen King and working with him for a very short time on this project. When I began work, Stephen did not have time to write the screenplay. Therefore, I was told to write a draft, and was assigned the producer's Italian language translator as the co-writer. This was a difficult task as the project was based on a calendar, *Cycle of the Werewolf*, and adapting it into a screenplay was difficult. Stephen would fly down from Maine and give us advice. In five minutes, he'd dash off six pages of notes which would solve all our problems with the script. Then he would leave, and the producer, who could hardly read English, would go through Stephen's list and arbitrarily eliminate most of King's great ideas. It was a pathetic situation, and I left the project soon after."

EASY

1.   *Silver Bullet* was one of four movies starring Corey Haim released in 1985. In one of the films, Haim costars with C. Thomas Howell, Kelly Preston, and Dee Wallace-Stone. What is this film?

2.   What is Marty's age?

3.   What is the name of the drive Jane collects bottles and cans for?

4.   Daniel Attias made his directorial debut with *Silver Bullet*. Attias' only prior directorial credits were episodes of a popular television series. What is this series?

5.   There is a picture on Brady's kite. What is this?

6.   The name of the cemetery where *Salem's Lot's* (1979) Danny Glick is buried shares its name with the graveyard where Brady is laid to rest. What is the cemetery?

7.   In Marty's first letter to Reverend Lowe, what does he suggest the minister do?

8.   Where was *Silver Bullet* filmed?

9.   Where does Milt Sturmfuller conclude "cripples" always end up?

10. Artwork by artist Berni Wrightson was included in Stephen King's *Cycle of the Werewolf*, which *Silver Bullet is* based upon. One year

before *Cycle of the Werewolf* was published, Wrightson adapted a King screenplay for a graphic novel published by Plume which tied in with the film. What is this film?

11. What time is the curfew in Tarker Mills?

12. How many films has Daniel Attias directed since *Silver Bullet*?

13. What is stenciled on the baseball bat Owen Knopfler wields?

14. How many times has Uncle Red been divorced?

15. What well-known horror/fantasy filmmaker was hired as screenwriter, but later resigned?

MEDIUM DIFFICULTY

1. According to Herb, there is no comfort, only what?

2. This cast member made a name for himself playing legendary criminal John Dillinger in the original 1945 version of *Dillinger*. Who is this actor?

3. What hymn do the townsfolk sing in Reverend Lowe's nightmare?

4. Armando Nannuzzi served as cinematographer on a second Stephen King adaptation the year after he worked on *Silver Bullet*. What is this film?

5. How many letters do Marty and Jane send Reverend Lowe before going to Uncle Red?

6. *Silver Bullet* was one of two films released in 1985 starring Gary Busey. The other (vastly superior) film was directed by Nicolas Roeg. What is this film?

7. What is Brady's surname?

8.   Who fires the silver bullet at the monocular werewolf?

9.   On what date was the Gala Fair scheduled (before its cancellation)?

10. Actor Everett McGill followed up *Silver Bullet* with a film directed by Clint Eastwood. What is this film?

11. What is the name of the Tarker Mills sheriff?

12. According to Red, when are psychotics the most active?

13. This cast member later gained fame as Jerry Blake in *The Stepfather* (1987) and *The Stepfather II* (1989). Who is this actor?

14. Jane finds something which belonged to one of the werewolf's victims inside the church garage. What is this?

15. What telltale sign of the Reverend's misdeeds does Uncle Red find on Marty's wheelchair?

HARD AS HELL

1.   Just before his death, Arnie Westrum sings the jingle from a beer commercial. What brand of beer is this?

2.   The year veteran actor Lawrence Tierney appeared in *Silver Bullet*, he also made a film with legendary filmmaker John Huston. Can you name this film?

3.   On what day of the week do Marty and Jane inform Uncle Red that they suspect Reverend Lowe of being a werewolf?

4.   *Silver Bullet* was nominated for an International Fantasy Film Award at Fantasporto in 1988. In what category was this nomination?

5.   Marty has a poster of a professional baseball player hanging over his bed. Who is this slugger?

6.   Carlo Rambaldi created the werewolf used in the film. On what 1968 film did Rambaldi and producer Dino De Laurentiis first collaborate?

7.   What does Uncle Red say will happen to him if Marty's mother discovers how fast the new-and-improved "Silver Bullet" wheelchair goes?

8.   *Silver Bullet* was one of two films composer Jay Chattaway scored in 1985. The other film was a shoot-'em-up actioner starring Chuck Norris. What is this film?

9.   *Cycle of the Werewolf* was originally conceived as a calendar. Who approached Stephen King with this idea in 1979?

10.   According to Jane, how much does a pair of Leggs brand pantyhose cost at the pharmacy?

11.   On what road did Andy's recent "fender bender" take place?

12.   Before directing *Silver Bullet*, Daniel Attias had served as assistant director on another Stephen King adaptation. What is this film?

13.   Director Daniel Attias was nominated for a Directors Guild Award in the category of Outstanding Directorial Achievement in a Dramatic Series in 2000. The title of the episode he was nominated for is "46 Long." What television series is this?

14.   What is the name of Marty and Jane's mother?

15.   *Silver Bullet* is one of four films edited by Daniel Loewenthal and scored by composer Jay Chattaway. What are the other three films?

QUIZ #12: THE WOMAN IN THE ROOM (1985)

Screenplay by: Frank Darabont
Directed by: Frank Darabont
Starring: Michael Cornelison, Dee Croxton, and Brian Libby
Granite Entertainment Group

Nearly a decade before crafting *The Shawshank Redemption* (1994), screenwriter/director Frank Darabont made a short film based on Stephen King's story "The Woman in the Room." With a budget of $35,000, Darabont cast actor Brian Libby, who had already appeared in a couple of films, including the Chuck Norris vehicles *The Octagon* (1980) and *Silent Rage* (1982). The resulting film is a masterwork at any cost. The film was released in 1985 as part of *Stephen King's Night Shift Collection*, which also included the lesser film *The Boogeyman*.

"The Woman in the Room" is one of the most personal works Stephen King has ever written. "It had been written as a kind of cry from the heart after my mother's long, losing battle with cervical cancer had finally ended," King recalls. "Her pain—the pointlessness of her pain—shook me in a deep and fundamental way; it made me see the world in a new and cautious way."

When the novelist viewed Darabont's short film for the first time, he was moved to tears. "[I] watched in slackjaw amazement," King later wrote. "*The Woman in the Room* remains, 12 years later, on my short list of favorite film adaptations."

Note: Because this is a short film with a running time of only 32 minutes, this quiz consists of a mere 15 general questions rather than the standard 45 of varying difficulty which appear in this book for the feature-length films.

1.   What is the name of John's mother?

2.   What cast member also appears in Frank Darabont's *Buried Alive* (1990), *The Shawshank Redemption,* and *The Green Mile* (1999)?

3.   John asks the prisoner how many people he's killed in his lifetime. What is his response?

4.   What form of cancer does John's mother suffer from?

5.   When John asks his mother to remove something from her purse, what does she take out?

6.   What is the name of John's brother?

7.   How many of his killings does the prisoner say meant something to him?

8.   What does John's mother keep inside "the Sucrets box by the night stand"?

9.   What's on the television the first time John visits his mother?

10.   What is the name of John's sister-in-law?

11.   The prisoner says the psychiatrist has Freud in one hand. What does he say is in the doctor's other hand?

12.   How old was John when his parents took him to Pacific Ocean Park?

13.   At what time on Monday will the prisoner's trial resume?

14.   John overdoses his mother with Darvon Compound. How many milligrams is this?

15.   In what Stephen King adaptation does director Frank Darabont appear as Dr. Daniel Edwards?

QUIZ #13: THE BOOGEYMAN (1985)

Screenplay by: Jeffrey C. Schiro
Directed by: Jeffrey C. Schiro
Starring: Michael Reid, Bert Linder, and Terence Brady
Granite Entertainment Group

Film student Jeffrey C. Schiro initially purchased the rights to adapt Stephen King's short story "The Boogeyman" for one dollar and a copy of the finished product, agreeing that he would not sell the film. However, this agreement had to be amended when an entrepreneur named Gerald Ravel sought to purchase the short film and distribute it through his Native Son Entertainment Company. Ravel's deal quickly fell through when distributors discovered that he didn't own the rights to the film. *The Boogeyman* was then picked up by Granite Entertainment Group and sold as part of *Stephen King's Night Shift Collection*, which also included the vastly superior *The Woman in the Room* (1985).

While the film no doubt garnered Schiro praise in the filmmaking class it was made for, it is too shoddy for such wide distribution. Its sound is bad, the acting is poor (most notably Michael Reid), and the production values are less than sufficient. Frank Darabont's above-average film *The Woman in the Room* vastly overshadows *The Boogeyman*, making the film's shortcomings all the more obvious.

Note: Because this is a short film with a running time of only 29 minutes, this quiz consists of a mere 15 general questions rather than the standard 45 questions of varying difficulty which appear in this book for the feature-length films.

1. After directing *The Boogeyman*, Jeff Schiro helmed episodes of a television series. What is this series?

2. At what time does Lester Billings tell Sgt. Garland he found the body?

3. What is Sgt. Garland's first name?

4. When the film was originally released in 1985, the title was misspelled on the videocassette cover. How was it spelled?

5. What is the name of the psychiatrist Lester speaks with?

6. What brand of beer does Lester drink as he completes a crossword puzzle?

7. Lester says he always kept the closet door shut because there was something dangerous inside. What is this?

8. After Lester's visit with the psychiatrist, he finds a note on the receptionist's desk. What does it say?

9. Although the film wasn't released until 1985, it was actually made much earlier. What year was *The Boogeyman* made?

10. Prior to Granite International's release of *The Boogeyman* and *The Woman in the Room*, a company named Native Son International had planned to release them. However, Native Son never purchased the rights to do so from Stephen King and Doubleday. What is the name of the entrepreneur behind Native Son International?

11. What is the name of Lester's wife?

12. What are the names of Lester's three children?

13. Where does Lester say he cannot go without "puking (his) guts out"?

14. Lester asks his wife why she taught their child a word. What is this word?

15. After the death of his first child, Lester says he noticed something strange. What is this?

QUIZ #14: MAXIMUM OVERDRIVE (1986)

Screenplay by: Stephen King
Directed by: Stephen King
Starring: Emilio Estevez, Pat Hingle, and Laura Harrington
Warner Bros.

Executive producer Dino De Laurentiis convinced Stephen King to try his hand at directing this adaptation of his short story "Trucks," for a salary of $70,000. As the best-selling novelist says in a trailer for the film, "If you want something done right, you have to do it yourself." With *Maximum Overdrive*, a film about trucks which begin running down humans, King set out to make an exploitation B-movie. "[I]t's not *My Dinner With Andre*," King commented before the release of the film. "And little Stevie is not rehearsing his Academy Award speech for this baby."

In terms of trash cinema, *Maximum Overdrive* was exactly what King had promised it would be: "a moron movie" in the tradition of *Rambo* (1985). To be fair, this was King's first (and only) film, and as bad as it may be, it is still tremendously better than any film in the *Children of the Corn* franchise.

Humorously, film critic Joe Bob Briggs offers an explanation for the film's shortcomings: "You're thinking, 'Oh, sure, Joe Bob, you're gonna say it's not Steve's fault when the movie starts peterin' out after about an hour, 'cause he's just a writer.' That's just so wrong it makes me want to puke. There's a good reason *Maximum Overdrive* drops its transmission after the first hour, and that's because Steve tried to direct a love scene. Think about it. Everything was fine up to that point, right? I mean, we got the machines slowly trying to take over the world. We got the bank sign flashing the f-word. We got the great scene where the drawbridge goes up by its own self and destroys eight, 10 motor vehicles, including the famous Watermelon Fu shot. ... Great stuff. Great flick. Then what happens? Emilio Estevez and Laura Harrington do this pathetic little kissing scene, and a couple of scenes later they start making the sign of the four-legged spouting walrus, and you know what that adds up to? A Perry Como music video."

EASY

1. What band performs all the songs in *Maximum Overdrive*?

2. What is Curt referring to when he quips, "Great smell, huh"?

3. Cinematographer Armando Nannuzzi worked on another Stephen King adaptation the year before he came to work on *Maximum Overdrive*. What is this film?

4. What name does Hendershot call all male characters?

5. What actor makes an early appearance as a man killed by a video game?

6. Actor Emilio Estevez's father, Martin Sheen, appears in two Stephen King adaptations. What are these?

7. In 1987, *Maximum Overdrive* received two Razzie nominations. In what categories was the film nominated?

8. What is the name of the toy store advertised on the side of the semi with the Green Goblin head on its hood?

9. Where is Brett heading when she hitches a ride with the Bible salesman?

10. What is the name of the waitress who screams, "We made you"?

11. Which of the truck stop's occupants is afraid of spiders?

12. Brett says that Billy is "not only a hero." What else does she say he is?

13. The Motion Picture Association of America handed *Maximum Overdrive* an "X" rating. According to Stephen King, how many specific points of violence had to be cut or trimmed to receive an "R" rating?

14. What do the trucks request via Morse code?

15. Why did director King sometimes find difficulty in relating his ideas to his cinematographer?

MEDIUM DIFFICULTY

1. When Brett gives Hendershot a "lesson in manners," what does she do?

2. Who appears in the appropriately titled role of Second Woman?

3. Actor Emilio Estevez made his directorial debut the same year *Maximum Overdrive* was released. What is this film?

4. Dean Gates served as special makeup effects artist on *Maximum Overdrive*. Before going his own way, Gates was an assistant to a makeup effects legend who appeared as an actor alongside Stephen King in both *Knightriders* (1981) and *Creepshow 2* (1987). Who is this?

5. How much did this film earn theatrically in the United States?

6. What does Brett say Billy does "like a hero"?

7.   What does Billy use to demobilize the machine gun?

8.   What magazine does Joey read while sitting on the toilet?

9.   What is the company name printed on the side of the killer ice cream truck?

10. *Maximum Overdrive* contains only one original song. What is the title of this song?

11. What fruit is dumped on the vehicles on the drawbridge?

12. Although editor Evan Lottman probably wasn't expecting an Oscar nomination for his work on *Maximum Overdrive,* he had been previously nominated for his work on another horror film. What is this film?

13. What is the name of the truck stop in which the film takes place?

14. Which *Maximum Overdrive* cast member also appears in *On the Waterfront* (1954), *Splendor in the Grass* (1961), and *Bloody Mama* (1970)?

15. What does the star on Billy's time card indicate?

HARD AS HELL

1.   What is Billy's surname?

2.   What does the drive thru intercom at Burger-Lean spout repeatedly?

3.   According to the postscript, how many days after the close of the film did a Russian "weather satellite" destroy the UFO?

4.   During filming, the crew took out an ad in a local newspaper. Why?

5.   During filming of *Maximum Overdrive*, Stephen King consulted a close friend and veteran filmmaker. Who is this?

6.   What is the date in which the machines come to life?

7.   What song does the killer ice cream truck play over its speakers?

8.   What is the name of the truck stop in the original Stephen King short story "Trucks"?

9.   What is the cost of the traveling salesman's Bibles?

10. What is the slogan on the side of the toy store semi?

11. Nine years after his appearance in *Maximum Overdrive*, actor Frankie Faison played Don Gaffney in a second Stephen King adaptation. What is this film?

12. In 1992, actors Emilio Estevez and Frankie Faison reunited in a second film. What is this film?

13. Before making *Maximum Overdrive*, co-producer Milton Subotsky had planned to make an anthology film based on three Stephen King short stories. This anthology, which would have been scripted by Edward and Valerie Abraham, was to have been titled *The Machines*. What three King stories would have comprised this anthology film?

14. Actress Yeardley Smith is best known for voicing a well-known animated character. Who is this?

15. Which prominent crew member lost an eye during the filming of *Maximum Overdrive*?

QUIZ #15: STAND BY ME (1986)

Screenplay by: Raynold Gideon and Bruce A. Evans
Directed by: Rob Reiner
Starring: Wil Wheaton, River Phoenix, and Corey Feldman
Columbia Pictures Corporation

Most Stephen King fans went into 1986 anxiously awaiting a Stephen King adaptation—*Maximum Overdrive*. While that film had been overhyped because of King's presence as the film's director, Rob Reiner's *Stand By Me* received little fanfare as it went into production. However, the two films quickly switched roles after their release. One *Newark Star-Ledger* reviewer wrote: "Considering what a disaster Stephen King's *Maximum Overdrive* is, directed by the best-selling horror novelist himself, it's a pleasure to report that *Stand By Me*, based on the novella *The Body*, is an almost unqualified success... [O]ne of the extremely rare films ever to convey a sense of what it is truly like to be a 12-year-old boy in rural America."

Because director Reiner had experienced difficulties in optioning the rights to King's novella, he screened the film for the author quite unsure what to expect from him. After the screening, a misty-eyed, genuinely-moved King said he had to take a few moments to compose himself. The film, based on a largely-autobiographical novella, had stirred up memories in the novelist. In his book *Stephen King Goes to Hollywood*, Jeff Conner writes, "[King] sadly noted that his three friends from that time period in his life were now all dead, unable to see themselves and their impact on his life on the screen."

EASY

1. Like his character in *Stand By Me*, actor River Phoenix died young. How old was Phoenix at the time of his death?

2. The body the boys travel to view is lying beside a river. What is the name of this river?

3. What is Gordie's last name?

4. Rob Reiner directed another King adaptation four years later. What is this film?

5. What is the name of Ace Merrill's gang?

6. What position did Gordie's brother play on the football team?

7. Like most of King's works, his novella *The Body*, which *Stand By Me* was adapted from, is set in Maine. This location was changed for the film. In what state does *Stand By Me* take place?

8. Gordie and his friends sing the theme song from a popular television series starring Richard Boone. What is this series?

9. What does Vern find lying in the street when he returns to Castle Rock?

10. Who appears in a cameo as Gordie's deceased brother?

11. *Stand By Me* was nominated for one Oscar in 1987. In what category was this nomination?

12. Whose breasts do Teddy believe to be "getting bigger"?

13. How old is Gordie when he goes on the journey with his friends?

14. Which cast members were awarded the Young Artist Awards' Jackie Coogan Award for their "outstanding contribution to youth"?

15. The name of the billiards club Ace goes to is named Irby's Billiards. What is this a reference to?

MEDIUM DIFFICULTY

1. Screenwriters Raynold Gideon and Bruce A. Evans began working as producers on their films after a spec script they had sold was reworked to the point of near-unrecognizability by director John Carpenter. What is this film?

2. How many hours do Billy Tessio and Charlie Hogan keep the body a secret from Ace?

3. What is the name of Milo Pressman's dog trained to "sic balls"?

4. Three of the four novellas in Stephen King's 1982 collection *Different Seasons* have been adapted as feature films. What is the name of the novella which has not been adapted?

5. What does Vern accidentally drop from the railroad bridge?

6. What is "Lard Ass" Hogan's first name?

7. In Stephen King's original novella, characters Royce and Steve share the surname of a filmmaker who has directed multiple King adaptations. What is this?

8. Vern wonders whether a superhero could defeat Superman in a battle. Who is this?

9. Cinematographer Thomas Del Ruth served as cinematographer on another King adaptation released one year after *Stand By Me*. What is this film?

10. What is Chris Chambers' occupation as an adult?

11. What is the name of the dead boy Gordie and his friends travel to see?

12. What is the nickname of Chris' brother?

13. What later keeps Teddy out of the military?

14. What is the name of Gordie's older brother who died in a jeep accident?

15. Producer Andrew Scheinman made his directorial debut in 1994. What film did he direct?

HARD AS HELL

1. In what year do Gordie and his friends travel to see the body?

2. What does Gordie say "friends come and go in your life" like?

3. What brand of cigarettes does Chris steal from his father?

4. On what television show did Billy Tessio learn about anonymous tip phone tracing?

5. What 1985 Albert Brooks comedy features *Stand By Me* scribe Raynold Gideon as a character named Ray?

6. What is the name of the driver Ace races while traveling to see the body?

7. What magazine does Gordie buy at the film's opening?

8. What is the name of the Catholic girl Billy Tessio complains will "only let me feel her tits"?

9. Who was the first director attached to this film?

10. What is the population of Castle Rock?

11. When combining their change, how much money do Gordie, Chris, Teddy, and Vern have collectively?

12. What is the name of the lunch lady Chris returned the stolen lunch money to?

13.   Screenwriter Bruce A. Evans made his directorial debut in 1992.
       What film did he direct?

14.   What film was actor River Phoenix making when he died on Oc-
       tober 31, 1993?

15.   What actress was River Phoenix's date the night he died at Los
       Angeles' The Viper Room?

QUIZ #16: CREEPSHOW 2 (1987)

Screenplay by: George Romero
Directed by: Michael Gornick
Starring: John Domenick, Tom Savini, and George Kennedy
New World Pictures

Creepshow 2 proved to be a misfire because of the diminished roles of both Stephen King and George Romero. Due to other obligations, neither was able to step back into their roles from the first film. Whereas George Romero had directed *Creepshow* (1982) and King had penned the script, *Creepshow 2* was adapted by Romero from stories written by King, and directed by Michael Gornick, who had served as cinematographer on the first film. In addition, the film was further damaged by shoddy animation which linked the stories. The result was a film that was high in campiness, but offered little in the way of terror, or even entertainment for that matter.

On his limited role with *Creepshow 2*, King said, "My philosophy about all this stuff is to keep out of people's way and let them do their jobs. That's pretty much what I do, and what I expect people to do for me."

Washington Post critic Richard Harrington observes, "In modern Hollywood, some films seem designed for the VCR, not for the theater. A case in point: *Creepshow 2*... Unfortunately, none of these episodes are as good as HBO's *The Hitchhiker* or the syndicated *Tales from the Darkside*. Bloodier, but not better. And yes, King makes a cameo appearance in *Creepshow 2*; his American Express ad is better."

EASY

1. Who appears in a cameo as the Creep?

2. Bill leads the bullies through a gate marked "Keep out." What is the name of the realty company who owns the land?

3. Who does Annie call "one screwed up broad"?

4. Who appears in a cameo as a semi driver?

5. After Rachel's death, why does Deke reason that the "oil slick" will leave them alone?

6. What was the destination of the doomed hitchhiker?

7. What does the undead hitchhiker repeat each time he sees Annie?

8. The actor who appears as Fatso Gribbens is the son of an actor who appeared in *Creepshow*. Who is this?

9. What does Annie rummage through her glove compartment for?

10. According to Sam White Moon, how long did it take to grow his hair?

11. Who owns the Firebird that Sam White Moon says will "fly us all to Hollywood"?

12. Which cast member was Miss New Orleans in 1931?

13. Randy and Rachel say they saw an oil slick prior to the events in "The Raft." How many years before was this?

14. After the "oil slick" attacks Deke, what is the only thing left of him?

15. Which cast member also appears in *The Sons of Katie Elder* (1965), *The Dirty Dozen* (1967), and *Cool Hand Luke* (1967)?

MEDIUM DIFFICULTY

1. In the closing credits, a 1949 article on comic books and their (lack of) effects on juvenile delinquency is quoted. In what publication did this article appear?

2. How much does Annie joke that her concussion will cost her?

3. Director Michael Gornick also worked on *Creepshow*. What was his role in that production?

4. An additional segment about a bowling team that returns from the dead was written for *Creepshow 2*, but not produced. What is the title of this segment?

5. What type of music does Annie dial on 106.5 FM?

6. How much does Annie joke that it will cost her to "make the car look like (she) just drove it out of the showroom"?

7. How many orgasms does Annie say she had?

8. What is the occupation of Annie's husband?

9. Who brings the tribe's "cherished treasures" to Ray?

10. What is Ray and Martha's surname?

11. What television show are the Cavanaughs, Fatso, and Sam White Moon all watching?

12. As the hitchhiker pulls himself up Annie's hood, he raises a sign. What does it read?

13. What does Annie's husband find lying across her dead body?

14. What does Sam White Moon speculate that the treasures of his people are worth?

15. What is Annie's surname?

HARD AS HELL

1.   What is the name of the town where Ray's store is located?

2.   *Creepshow 2* was filmed in three Maine cities. Can you name which cities?

3.   There is a picture of a cow hanging on Fatso Gribbens' wall. What is the name of the cow?

4.   What is the name of Annie's husband?

5.   What time does Annie wake up after having sex with the gigolo?

6.   One of the stories in the film was originally written for the first *Creepshow* as a possible replacement for "They're Creeping Up On You." Which story is this?

7.   Annie contemplates lying and telling her hubby that she was with another couple. What are their names?

8.   How much does Annie joke that the burned leather upholstery will cost to repair?

9.   On what highway does Annie run over the hitchhiker?

10. What does Martha say "tore this country down"?

11. What does Ray say he can smell in the air?

12. How much is the C.O.D. Billy receives?

13. What are Benjamin White Moon's final words to Old Chief Wood'nhead?

14. Where does Sam White Moon say there "ain't no dust"?

15. What does the tag on Annie's Mercedes say?

QUIZ #17: THE RUNNING MAN (1987)

Screenplay by: Steven De Souza
Directed by: Paul Michael Glaser
Starring: Arnold Schwarzenegger, Maria Conchita Alonso, and Yaphet Kotto
Taft Entertainment

Although both stories feature a man who is indeed running, this film hardly resembles the 1982 Stephen King novel (written under the pseudonym Richard Bachman) of the same title. Here King's story of one man's fight for survival is bastardized into an action film where protagonist Ben Richards (Arnold Schwarzenegger) dispatches the baddies without so much as breaking a sweat. "[The producers] obviously saw it as a book that could be adapted to fit an existing *Rambo/Terminator* kind of genre, where you're able to give Schwarzenegger the tag lines that he's known for, like 'I'll be back,'" King explained to *Cinefantastique* writer Gary Wood.

Stephen King would later discuss the film further in a *Writers' Journal* interview: "I didn't care for the way they made *The Running Man* very much. It was not very much like my book, and I liked that book a lot. I relate it to a period in my life that I enjoyed, and I remember the writing of it with great affection. I didn't like the movie, but I kept my mouth shut. Now the movie's gone, but the book rules."

EASY

1.   What is Richards' response when Killian tells him to "drop dead"?

2.   Who is the mystery guest on *The Running Man*?

3.   What are the three things Killian believes Richards possesses?

4.   What nickname is Richards unjustly given after the Bakersfield massacre?

5.   What is Richards' first name?

6.   When Richards says, "I'll be back," what is Killian's response?

7.   What does Richards use to strangle Professor Subzero?

8.   *The Running Man* is one of three films featuring both Arnold Schwarzenegger and Jesse Ventura. What are the other two?

9.   What rocker appears as Mic?

10.   What is the name of Richards' brother?

11.   Which stalker drags Richards behind a motorcycle?

12.   What does Killian say is being shipped in crates to the Justice Department?

13.   Who is the host of the aerobics show Amber watches?

14.   Which stalker is blown to pieces with dynamite?

15.   Which cast member appears in *The Dirty Dozen* (1967), *Fingers* (1978), and *Any Given Sunday* (1999)?

MEDIUM DIFFICULTY

1. What is the name of Killians' bodyguard played by Sven Thorsen?

2. What television series' reruns does Killian assure the network won't receive ratings as high as those of *The Running Man*?

3. How many people did Richards supposedly murder in Bakersfield?

4. What is the name of the game show where contestants are pursued by angry canines as they climb a rope?

5. Which cast member was an MTV veejay and composed the theme for *The Ben Stiller Show*?

6. What brand soft drink does Killian tell viewers "hits the spot"?

7. What is the name of the prisoner whose restraint collar causes his head to explode?

8. For how many years has the resistance been trying to jam the network's signal?

9. How many square blocks make up the "game zone" for *The Running Man*?

10. What is Killian's first name?

11. Who does Amber call a "dickless moron with a battery up his ass"?

12. What is the name of the fund which aids the families of fallen stalkers?

13. Who is the first stalker sent after Richards and company?

14. According to the announcer, what are "one and the same"?

15. When captured at the airport, where is Ben attempting to fly?

HARD AS HELL

1.   How many ratings points does Killian say *The Running Man* is up just after Richards' death is faked?

2.   How many rioters were present in Bakersfield?

3.   In 1988, *The Running Man* was awarded a Saturn Award. In what category was this award?

4.   What are the names of the previous season's three "winners"?

5.   What is Weiss' first name?

6.   What is Richards' identity number?

7.   What are the odds for Richards to make the next kill when he's first posted on the board in this category?

8.   Which cast member wrote the novels that *Straight Time* (1978) and *Animal Factory* (2000) were based on?

9.   What is the code to deactivate the perimeter?

10. Frank Darabont, who would later write and direct *The Shawshank Redemption* (1994) and *The Green Mile* (1999), cowrote an unproduced screenplay with *The Running Man* scribe Steven De Souza for a film which was to have starred Arnold Schwarzenegger. What is this screenplay?

11. Amy complains about the cost of a soft drink from a vending machine. How much is the can of soda she purchases?

12. What is Laughlin's first name?

13. The two "barrio foremen" are played by real-life brothers from Argentina. Who are these actors?

14. What is the name of the janitor who almost trips Killian?

15. What is the name of the prison where Richards is sent after refusing to take part in the Bakersfield massacre?

QUIZ #18: A RETURN TO SALEM'S LOT (1987)

Screenplay by: Larry Cohen and James Dixon
Directed by: Larry Cohen
Starring: Michael Moriarty, Ricky Addison Reed, and Andrew Duggan
Warner Bros.

Although filmmaker Larry Cohen has written and/or directed a number of solid, highly-entertaining films in his long and respectable career, *A Return to Salem's Lot* is not one of them. After viewing this "sequel," one has to wonder if Cohen and company ever even took the time to watch the original 1979 telefilm; this second installment has little to do with Tobe Hooper's film, and the acting is easily on par with the worst in the history of the medium.

In *Stephen King from A to Z*, author George Beahm describes *A Return to Salem's Lot* perfectly: "[A] King movie in name only, since the rights to the original *Salem's Lot* allowed a sequel. The result: This stake-in-the-heart cinematic excuse, trading largely on King's good name, in a vain attempt to draw an audience. Thankfully, this turkey never saw film release in the theaters, but in its video incarnation it comes back to life again and again. This one deserves the kiss of death."

As the tagline for *The Mangler* (1995) explains, there are fates far worse than death. Having to watch *A Return to Salem's Lot* is one of them.

EASY

1.   Filmographies sometimes confuse *A Return to Salem's Lot* writer/
     director Larry Cohen with the man who wrote *It* (1990), because
     of their similar names. Who is this screenwriter?

2.   What legendary filmmaker appears in the role of Van Meer?

3.   There is only one place in Jerusalem's Lot where the vampires can-
     not go. Where is this?

4.   Actor David Holbrook's father, Hal, appears in a film written by
     Stephen King. What is this film?

5.   What is Abner Becker's age when he is killed by Joe Weber?

6.   Prior to his return to the United States, how long has it been since
     Joe last saw his son?

7.   What is the name of Joe's ex-wife?

8.   Who is Judge Axel's grandson?

9.   What is the name of Judge Axel's wife?

10. Actor Michael Moriarty also appears on the television series *The
     Dead Zone*, based on the novel by Stephen King. What character
     does Moriarty play on the series?

11. The character Joe Weber shares his last name with the lead actor in
     another Stephen King film. Who is this?

12. Clara Hooper's surname is likely a nod to the director of *Salem's
     Lot* (1979). Who is this?

13. Two Stephen King adaptations were released the year *A Return to
     Salem's Lot* was produced. What are these?

14. When Aunt Clara says, "You make it sound so all-fire awful,"
     what is she referring to?

15. According to Van Meer, he's not a Nazi hunter. What does he then proclaim himself to be?

MEDIUM DIFFICULTY

1. Which cast member also appears in *Urban Legend* (1998), *Cruel Intentions* (1999), and *American Pie* (1999)?

2. At the airport, Joe says he has a job offer in another country. What country is this?

3. According to Judge Axel, what is the vampire race protected by?

4. What does Van Meer say keeps him alert?

5. In 1987, *A Return to Salem's Lot* was one of two Stephen King-related films featuring actor David Holbrook. What is the other film?

6. What is the name of the constable played by co-writer James Dixon?

7. How does Van Meer distract Judge Axel from impaling Jeremy?

8. How old was Joe when Cathy was seventeen?

9. Which cast member appeared in *Gone with the Wind* (1939)?

10. What is Joe's profession?

11. Joe is interested in purchasing a station wagon priced at $1,500. After Jeremy haggles with the dealer, how much does Joe wind up paying?

12. Judge Axel says if Joe loves the vampires, he will be his successor. What does he say will happen if Joe does not love them?

13. In 1973, *A Return to Salem's Lot* co-writer James Dixon served as an associate producer on two films directed by Larry Cohen. What are these?

14.   In what state was *A Return to Salem's Lot* filmed?

15.   The vampires want Joe to perform a service for them. What is this?

HARD AS HELL

1.   Director Larry Cohen's wife was delegated to producer during filming. What is her name?

2.   What is the name of the pond where Cathy takes Joe to make out?

3.   A poster for an upcoming play hangs on the wall inside the school. What is the play?

4.   *A Return to Salem's Lot* was one of four screenplays written or co-written by Larry Cohen that were produced in 1987. What are the other three films?

5.   How does Jeremy kill Cathy?

6.   What book is assigned at the high school in Jerusalem's Lot?

7.   Why does Judge Axel believe his wife has a drinking problem?

8.   The American version of the film is 101 minutes in length. How long is the Australian cut?

9.   What is the name of the man Van Meer is searching for when he arrives in Jerusalem's Lot?

10.   In what year was Clara Hooper born?

11.   Actor Michael Moriarty appears in four films written and directed by Larry Cohen. One of these is *A Return to Salem's Lot*. What are the other three films?

12.   When Joe flies home to the United States, what is his airport arrival gate?

13. *A Return to Salem's Lot* is one of twelve films written and/or directed by Larry Cohen which features actor James Dixon. What are the other eleven films?

14. Van Meer steals a bus and saves Joe and Jeremy. What bus line is advertised on the bus?

15. Jeremy stole his stepfather Alan's car. What kind of car was it?

QUIZ #19: PET SEMATARY (1989)

Screenplay by: Stephen King
Directed by: Mary Lambert
Starring: Dale Midkiff, Fred Gwynne, and Denise Crosby
Paramount Pictures

Stephen King was inspired to write *Pet Sematary*—a largely autobiographical story (except for the returning dead, of course)—after his daughter Naomi's feline was struck down on the highway. Even before he finished pulling the cat's flattened carcass from the road, King knew he was onto something. The resulting novel was one he felt too horrifying to publish. So, when he finished writing the novel in 1979, he promptly put it away in a drawer and moved on. It was not until 1983 that the novelist reconsidered and allowed Doubleday to publish *Pet Sematary*. George Romero was initially interested in directing an adaptation of the novel, but was contractually obligated elsewhere when the film was finally given a green light. Impressed with her previous work, King agreed to allow Mary Lambert to direct the film as long as it was shot in Maine and followed his screenplay.

Of the resulting film King said, "Mary did a good job. She went in and didn't flinch. In a way, that's a pretty good compliment to the way that I work... My idea is to go in there and hit as hard as you can. Mary understood that."

EASY

1. Who was the first director attached to *Pet Sematary*?

2. Louis Creed and *The Shining*'s Danny Torrance have the same nickname. What is this?

3. What does Louis do when he gets home after burying Gage in the Indian burial ground?

4. What does Ellie call Victor Pascow?

5. What was Rachel's maiden name?

6. What two things does Jud Crandall declare the Pet Sematary a "place of"?

7. What does Ellie vow to save her allowance to pay for?

8. Who appears in a cameo as "Minister"?

9. Rachel hitches a ride home in a tanker truck. What is the truck's number?

10. Where does Jud say the pain stops and the good memories begin?

11. Whose cat does Ellie say Church is not?

12. In 1990, *Pet Sematary* was nominated for a Razzie Award. In what category was this nomination?

13. What is Church's full name?

14. What does Jud predict Ellie will be as happy as?

15. How many cats were used for the role of Church in *Pet Sematary*?

MEDIUM DIFFICULTY

1. What famed musician has been portrayed by *Pet Sematary's* Dale Midkiff and *Firestarter* (1984) actor David Keith?

2. How old was Rachel when her sister died?

3. At what time does the returned-from-the-dead Rachel arrive home?

4. What is the name of Rachel's father?

5. When Jud tells Gage, "I brought you somethin'," what is he referring to?

6. Producer Ralph Singleton made his directorial debut with another King adaptation the year after *Pet Sematary* was released. What is this film?

7. What is the name of Rachel's mother?

8. On what holiday is Church killed?

9. What does Victor Pascow say the "soil of a man's heart" is?

10. What does the bumper sticker on Louis Creed's car read?

11. When Rachel attempts to telephone Louis, she gets no answer. Where does Rachel's mother suggest Louis might have gone?

12. What is the name of the Creeds' housekeeper?

13. What does Jud "step over yonder" to do as Louis buries Church?

14. Which cast member went on to appear in *Kindergarten Cop* (1990), *Apollo 13* (1995), and *Mercury Rising* (1998)?

15. Actress Denise Crosby would later appear as a recurring character named Mary Speakes on a popular television series. Prior to Crosby's arrival, Stephen King had penned an episode of this series entitled "Chinga." What is this series?

HARD AS HELL

1.   In what year was Biffer born?

2.   What is the name of Rachel's dead sister?

3.   Mary Lambert directed only one film between *Pet Sematary* and *Pet Sematary II* (1992). What is this film?

4.   Louis says his father had a saying about God. What was this?

5.   Who does Jud say introduced him to the Indian burial ground?

6.   From what disease does the Creeds' housekeeper suffer?

7.   In 2000, producer Richard P. Rubinstein served as executive producer on a film written and directed by *Tales from the Darkside: The Movie* (1990) helmer John Harrison. The film stars William Hurt, Alec Newman, and Saskia Reeves. What is this film?

8.   During World War II, Bill Baterman buried his son in the Indian burial ground. What was the name of Bill Baterman's son?

9.   What does Louis conclude to be the odds that Church will die "under the gas" while being neutered?

10.   In what year did Jud's dog Spot die (for the second time)?

11.   Brad Greenquist appears in the film as Victor Pascow. Two years after the release of *Pet Sematary*, the actor appeared in another project scripted by Stephen King. What is this film?

12.   What is the company name printed on the side of the semi that runs over Gage?

13.   Who convinced the men in town that Bill Baterman's son had to be stopped?

14.   In what city do Rachel's parents reside?

15.   Who informed Rachel Creed of her housekeeper's suicide?

QUIZ #20: TALES FROM THE DARKSIDE: THE MOVIE (1990)

Screenplay by: George Romero and Michael McDowell
Directed by: John Harrison
Starring: Deborah Harry, Christian Slater, and Steve Buscemi
Paramount Pictures

Tales from the Darkside: The Movie is an anthology film containing three tales connected by a wraparound story about a young boy who is about to be cooked by a suburban witch. One of these stories, "The Cat from Hell," was adapted from a Stephen King short story by George Romero. The other two tales and the wraparound story were fashioned by screenwriter Michael McDowell; "Lot 249" was adapted from a short story by Arthur Conan Doyle and the others are originals conceived by McDowell. Sadly, the King/Romero collaboration is the weakest of the tales, not counting the wraparound story, which is a modern day reworking of "Hansel and Gretel." McDowell's own story, "Lover's Vow," is by far the most effective of the lot.

"On television, where the syndicated *Darkside* series has been popular for some years, such tales stand alone: video-ized short stories, usually from master genre craftsmen and women," *Washington Post* critic Richard Harrington observes. "Here, three disparate tales are lumped together, with a wraparound story to excuse their telling. Unfortunately, the fact that these particular stories come from the likes of Arthur Conan Doyle and Stephen King can't overcome the direction of John Harrison and the movie's basic television-level aspirations."

EASY

1. Who is the cat's first victim in the Drogan mansion?

2. What is the name of the bartender in "Lover's Vow"?

3. "The Cat from Hell" was originally planned for another film, but was never used. What is this film?

4. Who does Lee jokingly say the mummy looks like?

5. *Tales from the Darkside: The Movie* composer/director John Harrison had previously scored two Stephen King adaptations. What were these?

6. What type of tales does captor Betty say she enjoys most?

7. In 1985, actress Rae Dawn Chong appeared alongside *The Running Man* (1987) star Arnold Schwarzenegger in a film directed by *Firestarter* (1984) helmer Mark Lester. What is this film?

8. Actor William Hickey later appeared on a television series with *Stephen King's The Shining* (1997) star Steven Weber. What is this sitcom?

9. What beverage does Edward Bellingham offer Susan?

10. How much does Drogan offer Halston to whack the cat?

11. When the mummy slices Susan's back open, what does he stuff inside her wound?

12. Where is the cat hiding when Drogan returns to the mansion?

13. The feline kills Carolyn by "stealing her breath" in "The Cat from Hell." This same occurrence is discussed in a 1985 Stephen King adaptation. What is this film?

14.   What "weapon" does Lee wield against the mummy?

15.   In "Lot 249" Lee is awarded a scholarship he earns through duplicitous means. What is the name of this scholarship?

MEDIUM DIFFICULTY

1.   What does Edward Bellingham say he was not born with?

2.   What does Wyatt say Preston's children have the metabolism of?

3.   In "The Cat from Hell," the cat's third victim shares his name with a character from *Pet Sematary* (1989). What is his name?

4.   Where does Pellingham say he saw Lee's photograph?

5.   Halston becomes angry when the demonic cat stains his shirt with blood. How much did the shirt cost Halston?

6.   What does art agent Wyatt say sincerity is bad for?

7.   Actor David Johansen had a successful career as a pop singer in the early1990s under a different name. What is this name?

8.   What does Drogan request that Halston bring him so he can watch it burn?

9.   Christian Slater's character Andy saws the mummy's limbs off. In what 1998 film does a character played by Slater saw the limbs from the bodies of a dead prostitute and a security guard?

10.   Andy is talking on the telephone just before he is killed. Who is he talking to?

11.   According to Preston's agent Wyatt, what is "being a monster"?

12.   As Andy is about to burn Edward Pellingham, what does he use for kindling before searching for the scroll?

13. What does Andy say the mummy smells like?

14. George Romero adapted Stephen King's short story "The Cat from Hell." Among Romero and King's numerous collaborations is a 1981 film which features King as a character named Hoagie Man. What is this film?

15. *Tales from the Darkside: The Movie* is one of three films released in 1990 which credits George Romero as a screenwriter. One of the others was directed by *Creepshow 2* (1987) actor/special effects makeup artist Tom Savini. What is this film?

HARD AS HELL

1. What is the name of the curator of the university museum in "Lot 249"?

2. How much does Victorine sell Preston's painting for in "Lover's Vow"?

3. What is Edward Bellingham's apartment number?

4. In what film did director John Harrison act alongside Stephen King, playing a character named Pellinore?

5. What does Wyatt say is not a "marketable commodity"?

6. What is the name of the man who referred Halston the hitman to Drogan?

7. The segment "Lot 249" is based on a story by Arthur Conan Doyle. Stephen King has penned a short story featuring Doyle's most famous creation, Sherlock Holmes. The story first appeared in *The New Adventures of Sherlock Holmes*, edited by Martin Greenberg and Carol-Lynn Rossel Waugh. What is the name of this story?

8. How many cats were killed by Drogan Pharmaceuticals in the five years they tested their wonder drug?

9.   In 1999 and 2000, actor James Remar appeared in two films directed by *Firestarter* director Mark Lester. What are these?

10. On what street is the gallery owned by Carola's friend located?

11. How many people will be in attendance at Betty's dinner party in "Wraparound Story"?

12. How long overdue are Susan's library books in "Lot 249"?

13. Director John Harrison served as first assistant director to George Romero on two films. What are these?

14. Deborah Harry appeared in another anthology film the year before *Tales from the Darkside: The Movie* was released. What is this film?

15. What medical condition did Carolyn have, which Drogan says the cat aggravated?

QUIZ #21: IT (1990)

Screenplay by: Lawrence D. Cohen and Tommy Lee Wallace
Directed by: Tommy Lee Wallace
Starring: Harry Anderson, Dennis Christopher, and Richard Masur
Warner Bros.

It took Stephen King four years to complete the 1,138 page magnum opus *It*. "I knew *It* would be long since I was trying to focus and understand all the things I had written before," King explained. "You see, my preoccupation with monsters and horror has puzzled me, too. So, I put in every monster I could think of and I took every childhood incident I had ever written of before and tried to integrate the two. And *It* grew and grew and grew..." Because of the book's length, the only way *It* could be properly adapted was in the television miniseries format.

Despite a longtime leeriness toward horror adapted to television, King sold the rights for *It* to ABC television, which would ultimately lead to a long-term relationship between the network and the author.

"I'm pleased with the way *It* turned out," King told *Fangoria*. "If I had a problem with the movie, it was that we get all the way to the end and there's this sort of Tonka toy spider. I didn't really get too behind that. But on the other hand, I suppose it would be hard to find a real one that big. So I have some sympathy for that."

EASY

1.   The Losers Club watch a 1957 horror film directed by Gene Fowler, Jr. About this film, Stephen King wrote in *Danse Macabre*: "Undoubtedly part of the reason for the movie's meteoric takeoff at the box office had to do with the liberating, vicarious feelings the movie allowed these war babies who wanted to be good... [O]n the psychological level, the picture is a series of object lessons on how to get along—everything from 'shave before you go to school' to 'never exercise in a deserted gym.'" What is this film?

2.   Where was Mike Hanlon's father stationed during World War II?

3.   Which member of the Loser's Club had aspirations of becoming a painter?

4.   What is the name of Bill's dead brother?

5.   On what 1982 horror film did *It* helmer Tommy Lee Wallace make his directorial debut?

6.   What does Pennywise take the form of the first time Ben sees him?

7.   Which cast member also appears in *The Rocky Horror Picture Show* (1975), *Legend* (1985), and *Congo* (1995)?

8.   What is Ben Hanscom's occupation?

9.   What is Mike Hanlon's occupation?

10.   What disease killed Eddie's father?

11.   What is Richie's surname?

12.   Richie's biggest fear is a werewolf. On the television series *Buffy the Vampire Slayer*, actor Seth Green, who plays Richie, plays a werewolf. What is his character's name?

13.   Ben has the cover from a magazine on which he appeared hanging inside his home. What is this magazine?

14.   Which of the Losers occasionally stutters?

15. What show is Richie scheduled to guest host before returning to Derry?

MEDIUM DIFFICULTY

1. The title of a novel by Bill Denbrough is a nod to Stephen King's *The Shining*. What is the title of this fictitious novel?

2. In what city does the adult Stan Uris reside?

3. Whose body does Officer Nell say was found near the canal?

4. From 1973 to 1976, *It* cast members John Ritter and Richard Thomas both appeared as regulars on *The Waltons*. What is the name of the character Ritter played on the series?

5. In what war was Ben's father killed?

6. Which cast member is the author of a book entitled *Games You Can't Lose: A Guide for Suckers*?

7. What is "lucky seven"?

8. Who leaves a poem on Beverly's doorstep?

9. In what city did Ben Hanscom and his mother reside before relocating to Derry?

10. Who is Henry Bowers and his gang chasing when the Losers pelt them with stones?

11. In 1981, screenwriter Lawrence Cohen adapted a novel written by Stephen King's *The Talisman* collaborator Peter Straub. What is this film?

12. What is the name of Bill's wife?

13. What nickname does Eddie insist that Richie not call him?

14. In what city does Eddie reside as an adult?

15. Who pours their soft drink on Henry Bowers at the movies?

HARD AS HELL

1.   What is the name of the movie theater in Derry?

2.   What is the name of Eddie's mother?

3.   In 1989, a horror film directed by Tommy Lee Wallace was nominated for Best Film at Fantasporto. What is this film?

4.   By what name is the film producer Bill is working for referred to?

5.   What is the name of Ben Hanscom's mother?

6.   An Easter egg hunt was held at the iron works. The iron works exploded during this event, killing many people. In what year was this tragedy?

7.   In 1991, *It* won an Emmy. In what category was this victory?

8.   What is the name of Stan Uris' wife?

9.   What time is Eddie's flight to Boston?

10. What is Georgie's middle name?

11. Brandon Crane was nominated for a Young Artist Award for his performance in *It*, but lost. Who defeated him?

12. What is the name of Beverly's father?

13. Where do Bill Denbrough and his wife reside?

14. How many Derry settlers "disappeared without a trace"?

15. When Beverly is confronted by the blood-filled balloon which emerges from the bathroom sink, her father is watching television. What series is he watching?

QUIZ #22: MISERY (1990)

Screenplay by: William Goldman
Directed by: Rob Reiner
Starring: James Caan, Kathy Bates, and Richard Farnsworth
Castle Rock Entertainment

While most people wouldn't consider *Misery* a horror novel, its subject matter is one which terrifies Stephen King. "The occupational hazard of the successful writer in America is that once you begin to be successful, then you have to avoid being gobbled up," King explained in a 1980 interview with Michael Kilgore. "America has developed this sort of cannibalistic cult of celebrity, where first you set the guy up, and then you eat him. It happened to John Lennon; it has happened to a lot of rock stars. But I wish to avoid being eaten. I don't want to be anybody's lunch. In other words, I'd love to be on the cover of *Newsweek*, but I don't want to be on the cover of *Newsweek* because I died."

Because of his strong feelings about the book, King was hesitant to sell the film rights to *Misery*. Rob Reiner, who had previously directed *Stand By Me* (1986), initially planned to executive produce the project. Reiner's decision to helm *Misery* was largely a result of King's fears of the project being botched.

"The thing that drew me to the film was not that it was a suspense thriller genre," Reiner told a *Hartford Courant* journalist in 1990. "That's not what I was interested in doing next. What I was drawn to was the theme of it, the artist's dilemma of attaining a certain success doing something, and the fear of breaking away from that in an attempt to grow and change, the fear that you'll lose your audience."

EASY

1.   What is the full name of the heroine from Paul Sheldon's "Misery" series?

2.   What does Paul say one cannot purchase in a New York City restaurant?

3.   What beverage does Annie offer Buster?

4.   What word does Paul type to show Annie that the paper she has purchased smudges?

5.   William Goldman has written or co-written four Stephen King adaptations. One of these is *Misery*. What are the other three films?

6.   What does Annie say has "no nobility"?

7.   What is the title of Paul's never-to-be-published tenth "Misery" novel?

8.   *Misery* was director Rob Reiner's second King adaptation. What was the first?

9.   Director Rob Reiner and screenwriter William Goldman collaborated for the second time on *Misery*. On what film had they previously worked together?

10. What is the name of the character Paul names after his captor in his tenth "Misery" novel?

11. What kind of car does Paul drive?

12. The line about a "guy who went mad in a hotel nearby" is a reference to another novel by Stephen King. What is this?

13. What is the name of Annie's pet pig?

14. Why does Annie reason that she's never been "so popular"?

15. Which cast member also appears in *The Big Sleep* (1946), *Key Largo* (1948), and *The Shootist* (1976)?

MEDIUM DIFFICULTY

1. The film's cinematographer would later become a successful film-maker. His directorial credits include *The Addams Family* (1991), *Get Shorty* (1995), and *Men in Black* (1997). Who is this?

2. How many days does Paul lie unconscious after his accident?

3. Who appears in an uncredited role as the helicopter pilot?

4. What does Annie say gives her the blues?

5. Warren Beatty was the first actor cast to play Paul Sheldon. However, Beatty removed himself from the project to appear in another film. What is this film?

6. Actor J.T. Walsh makes an uncredited cameo appearance as a state trooper. Three years after the release of *Misery*, Walsh would appear in a second King adaptation. What is this film?

7. What three things does Paul request upon completion of his soon-to-be-destroyed novel?

8. The scene in which Annie breaks Paul's ankles to keep him from escaping is horrifying. However, her method in King's original novel is far more gruesome. What does Annie do to keep Paul from running in the novel?

9. What is the title of Paul's "serious" novel published after his kidnapping?

10.   What was Paul's age when he published his first book?

11.   What was the "Misery" line Annie quoted when she was jailed in connection with the infants' deaths?

12.   In his first credited appearance in a film, actor James Caan played a hoodlum who helped keep a wealthy widow imprisoned on an elevator. What is this film?

13.   Who is Annie's "all-time favorite" musician?

14.   The first time Paul sits down to type on the typewriter Annie has purchased him, he repeatedly types one word. What is this?

15.   What is the title of the book in which Misery dies?

HARD AS HELL

1.   A poster for another film directed by Rob Reiner is visible inside the general store. What is this film?

2.   Annie says the practice of "hobbling" began as a means to keep enslaved miners from fleeing. Where was this?

3.   What was the occupation of Carl Wilkes?

4.   Kathy Bates originated the role of a character named Jessie Bates on stage. When this play was adapted to film, Carrie (1976) actress Sissy Spacek took over the role. What is this film?

5.   One letter is missing from the typewriter Annie purchases for Paul. What is this letter?

6.   In 1990, actress Francis Sternhagen also appeared in a film directed by Rob Reiner's father, Carl Reiner. What is this film?

7.   In Stephen King's novel, Paul parodies his work in a short story written for his closest friends as an April Fool's Day gift. In this

humorous short story, Misery has a sexual encounter with an Irish Setter. What is the title of this story?

8.   Who was Annie's favorite serial character?

9.   What is the name of the shopkeeper in Silver Creek who does not like people sitting on the benches in front of his store?

10. In what city was Annie "on the witness stand"?

11. What is the name of the lodge where Paul writes his novels?

12. What is the name of the highway patrolman played by J.T. Walsh?

13. On October 6, 2000, actor Richard Farnsworth committed suicide. Why?

14. Annie says there are only "two divine things in this world." What are these?

15. Producer Andrew Scheinman made his directorial debut in 1994 with a film featuring Timothy Busfield of *Trucks* (1997). What is this film?

QUIZ #23: GRAVEYARD SHIFT (1990)

Screenplay by: John Esposito
Directed by: Ralph S. Singleton
Starring: David Andrews, Kelly Wolf, and Stephen Macht
Paramount Pictures

Stephen King sarcastically refers to *Graveyard Shift* as a "honey of a movie if there ever was one." And he's right—the film is downright bad. Despite the best intentions of director Ralph Singleton, screenwriter John Esposito, and producer William J. Dunn, *Graveyard Shift* is a poorly-executed film which would have been more effective in a shorter format; stretching a 20-page short story into a full-length film is not the best way to produce a solid project.

King authority Stephen J. Spignesi suggests that the film's biggest flaw "is that it's too slow-paced. Also, King's characters again come off like cartoon people, and I found myself checking my watch throughout the seemingly interminable 86-minute running time of the film. Overall, I'd call the film a qualified failure (some of the performances and the sets redeem it), but its final grade can't be more than a C-." Fellow King expert George Beahm concurs: "*Graveyard Shift's* oppressively dark cinematography, its dismal location, and its subject matter makes this film a one-time viewing."

Film writer Leonard Maltin takes the criticism a step further, calling *Graveyard Shift* a "bottom-of-the-barrel, cliché-ridden shocker" that is "poorly directed, with even worse special effects."

EASY

1. The cleanup crew works in the basement during a holiday. What is this holiday?

2. When John Hall tells Warwick that he mistook him for a rat, what is Warwick's reply?

3. A mill worker names the rat that urinates on a chair. What is the name of this rat?

4. Who attacks Warwick's car with an axe?

5. What is the name of the mill's only African-American employee?

6. What is the name of the textile mill in which this story takes place?

7. What state is John Hall originally from?

8. What is the name of the exterminator's "rat terrier"?

9. The film's executive producers are married to each other. Who are they?

10. When Warwick catches Ippeston impersonating him, he advises him to audition for a television show. What is this show?

11. Actor Andrew Divoff later earned cult status when he appeared as the title character in a 1997 film and its 1999 sequel. What is the title of this Wes Craven-produced film?

12. After John Hall discovers the trapdoor, Warwick tells him to choose someone to accompany him into its corridors. Who does Hall choose?

13. What hours does the graveyard shift run at the mill?

14. One of the employees is told to clock out "permanently" after saying that he is not an exterminator. Who is this employee?

15. *Graveyard Shift* director Ralph S. Singleton has also served as a producer on two other King-related films. Can you name them?

MEDIUM DIFFICULTY

1. How much does Warwick bribe the safety inspector?

2. What is Jane's last name?

3. Six years after the release of *Graveyard Shift*, screenwriter John Esposito served as co-producer on a film written by Quentin Tarantino and Robert Kurtzman. What is this film?

4. What is the name of the agency the exterminator works for?

5. How many female characters appeared in Stephen King's original short story?

6. What does Warwick conclude that the fire hose "sure beats nailin' 'em with"?

7. What fictitious Maine town is Jane from?

8. What is the name of the second worker killed at the mill?

9. Who does Danson call "a regular bug light"?

10. What is the significance of Warwick's dialogue in the film?

11. In an obvious case of product placement, John Hall always shoots the same brand of soft drink through his slingshot. What is this brand of soft drink?

12. What does the sign beside the picker-machine advise workers to keep their hands out of?

13. What is the exterminator's name?

14. From what does Warwick say he can get "no guarantees"?

15. How much did Stephen King charge producer William J. Dunn for the rights to "Graveyard Shift"?

HARD AS HELL

1.   Whose car carries the Maine license plate number 3897N5?

2.   Jane's character did not exist in Stephen King's original short story. However, a male character with the same surname appeared. Who was this?

3.   To horror film aficionados, actor Brad Dourif is probably best known for his role in the first three installments of a popular film series. In these films, Dourif voices the evil leading character. Who is this?

4.   In what publication did King's original short story first appear?

5.   Prior to his producing *Graveyard Shift*, William J. Dunn had scouted locations for two other King adaptations. What are these?

6.   According to Jane, Warwick once offered her a promotion in exchange for sexual favors. What position did he offer her?

7.   As members of the cleanup crew spray the rats with the fire hose, a Beach Boys tune plays over the soundtrack. What is this song?

8.   *Graveyard Shift* was one of two films featuring actress Ilona Margolis in 1990. The other film features Julia Roberts and earned more than $60 million in the United States. What is this film?

9.   How long is the nonunion probationary period at the mill?

10. What was John's occupation when he was in Miami?

11. According to Warwick, when was the last time the basement was touched?

12. When the film aired on network television, it featured an alternate ending. What does John do at the close of the film in this alternate ending?

13. According to Jane, Warwick had proposed to have sex with her twice a week in exchange for a promotion. What days had he suggested?

14. Before coming to Maine, John had been employed at another textile mill. What is the name of this mill?

15. What is the name of the employee killed at the opening of the film?

QUIZ #24: SOMETIMES THEY COME BACK (1991)

Screenplay by: Lawrence Konner and Mark Rosenthal
Directed by: Tom McLoughlin
Starring: Tim Matheson, Brook Adams, and Robert Rusler
Paradise Films

Not content with the lackluster Stephen King adaptations he had already made, executive producer Dino De Laurentiis decided to produce King movies for television. After choosing to make *Sometimes They Come Back*, De Laurentiis hired veteran director Tom McLoughlin. The results were mixed. McLoughlin's direction was on-point, and the acting was above par, but *Sometimes They Come Back* was hampered by the same problems *Graveyard Shift* (1990) and *Children of the Corn* (1984) had faced before it: a short story is not generally sufficient base material for a feature-length film; adapting short stories this way often leads to the addition of unneeded fluff.

The 11th Hour film critic Linda Najera says, "My reaction to this movie—once the credits started rolling that is—was, Stephen King writes for Lifetime? I mean sure, there were really bad guys who come back from the grave and wreak havoc, but the whole point of the movie turned out to be some touchy-feely morality tale about facing up to your fears, something I still don't think the lead character did very well. But what do I expect from a TV movie, right?"

EASY

1. What is the surname of the former owners of the property on which Kate's body is discovered?

2. *Sometimes They Come Back* was the third Stephen King adaptation co-produced by Milton Subotsky. What two King films had Subotsky already made?

3. What year is Chip's graduating class?

4. What is the name of the high school where Jim Norman teaches?

5. In what city does this story take place?

6. Dino De Laurentiis executive produced *Sometimes They Come Back*. In one scene, Jim is watching another film produced by De Laurentiis. What is this film?

7. The street toughs are killed by the train because they cannot find their keys. What object adorns their key chain?

8. Actor Nicholas Sadler appeared in two films in 1991. One of these was *Sometimes They Come Back*. In the other film, Sadler appeared on-screen with Christian Slater and Anthony Quinn. What is this film?

9. How much does Lawson say he bet Vinnie that Jim's van wouldn't burn?

10. How many years elapsed between the time Jim and his family moved out of his childhood home and his return?

11. In Billy's last conversation with Jim, what does he say he does not want to end up being?

12. Brooke Adams' turn as Sally Norman marked her second appearance in a Stephen King adaptation. What was the first King film Adams starred in?

13. While staring at one of Scott's toys, Jim has a flashback. What is the toy?

14. In what city did Jim teach before moving back to his childhood hometown?

15. Finish this tagline: "With *Pet Sematary* and *Misery*, Stephen King scared you to death..."

MEDIUM DIFFICULTY

1. Before making *Sometimes They Come Back*, actors Tim Matheson and William Sanderson had already appeared together in another film. What is this film?

2. Charles Bornstein served as editor on *Sometimes They Come Back*. That same year, Bornstein edited a film directed by frequent Stephen King collaborator Mick Garris. What is this film?

3. Officer Nell's first name is changed in the film. In Stephen King's short story his name is Don. What is his name in the film?

4. What was the name of Jim and Wayne's father?

5. What "high school" are the new students said to be transfers from?

6. Screenwriters Mark Rosenthal and Lawrence Konner received a story credit on a big-budget science fiction film the same year *Sometimes They Come Back* was aired. What is this film?

7. In the film, Jim's son is named Scott. What is the name of his son in the original King short story?

8. What is the name of the first mysterious "new student" to appear in Jim's class?

9. On what short-lived television series had Robert Rusler appeared

as a regular cast member the year before *Sometimes They Come Back* was released?

10. In what magazine was the short story "Sometimes They Come Back" first published?

11. There is a major difference in the storyline between the original King short story and the film regarding the character Sally Norman. What is this?

12. How much is Wayne's library fine?

13. What significant event happened to co-producer Milton Subotsky 24 days after *Sometimes They Come Back* aired on CBS for the first time?

14. William Sanderson plays the only survivor of the street gang. What is the name of this character?

15. Officer Nell informs Jim what Milford is. What is it?

HARD AS HELL

1. In the film, Wayne's death occurred in 1963. What year did Wayne die in the original short story the film is based upon?

2. *Sometimes They Come Back* helmer Tom McLoughlin appears as "Church Guard" in a film directed by *The Stand* (1994) director Mick Garris. What is this film?

3. In 1985, actress Brooke Adams was directed by *A Return to Salem's Lot* (1987) helmer Larry Cohen. On what film did Adams and Cohen collaborate?

4. Both *Sometimes They Come Back* and *It* (1990) feature characters named Officer Nell. In *Sometimes They Come Back*, this character is played by Duncan McLeod. What actor appears as Nell in *It*?

5. What is painted on the walls of Jim and Sally Norman's bath-room?

6. On what date was Wayne killed?

7. What is the high school mascot which appears on the back of Chip's letter jacket?

8. This was the sixth King adaptation produced by Dino De Laurentiis. What was the first?

9. What is Chip's number on the football team?

10. In what three cities was *Sometimes They Come Back* filmed?

11. In what city does Chip say his brother resides?

12. Three years after appearing in this film, actor Tim Matheson made his directorial debut with a telefilm starring Peter Coyote and Courtney Thorne-Smith. What is the title of this telefilm?

13. Director Tom McLoughlin's wife, Nancy, appears in the role of Dr. Bernardi. In how many films directed by her husband does Nancy McLoughlin appear?

14. Composer Terry Plumeri scored three films in 1991. One of these was *Sometimes They Come Back*. What are the other two films?

15. Jim finds the ghosts' keys stashed away in an old cigar box. What brand of cigars is printed on the box?

QUIZ #25: GOLDEN YEARS (1991)

Screenplay by: Stephen King and Josef Anderson
Directed by: Kenneth Fink, Allen Coulter, Michael Gornick, and Stephen Tolkin
Starring: Keith Szarabajka, Felicity Huffman, and Frances Sternhagen
Laurel Entertainment

When CBS suggested that Stephen King conceive an original series for their network lineup, they envisioned something along the lines of *The Twilight Zone*. Instead, King delivered *Golden Years*, a series about an elderly man who accidentally stumbles across the proverbial fountain of youth and is then hunted by government agents.

"I envisioned this as a 14 or 15-hour series—something that would run for one entire season, with a two-hour opening episode and a bang-up two-hour finale," King explained. "I began to discuss the idea and actually show some of the work after I had written four hours' worth of script. No one was very interested." Perhaps it was this lack of interest at CBS which prompted the network's decision not to renew the series for the 1991 fall season.

On the cancellation of *Golden Years*, King says, "We were disappointed, but I was a little bit relieved too, because I had books to rewrite and a bunch of other stuff that would've had to hang fire longer if the show had been renewed. But, nobody likes to lose; nobody likes to be told, 'Go peddle your papers, this doesn't work,' when for a large segment of the audience, it actually did work."

The seven completed episodes of the series were then edited together (with a new ending slapped on) into a four-hour film for DVD release.

EASY

1. What is Harlan's age?

2. What is the name of the project spearheaded by Dr. Todhunter?

3. Who performs the theme song, "Golden Years"?

4. Actor Ed Lauter is most often associated with the film *The Longest Yard* (1974). What character did Lauter play in this film?

5. Harlan says things could be worse and that he could be "turning into a human alligator." In what Stephen King adaptation is a man transformed into a lizard?

6. What is the name of the doctor whose car is wired with explosives?

7. What is the name of Harlan Williams' wife?

8. Who appears in a cameo as an impatient bus driver?

9. Frances Sternhagen appeared in a Stephen King adaptation the year before *Golden Years* aired on television. What is this film?

10. The name of a character played by Jonathan Teague Cook references Stephen King's novel *The Stand*. What is the name of this character?

11. Who does Terry say agents of The Shop called the "best field operative who ever lived"?

12. Before being whittled into a video movie, seven episodes of *Golden Years* were filmed. How many of these were written by Stephen King?

13. What are kept in a metal box buried at the grave of Dr. Todhunter's father?

14. Director Michael Gornick had directed a Stephen King adaptation prior to his work on *Golden Years*. What is this film?

15. Which cast member also appears in *Missing* (1982), *Protocol* (1984), and *A Perfect World* (1993)?

MEDIUM DIFFICULTY

1. What is the name of the "agricultural testing facility" where Harlan is employed?

2. What is the name of General Crewes' pencil-sharpening secretary?

3. How long did it take to apply the "elderly" makeup to actor Keith Szarabajka each day?

4. What is Dr. Todhunter's first name?

5. What college did Dr. Todhunter attend?

6. What is Harlan Williams' middle name?

7. Who makes a cameo as a janitor?

8. What does Mrs. Williams conclude is not one of Terry's strong points?

9. What word does Terry define as being "too damned big and improbable to be what you're looking for"?

10. What is McGiver's rank?

11. What is the name of Harlan's ophthalmologist?

12. Terry leaves a note on a mirror in the Williams' home written in lipstick. What does it read?

13. Which cast member also appears in *Reversal of Fortune* (1990), *Hackers* (1995), and *Magnolia* (1999)?

14. What is the name of the Williams' daughter who resides in Chicago, Illinois?

15. What does Terry conclude that she and Mrs. Williams are "excellent candidates" for?

HARD AS HELL

1. When is Harlan's birthday?

2. What is the name of the gatekeeper where Harlan is employed?

3. What is Harlan's tech number?

4. What is the name of Dr. Todhunter's deceased father?

5. What is the name of Mrs. Williams' cousin who resembles the abducted corpse?

6. What is General Crewes' first name?

7. What does Dr. Todhunter call the "green stuff"?

8. What is the name of the assistant who informs investigators that Dr. Todhunter ordered him to ignore override warnings?

9. On what highway do Pennsylvania state troopers find three kids joy riding in Terry's car?

10. Who was Terry Spann's partner when she was employed by The Shop?

11. In what year was Harlan married?

12. What is the name of Francie's seeing-eye dog?

13. What two movies are showing at the mall where Terry switches cars?

14. What does Terry remark will "boil your eyeballs"?

15. What is the name of the mall where Terry steals the hearse?

QUIZ #26: SLEEPWALKERS (1992)

Screenplay by: Stephen King
Directed by: Mick Garris
Starring: Brian Krause, Madchen Amick, and Alice Krige
Columbia Pictures Corporation

Sleepwalkers was the first story Stephen King wrote expressly for film. Having seen helmer Mick Garris' work on *Psycho IV: The Beginning* (1991)—another film which dealt with an incestuous mother-son relationship—King campaigned to work with Garris, who he later discovered was a fan of his. King and Garris worked well together and developed a working relationship which would continue for (at least) another decade. However, *Sleepwalkers* didn't turn out the way King and Garris had envisioned it due to scissor-happy executives at Columbia Pictures.

"In its original cut, it was a fantastic horror movie," King later said. "Mick didn't have enough power, and I didn't have enough time, to stop Columbia from whittling it down to something about two critical cuts above *Dr. Giggles.*" On his collaborator King observes, "Mick has an understanding of Americana, and I like that. He has as good a visual sense as Steven Spielberg, and I like that too."

Cuts or no cuts, film critics had little if anything positive to say about *Sleepwalkers*. *USA Today* critic Susan Wloszczyna was especially harsh: "One can understand why horror honcho Stephen King was tired of screenwriting hacks turning his mega-selling stories into multiplex sludge. After all, as *Sleepwalkers* amply demonstrates, ol' Cujo breath can come up with his own lousy script, thank you."

EASY

1.   Who appears in the film as Captain Soames?

2.   Producer Michael Grais cowrote a 1982 film directed by *Salem's Lot* (1979) helmer Tobe Hooper. What is this film?

3.   Charles writes a story about his plight. In the story, what is the name of the character who represents Charles?

4.   What type of animals gather outside the Brady's home?

5.   How many films directed by Mick Garris feature Stephen King as an actor?

6.   In Charles' class, a student is caught passing a drawing of two people having sex. What three word proposal is written on this picture?

7.   Mick Garris' wife Cynthia appears in the film as a dispatcher. What is the dispatcher's name?

8.   John Landis appears as an actor in three films released in 1992. One of these is *Sleepwalkers*. Another, written and directed by Henry Jaglom, is about a filmmaker named Dean. What is this film?

9.   What do police find in the hair of the film's first human victim?

10.   What is Deputy Simpson's first name?

11.   What is Charlie's favorite song?

12.   Where in California does the film begin?

13.   What is the name of the Indiana town where the Bradys have just moved?

14. Filmmaker John Landis has appeared in three Stephen King films. One of these is *Sleepwalkers*. What are the other two films?

15. Who appears in the film as a cemetery caretaker?

MEDIUM DIFFICULTY

1. Who says, "Nobody likes a smartass"?

2. Actress Madchen Amick came to the public's attention after a stint on a television series which has since developed a tremendous cult following. On this series, Amick played Shelly Johnson. What is this series?

3. As he is chased by Deputy Simpson, Charles speeds past a school bus, almost running down a student. What is the name of the school stenciled on the side of the bus?

4. What two filmmakers appear in cameos as forensic technicians?

5. Actress Alice Krige was no stranger to horror aficionados. She played the memorable Eva Galley in a 1981 horror film featuring Fred Astaire, Melvin Douglas, and Douglas Fairbanks, Jr. What is this film?

6. What does Charles ram into Deputy Simpson's ear, making what he calls "cop-kabob"?

7. What is the name of the fictitious Ohio city where Charles claims he's from?

8. *Sleepwalkers* won four awards at the 1992 Fantafestival. In what categories were these awards?

9. Who teaches Charles' fourth-hour English class?

10. Who appears in a cameo as a lab technician?

11. Who appears in a cameo as a lab assistant?

12. Five years after his appearance in *Sleepwalkers*, Clive Barker played an anesthesiologist in another King film. What is this film?

13. *Scream Dreams* is part of a double bill at the local theater. What is the second film on the bill?

14. Producers Michael Grais and Mark Victor share screenwriting credits on a number of films. One of these is a Steven Seagal actioner directed by Dwight H. Little. What is this film?

15. At the beginning of the film, who is Charles gazing at in the high school yearbook?

HARD AS HELL

1.   When the film aired on television in Hong Kong, its title was changed. What was the new title?

2.   What book defines "sleepwalker" at the opening of the film?

3.   At what address do Charles and Mary Brady reside?

4.   The house shown as the exterior of the Brady's home was used on a popular seventies' television series. What is this series?

5.   What is the name of the theater where Tanya works?

6.   What is the name of the graveyard where Charles attacks Tanya?

7.   Mark Hamill makes an uncredited cameo appearance as a police officer. What is the name of this police officer?

8.   What does Charles' English instructor call "mercenary"?

9.   Who appears in a cameo as Officer Wilbur?

10. What does Charles order at the theater snack bar?

11.   Cynthia Garris, who plays Laurie, appears in eight films. How many of these were directed by her husband, Mick Garris?

12.   What is the name of Deputy Simpson's cat?

13.   What is the name of the cat that appears in the film as Deputy Simpson's cat?

14.   Mary cooks roasted chicken with cranberry sauce. What does she prepare for dessert?

15.   King has stated that *Sleepwalkers* was inspired by a member of his family. Who was this?

QUIZ #27: PET SEMATARY 2 (1992)

Screenplay by: Richard Outten
Directed by: Mary Lambert
Starring: Edward Furlong, Anthony Edwards, and Clancy Brown
Paramount Pictures

Three years after the $60 million success of *Pet Sematary* (1989), director Mary Lambert returned with this second installment, this time unassisted by Stephen King. Here, screenwriter Richard Outten simply plants a new family into the town of Ludlow, leading them down the familiar path the Creed family had taken before them.

As far as sequels to King adaptations go, *Pet Sematary 2* ranks among the best of them. However, this dubious distinction was hardly enough to satisfy critics. *Washington Post* scribe Richard Harrington wrote that the film "feels like an elongated *Tales from the Crypt*, though the annoying heavy-metal soundtrack feels like a seepage from *Headbanger's Ball*. The first time around, Lambert went for terror; this time it's mostly hardy-har-horror." The authors of *Variety Portable Movie Guide* took their criticism a step further, saying, "*Pet Sematary 2* is about fifty percent better than its predecessor, which is to say it's not very good at all."

EASY

1. What is the name of Jeff's kitten?

2. When Drew's mother allows him to go out on Halloween night, she imposes a curfew. What time must Drew be home by?

3. Chase Mathews asks Gus why he dug up the corpse of his wife. What is the sheriff's reply?

4. In 1985, actor Anthony Edwards appeared alongside *The Shawshank Redemption* (1994) star Tim Robbins in a film directed by *Misery* (1990) helmer Rob Reiner. What is this film?

5. What is Chase Mathews' occupation?

6. As Jeff chases Clyde on his bicycle, they pass a mailbox which bears a familiar surname. This name is also visible on a headstone in the cemetery. What is this name?

7. In what county is Gus sheriff?

8. Stephen King insisted *Pet Sematary* be filmed in Maine. What state was this sequel filmed in?

9. Edward Furlong appeared alongside *The Running Man* (1987) actor Arnold Schwarzenegger and *Children of the Corn* (1984) star Linda Hamilton in a film which grossed more than $500 million worldwide the year before *Pet Sematary 2* was released. What is this film?

10. For Halloween, Jeff dresses like a famous film character. Who?

11. What is Renee Mathews' maiden name?

12. Two years before serving as producer on *Pet Sematary 2*, Ralph S. Singleton made his directorial debut helming a Stephen King adaptation. What is this film?

13.   What is Drew's Halloween costume?

14.   What is Chase's reasoning for Zowie's not having a heartbeat?

15.   Two years after *Pet Sematary 2*, actor Clancy Brown appeared as Byron Hadley in a Stephen King adaptation. What is this film?

MEDIUM DIFFICULTY

1.   What is the name of the Mathews' maid?

2.   What is Stephen King's title on *Pet Sematary 2*?

3.   What is Drew's reasoning for Zowie's not having a heartbeat?

4.   What part of Jeff's anatomy does Clyde threaten to remove with the spinning spokes of a bicycle?

5.   The name Clyde Parker pays homage to a popular 1967 film about a character named Clyde and a character with the surname Parker. What is this film?

6.   What is the cargo of the truck that hits Drew and his mother?

7.   According to Clyde, Ellie Creed could only say two words after the death/rebirth of her family. What were they?

8.   *Pet Sematary 2* was one of two films produced by Ralph S. Singleton in 1992. What is the other film?

9.   When reciting the Miranda Law to Drew, he informs the youngster that he won't need an attorney. Why?

10.   On Gus' sign advertising his rabbits, he suggests three uses for the hares. What are these?

11.   *Pet Sematary 2* was one of two Stephen King-related films on which Russell Carpenter served as cinematographer in 1992.

However, King had nothing to do with either story. What is the other film?

12. How many boxes containing the wardrobe of the dead Renee Mathews do movers carry into the house?

13. What is Gus' last name?

14. Drew makes Jeff promise something. What is this?

15. What is the name of Drew's mother?

HARD AS HELL

1. In what year was Renee Mathews born?

2. According to Gus, what is life full of?

3. How much does one of Gus' rabbits cost?

4. What is the name of the vet who tells Chase about the dead cat, Church?

5. What is the name of the lab specialist who examines Zowie's blood?

6. Producer Ralph S. Singleton won an Emmy for his work on a hit television series in 1986. What is this series?

7. Shortly after shooting *Pet Sematary 2*, actor Anthony Edwards married someone else involved with the production. Who is this?

8. *Pet Sematary 2* is one of two films written or co-written by Richard Outten that was released in 1992. On the other film, Outten shared writing credits with several scribes, including Ray Bradbury. What is this film?

9. A song by rock group L7 appears in *Pet Sematary 2*. This song would later appear in *Natural Born Killers* (1994), which was produced by *Apt Pupil* (1998) producer Don Murphy. What is this song?

10. Director Mary Lambert's sister is a United States Senator from Arkansas. What is her name?

11. *Pet Sematary 2* was nominated for an award at the 1993 Avoriaz Fantastic Film Festival. What award was this?

12. One year after appearing as a priest in *Pet Sematary 2*, actor Robert Easton played Lester Pratt in a Stephen King adaptation. What is this film?

13. Zowie attacks Gus in the pet cemetery just as Gus is about to strike Drew. What was Gus about to strike his stepson with?

14. In 1976, producer Ralph S. Singleton served as assistant director on two films which were later named to the American Film Institute's list of the top 100 American films ever made. What are these films?

15. Jeff has a nightmare that someone is peering in his bedroom window. Who is this?

QUIZ #28: THE DARK HALF (1993)

Screenplay by: George Romero
Directed by: George Romero
Starring: Timothy Hutton, Amy Madigan, and Michael Rooker
Orion Pictures Corporation

The Dark Half is a very personal novel for Stephen King (and likely thera-peutic in some ways) because it deals with a best-selling author who is blackmailed when a fan discovers that he's been writing books under a pseudonym. The novelist then decides to kill off his pseudonym, George Stark, but quickly finds that George is not pleased with this idea. On the conception of the novel King says, "I started to play with the idea of multiple personalities and then I read somewhere, probably in the case of the twin doctors that the film *Dead Ringers* was based on, that sometimes twins are imperfectly absorbed in the womb and I thought, 'Now wait a minute. What if this guy is the ghost of a twin that never existed?' After that, I was able to wrap the whole book around that spine and it made everything a lot more coherent."

When King's friend and former collaborator George Romero sug-gested that he adapt *The Dark Half*, the novelist happily agreed. The re-sult is a highly-entertaining adaptation which is loyal to King's original source material. "I tried to be as faithful as possible to the book, but there are a few changes," Romero said. "For instance, Tim (Matheson) plays both Beaumont and Stark, but that change was done with Steve's input. I told him we were going to do it, that the studio liked the idea too, and he agreed. It makes it visually clearer in a two-hour time frame to have one actor play both roles. It's a difficult concept to accept—just who is George Stark? Most people, when I tell them the story, are not sure if Stark is a monster or his twin. This approach locks it in harder without having any negative effects on the internal workings of the story."

EASY

1.   How many years has it been since Thad stopped smoking?

2.   What is the significance of Thad's short story, "Here There Be Tygers"?

3.   Cinematographer Tony Pierce-Roberts was nominated for the Best Cinematography Oscar twice. For what films was he nominated?

4.   What Greek word does Reggie DeLesseps define as "conductors of souls between the land of the living and the kingdom of the dead"?

5.   During filming, there was one more trailer on the lot than there were actors assigned trailers. Why was this?

6.   A film released the year before *The Dark Half* also features both Timothy Hutton and Amy Madigan. What is this film?

7.   Who do the NYPD officers find stuffed inside Fred Clawson's mouth?

8.   What song plays in Thad's dream as he meets George Stark for the first time?

9.   *The Dark Half* editor Pasquale Buba appears as an actor in two films directed by George Romero. What are these?

10.   The film was shot in 1990, but was not released until 1993. Why?

11.   What is the inscription on Stark's grave?

12.   What is the phrase that appears on the back of Stark's automobile?

13. Rohn Thomas and Larry John Meyers, the actors who appear as Doctors Albertson and Pritchard, appeared together in a second film in 1999. What is this film?

14. While typing his short story, "Here There Be Tygers," Thad experiences his first attack. In what year is this?

15. Actor Rohn Thomas appeared in a second King adaptation the following year. What is this film?

MEDIUM DIFFICULTY

1. Which of Thad's children does he label a "born editor"?

2. What is the name of Thad's wife?

3. What significant change did screenwriter George Romero make from the novel regarding the character Reggie DeLesseps?

4. Who appears in a cameo as Trudy Wiggins?

5. *The Dark Half* was one of three films released in 1993 on which Tony Pierce-Roberts served as cinematographer. One of these films was nominated for eight Academy Awards the following year, including Best Picture, Best Director, and Best-Adapted Screenplay. What is this film?

6. What Mississippi town is the home of George Stark?

7. Timothy Hutton made his feature directorial debut in 1998 on a film starring Kevin Bacon and Mary Stuart Masterson. What is this film?

8. Thad explains to his lecture group that each person has two people inside them. According to Thad, who are these two people?

9. According to his gravestone, what year was George Stark born?

10. What does Reggie ask Thad to wear when he returns to work so she can recognize him?

11. What do the police find scrawled in blood on Clawson's wall?

12. Fred Clawson discovers that George Stark is a pseudonym for Thad Beaumont. Who is erroneously credited with the discovery that Richard Bachman was a pseudonym for Stephen King?

13. What are the names of Thad Beaumont's two children?

14. The window washer outside Rick Cowley's apartment window is holding a sign. What does it read?

15. Which of the following actors was not considered for the role of Thad Beaumont: Ed Harris, Gary Oldman, Tom Hanks, or Willem Dafoe?

HARD AS HELL

1. Timothy Hutton received his first writing and directing credits for an episode of *Amazing Stories* (on which frequent King-director Mick Garris worked as story editor). What is the title of this episode?

2. What is the full name of the "Machine" character who appears in George Stark's novels?

3. In *The Dark Half*, there is a discussion regarding Thad Beaumont's use of a fake author photograph on the George Stark books. Stephen King's pseudonym, Richard Bachman, also used a phony photo on the hardcover edition of *Thinner*. The man whose photograph appears on that work is actually a real estate broker from St. Paul, Minnesota. What is his name?

4. *The Dark Half* won three awards at the 1993 Fantafestival. In what categories were these victories?

5. What are the names of the real-life twins who appear in the film as Thad Beaumont's children?

6. A framed poster from a Broadway play hangs inside Miriam Cowley's apartment. What is this play?

7. What is the title of the novel George Stark forces Thad to collaborate on?

8. What is the name of the convenience store clerk who overhears Thad speaking on the telephone with George Stark?

9. What is the address of Miriam's apartment?

10. What is the address of Rick Cowley's apartment?

11. An intern becomes ill during Thad's brain surgery. What is the name of this intern?

12. *The Dark Half* was the second film on which George Romero's wife, Christine, served as an associate producer. What was the first?

13. What is the name of the photographer who is beaten to death with his own prosthetic leg?

14. What is the name of the *People* scribe who interviews Thad Beaumont?

15. What time was Thad's flight from Bangor to New York City?

QUIZ #29:
THE TOMMYKNOCKERS (1993)

Screenplay by: Lawrence D. Cohen
Directed by: John Power
Starring: Jimmy Smits, Marg Helgenberger, and John Ashton
Konigsberg/Sanitsky Company

Few Stephen King fans will list *The Tommyknockers* as one of their favorite novels. The author's "gadget novel"—a morality play about the evils of technology—is one of few missteps in his extremely prolific career. *Publishers Weekly* blasted the work: "Taking a whole town as his canvas, King uses too-broad strokes, adding cartoonlike characters and unlikely catastrophes like so many logs on fire; ultimately, he loses all semblance of style, carefully-structured plot or resonant meaning, the hallmarks of his best writing." But let's be honest here, flawed King is better than most writers' finest work.

After the success of the miniseries *It* in 1990, King and ABC Television agreed to adapt *The Tommyknockers* with the same production company. *It* screenwriter Lawrence D. Cohen also returned to take on the writing chores. *DVDLaser* critic Doug Pratt comments, "The special effects could have been a little stronger, but the conclusion is quite satisfying and there are many interesting characters and moments of tension to keep the viewer attentive during the interim."

EASY

1. *The Tommyknockers* marked E.G. Marshall's second appearance in a Stephen King adaptation. What is the other film Marshall appeared in?

2. What is the unanimous decision regarding Joe made by the three television panelists?

3. In 1993, actor Robert Carradine also appeared in a made-for-television film directed by John Carpenter. What is this film?

4. What is the name of Bobbi's dog?

5. Nine years before appearing in *The Tommyknockers*, actress Joanna Cassidy won a Golden Globe award for her performance on a comedy television series. What is this series?

6. What is Bobbi's nickname for Jim Gardner?

7. Nancy Voss says that some people refer to her lipstick as "Final Passion." However, she calls it something else. What?

8. What is the name of the magician Hilly aspires to be like?

9. In what country was *The Tommyknockers* filmed?

10. The actress who plays Nancy Voss appeared in more than eighty adult films between 1984 and 1986. Who is this?

11. In 1981, screenwriter Lawrence D. Cohen adapted a novel by Stephen King's *The Talisman* collaborator Peter Straub. What is this film?

12. Nancy Voss erases a policeman named Jingles. In another Stephen King adaptation, Mr. Jingles is the name of a mouse. What is this film?

13. In a February 1997 episode of a popular television series, actor Robert Carradine reunited with *Tommyknockers* costar Jimmy

Smits. In this episode, Carradine plays a character named Gerard Salter. What is this series?

14. The scene in which a soft drink vending machine murders Butch Duggan is reminiscent of a scene in another King adaptation in which a soft drink vending machine attacks a little league baseball team. What is this film?

15. After writing the novel *Misery*, Stephen King experienced the worst bout of writer's block in his career. However, this writer's block ended when King sat down and penned a short story in a single sitting. What was this short story which first appeared in *Midnight Graffiti*?

MEDIUM DIFFICULTY

1. What is Bryant Brown's nonsensical motto?

2. Before Stephen King integrated elements of it into *The Tommyknockers*, a short story featuring the character Becka Paulson was published in *Rolling Stone* magazine in 1984. What is the name of this story?

3. Elt Barker modifies a soft drink vending machine. What fictitious brand of soft drink is advertised on the machine?

4. What two things does Hilly say he hates?

5. One of the film's two cinematographers made his debut working on *Mad Max* (1979). Who is this?

6. What does Nancy Voss leave on Joe Paulson's grave?

7. What are the Big Injun Woods also now known as?

8. *The Tommyknockers* was the fourth collaboration between director John Power and cinematographer Dan Burstall. What are the other three films they had worked together on previously?

9.   Which cast member also appears in *Beverly Hills Cop* (1984), *King Kong Lives* (1986), and *Midnight Run* (1988)?

10.   What reason does Joe give for leaving the search party?

11.   What is Raging Angel?

12.   Davey insists he be paid for his assisting Hilly with his big magic trick. What does Hilly agree to pay Davey?

13.   Who appears as Pearl?

14.   Ruth Merrill's dolls chant something repeatedly as they close in around her. What is this?

15.   Which cast member also appears in *The Caine Mutiny* (1954), *12 Angry Men* (1957), and *Interiors* (1978)?

HARD AS HELL

1.   What is the name of the town in which the story takes place?

2.   Where does Nancy Voss say her gadget sent the two state troopers?

3.   A news anchor appears in the film as Chaz Stewart, the game show host who convinces Becka to murder her husband. Who is this?

4.   In what year was Joe Paulson born?

5.   What does Nancy Voss say she likes a man who knows the value of?

6.   The version of the film released on video runs 120 minutes. How long was the original version which aired on television in 1993?

7.   The townsfolk chant something repeatedly as Bobbi addresses them at the Town Hall. What is this?

8.   What does Bobbi call her "telepathic typewriter"?

9.   Actor Cliff De Young once performed a song which climbed to number seventeen on the *Billboard* Hot 100 pop charts in 1974. The song, "My Sweet Lady," was written for a popular telefilm the actor/musician appears in. What is this film?

10. Who is "One More Mile" dedicated to?

11. Prior to working with Jimmy Smits on *The Tommyknockers*, actress Annie Corley had appeared on two television series with him. What are these?

12. What is the name of the novel Bobbi dictated mentally?

13. In 1995, actress-turned-musician Traci Lords saw two of her songs, "Fallen Angel" and "Control," selected to appear on the soundtrack albums of two Hollywood films. What are these?

14. The producer of *As Summers Die* (1986) and *The Last Don* (1997) appears in a cameo as a neurologist. Who is this?

15. What is Joe Paulson's occupation?

QUIZ #30: NEEDFUL THINGS (1993)

Screenplay by: W.D. Richter
Directed by: Fraser Clark Heston
Starring: Max von Sydow, Ed Harris, and Bonnie Bedelia
Columbia Pictures/New Line Cinema

Stephen King was driving down a country road through the small town of Brewer, Maine, when the initial idea for *Needful Things* came to him. "For a long time, I worked with simply one image," King said. "A little boy throwing mud at sheets. And I knew that whoever came home and discovered the mud on the sheets was going to think someone else did it. That was all I really had to work with." From there *Needful Things* grew into a morality play about the value (or the lack thereof) of possessions.

The film adaptation of *Needful Things* landed in theaters just two years after King's novel had first appeared in bookstores. The film was written by W.D. Richter and marked the directorial debut of Fraser Clarke Heston, the son of Charlton Heston. While Richter's script remained faithful and Heston's direction was passable, the film fell victim to severe cuts. (A "director's cut" containing restored footage later aired on television.)

Needful Things was far from a critical favorite. *Chicago Sun-Times* writer Roger Ebert called the project "yet another one of those films based on a Stephen King story that inspires you to wonder why his stories don't make better films. For every one that does, there are three that don't. In this case, the problem is that the characters are unattractive and the plot, once it reveals itself, lacks any surprises. You know you're in trouble when a movie's about Satan, and his best lines are puns."

EASY

1. Why isn't Brian Rusk in school the day Leland Gaunt's shop opens?

2. Who does Norris Ridgewick believe Gaunt looks like?

3. What does Polly say she has to know?

4. What nickname does Danforth Keeton III despise?

5. What 1965 film features both Max von Sydow and director Fraser Clarke Heston's father, Charlton Heston?

6. What is Nettie's surname?

7. *Needful Things* was the second Stephen King adaptation actor J.T. Walsh appeared in. What was the first?

8. *Needful Things* was the second Stephen King adaptation actress Bonnie Bedelia appeared in. What was the first?

9. Who splatters turkey feces all over Wilma Jerzyck's clean sheets?

10. What is the name of Nettie's dog?

11. Who hangs tickets "signed" by Norris Ridgewick inside Danforth's home?

12. What does Brian Rusk scream before attempting suicide?

13. Why doesn't Polly Chalmers shake hands?

14. What is the name of the baseball announcer Brian imagines as he pelts Wilma's home?

15. Who does Gaunt say he knew well that "died badly"?

MEDIUM DIFFICULTY

1.   Whose baseball card does Brian Rusk say is worth "over $65"?

2.   What is the name of Danforth Keeton's business?

3.   Who kills Nettie's dog?

4.   What does Gaunt say a young woman is entitled to?

5.   What is Brian Rusk's age?

6.   What is the name of the bartender who throws Hugh Priest out of the bar?

7.   *Needful Things* was awarded a Saturn Award in 1994. In what category was this award given?

8.   The character Alan Pangborn also appears in *The Dark Half* (1993). What actor appears as Pangborn in that film?

9.   From what country does Gaunt say the necklace he gives Polly originated?

10.   What does the note that accompanies the rat trap Norris receives say?

11.   What is the name of Nettie's deceased husband?

12.   What announcer lends his voice for Danforth's imaginary horse races?

13.   What year is the Topps Mickey Mantle card Brian Rusk purchases?

14.   What does Wilma Jerzyck accuse Nettie of breaking just before attacking her with a meat cleaver?

15.   What does the bumper sticker Father Meehan asks Gaunt to hang in his window read?

HARD AS HELL

1. What slogan is printed on the "welcome to Castle Rock" sign?

2. What year does Gaunt tell Hugh it is "all over again"?

3. Actress Bonnie Bedelia's picture appears on the cover of the book, *The Films of Don Shebib*, by Piers Handling. On what 1973 film did Bedelia collaborate with Shebib?

4. What Bible verse is quoted on the letter from the "Concerned Baptist Men of Castle Rock"?

5. What is the name of the Catholic church where Father Meehan resides?

6. *Needful Things* is one of two films featuring actors Ed Harris and J.T. Walsh. What is the other film?

7. What does Alan Pangborn find with the money on the desk in his boat?

8. How much did Danforth borrow from the town's petty cash fund?

9. On what 1996 film did *Needful Things* helmer Fraser Clark Heston direct his father, Charlton Heston?

10. What city does Gaunt say he's from?

11. How much does Gaunt call "half the price" for Brian's baseball card?

12. A year after his turn in *Needful Things* as Deputy Norris Ridgewick, actor Ray McKinnon appeared in another Stephen King adaptation, *The Stand* (1994). What character does McKinnon play in *The Stand*?

13. In what city was Pangborn a police officer before relocating to Maine?

14. A headline is shown reading: "Two Killed in Castle Rock Double Murder." What is the name of the newspaper?

15. What 1984 cult film was directed by *Needful Things* scribe W.D. Richter?

QUIZ #31: CHILDREN OF THE CORN II: THE FINAL SACRIFICE (1993)

Screenplay by: Gilbert Adler and A.L. Katz
Directed by: David Price
Starring: Terence Knox, Paul Scherrer, and Ryan Bollman
Dimension Films

In this second installment, authorities finally discover that the good folks of Gatlin, Nebraska, have been murdered by their children (only eleven years after the massacre!). When a tabloid reporter and his son arrive in Gatlin, they soon discover that the terror is far from over. In his *Movie & Video Guide*, critic Leonard Maltin writes, "Once again, the kids of an isolated Nebraska farming community are killing the adults and nobody knows why. Nobody knows the reason for this movie's existence, either."

When asked by an *Entertainment Weekly* reporter about his thoughts on the *Children of the Corn* franchise, Stephen King asked, "The long answer or the short answer?" When the reporter requested the long answer, King responded flatly, "They all sucked." Who can argue with that?

EASY

1.   How were Lacey's parents killed?

2.   What is Lacey's mode of transportation?

3. Who calls the children "bastards" and "little shits" when they burn the church?

4. How does Frank Redbear know John Garrett's identity the first time they meet?

5. What does Reverend Hollings say "is a pestilence"?

6. During the town meeting, who suggests that something might have taken control of the children?

7. Where is Danny from?

8. What is Mrs. Burke's first name?

9. According to Micah, what must the "sower of seeds" be?

10. What is the name of the boy who strikes Doc Appleby with a baseball bat?

11. What is the name of Angela's deceased aunt?

12. While Lacey and Danny are making out in the cornfield, Lacey complains that she is lying on top of something. What is this?

13. What is the name of the bed and breakfast where John and Danny stay?

14. According to Danny, his mother only curses when talking about one subject. What is this?

15. What is Doc Appleby's first name?

MEDIUM DIFFICULTY

1. What does Micah ask Danny to chant with the other children?

2. Something is put inside Doc Appleby's mouth after he is killed. What is this?

3. What is the film's alternate title?

4. What is the name of the man Micah causes to bleed during a church service?

5. Actor Terence Knox made his big screen debut playing a character known as "Roose" in a 1980 film directed by Robert Zemeckis. What is this film?

6. John wrote a "news" story about President John F. Kennedy's "secret marriage." Who did the story allege Kennedy was wed to?

7. What does Doc Appleby say is John's problem?

8. On what short-lived television series did actor Paul Scherrer appear as a regular named Eric Olander?

9. What happened to Mrs. Burke fifteen years ago?

10. How much did Angela earn per year working as a sales executive?

11. What did Micah's father say every sin deserved?

12. Inside what towering structure does Danny remember vomiting?

13. What was John's age when Danny's mother was impregnated?

14. How many miles is Hemingford from Gatlin?

15. What is the name of the Channel 12 cameraman murdered in the cornfield?

HARD AS HELL

1. What is the scientific name John Redbear provides for the "green stuff" on the corn?

2. Who does Doc Appleby immediately telephone after his visit from John?

3. What is the name of Mrs. Burke's cat?

4. What will John's age be in April?

5. According to Doc Appleby, Mrs. Burke's husband left her for a waitress. Where was the waitress from?

6. How much does John say he paid for his shoes?

7. What is the name of Danny's "shithead" stepfather?

8. What is the cost to stay for one night at Angela's bed and breakfast?

9. What is the name of the tabloid newspaper John writes for?

10. On what day does Lacey inform Danny the next bus will arrive in Hemingford?

11. Frank Redbear is a college professor. In which department does he work?

12. How much does John Garrett weigh?

13. *Children of the Corn II: The Final Sacrifice* was nominated for an International Fantasy Film Award in 1993. In what category was this nomination?

14. On what cable television series did actor Terence Knox make a cameo on in 2001 as a porn star named Larry Wad?

15. What is the name of the publication for which John wrote before having a "difference in opinion" with his editor?

QUIZ #32: THE STAND (1994)

Screenplay by: Stephen King
Directed by: Mick Garris
Starring: Gary Sinise, Molly Ringwald, and Jamey Sheridan
Laurel Entertainment

For many years, various filmmakers, from George Romero to John Boorman, discussed bringing Stephen King's most beloved work, *The Stand*, to the screen. However, the filmmakers were always faced with one challenge: because of the length of King's book (823 pages when originally published in 1978, 1,153 pages in the "uncut" version released in 1990) and the number of central characters, there was no way to properly adapt *The Stand* into a two-to-three-hour film. For a while, King and Romero considered making the film in two separate installments. However, this was decided against because of the danger that audiences might not like the first film, and then a second would never be produced. Finally, ABC Television offered to produce *The Stand* as a $28 million miniseries, and King agreed.

By all accounts, *The Stand* would ultimately be a success. Perhaps one of the reasons the film rises above the medium is because of director Mick Garris' dislike for television movies. "[B]efore I did *The Stand*, I'd maybe watched one miniseries in my life," Garris said. "After *The Stand*, I've watched that and *The Shining*, and maybe one other miniseries. I know it's biting the hand that feeds me, but I'm hoping that not being a TV watcher can possibly elevate, or at least remove it, from the standards of television."

EASY

1. What pricey actor was first approached to play the role of Flagg?

2. What hymn does Fran Goldsmith sing after the death of her father?

3. Actor Sherman Howard, who appears as Dr. Dietz, is perhaps best known to horror aficionados for his role in George Romero's *Day of the Dead* (1985). What character does Howard play in that film?

4. What is the name of Ray Booth's sister?

5. In what city is the R.E.M. concert Fran and Amy plan to attend?

6. On what highway do Fran and Stu see crosses in their dreams?

7. What does Stu say "country don't mean"?

8. When director John Boorman was attached to *The Stand*, he brought in a screenwriter he had worked with a couple of times already. This writer then proceeded to adapt *The Stand* in an unorthodox manner, writing the script backwards. Who was this?

9. Stephen King appears as Teddy Weizak. Another character named Weizak appears in an earlier King (novel and) adaptation. What is this film?

10. What pro basketballer plays a character known as "The Monster Shouter"?

11. Of what does Larry Underwood comment, "We like to call 'em scouts"?

12. In what East Texas town is Hap's Service Station located?

13. What actor appears uncredited as General Starkey?

14. Kathy Bates' character Rae Flowers is depicted quite differently in Stephen King's original novel. What is the most significant difference?

15.   *The Stand* was voted best all-time miniseries in an *Entertainment Weekly* poll, receiving twenty-seven percent of the votes. What miniseries was voted as the second best all-time miniseries with seventeen percent of the votes?

MEDIUM DIFFICULTY

1.   Who hypnotizes Tom Cullens?

2.   Stephen King, Ed Harris, and Ossie Davis all appear in another project which aired the same year as *The Stand*. What is this?

3.   A note is found on the dead General Starkey's lapel. What does it read?

4.   In what city does Mother Abigail finally meet Fran, Stu, and the others?

5.   John Bloom appears in a cameo as Deputy Brentwood. Bloom is better known to film buffs by his pseudonym. What is this?

6.   When is Tom Cullen to return home from his reconnaissance mission?

7.   Who appears in a cameo as Henry Dunbarton?

8.   What is Trashcan Man's real name?

9.   What 1974 Blue Oyster Cult tune plays during the film's opening credits?

10.   What fictitious product asks, "Do you need a buddy?"

11.   Who does Flagg order to seduce Harold Lauder?

12.   In what month is Fran's baby due?

13.   What is Tom Cullen to say if asked why he left the group?

14.   Where is "Blue Base" located?

15.   What was the first film Ossie Davis and Ruby Dee appeared in together?

HARD AS HELL

1. The character John Landis plays shares his name with the person Stephen King dedicated the novella *Rita Hayworth and the Shawshank Redemption* to. Who is this?

2. Cast members Ruby Dee and Ossie Davis had three children together. One of them is an actor who appears in *Beat Street* (1984) and *Def By Temptation* (1990). Who is this?

3. What is the name of Larry Underwood's mother?

4. Who actually sang the Larry Underwood tune "Baby Can U Dig Your Man" for the film?

5. Where is Marcy Halloran from?

6. *The Stand* was awarded three Emmys in 1994. In what categories were these wins?

7. In what Maine town does Fran reside?

8. What does Larry Underwood's mother sarcastically ask if West Coast leg-breakers provide before they begin hurting you?

9. What is the name of Harold's published poem?

10. What is General Starkey's first name?

11. According to Glen Bateman, what "was a death trip"?

12. What is the scripture verse Mother Abigail writes at the bottom of her farewell letter?

13. Where is Nick Andros from?

14. Who appears as Susan Stern?

15. What filmmaker appears in a cameo as Bobby Terry?

QUIZ #33: THE SHAWSHANK REDEMPTION (1994)

Screenplay by: Frank Darabont
Directed by: Frank Darabont
Starring: Tim Robbins, Morgan Freeman, and Bob Gunton
Warner Bros.

When Frank Darabont, who had already directed the short Stephen King adaptation *The Woman in the Room* (1985), asked the author for permission to adapt the novella *Rita Hayworth and the Shawshank Redemption,* the author was interested to see what Darabont could make of it. Like *The Woman in the Room*, this wasn't a work filmmakers had been beating King's door down for.

The resulting film is easily the finest Stephen King adaptation ever filmed, one of the few instances where a screenwriter's voice and the voice of the original novelist sync together in perfect harmony. While the novella was hardly one of the author's finest pieces, Darabont improved upon King's work tremendously, crafting a film that is arguably a masterpiece.

Of *Shawshank's* director, King praises, "Frank Darabont is one of four or five guys out there who know what they're doing. I've worked with some people, or attempted to work with some people, who are totally insane, and they get ahead out there... Frank is not interested in everybody knowing that this is a Frank Darabont movie. He is not out there dancing and singing in front. He knows exactly what he's doing. He knows what every shot is supposed to be, and what it's supposed to do."

EASY

1.   What is the first item Andy asks Red to obtain for him?

2.   Who does Andy say kept him company in solitary?

3.   The word "mother" is scrawled on the wall of Andy's cell just above his poster. In 1985, Robbins appeared in a film as a character named "Mother." What is this film?

4.   What is Andy's favorite passage from the Bible?

5.   Who was Brooks Hatlen named after?

6.   What happened to Brooks in 1912?

7.   Gill Bellows appears as Thomas ("Tommy") Williams. On *Ally Mc-Beal* Bellows played a character with a similar name. What was this?

8.   How many times was Andy's wife shot?

9.   What embroidered Biblical phrase hangs on Warden Norton's office wall?

10. How long does Andy write letters before receiving the $200 to improve the prison library?

11. What is Warden Norton's first name?

12. What contraband does Hadley ask Andy to explain after the first inspection?

13. Warden Norton says he believes in two things. What are these?

14. What is the name of the grocery store where Brooks and Red are employed?

15. How many cigarettes does Red wager that Andy will be the first "new fish" to break down and weep?

MEDIUM DIFFICULTY

1.   Andy locks one of the guards in the restroom. The guard is read-
     ing a comic book. What is the title of this comic book?

2.   King fans will remember actor Brian Libby from *The Woman in
     the Room*. What is the name of Libby's character in *The Shawshank
     Redemption*?

3.   After Andy gets beer for his coworkers on the rooftop, who offers
     him a beer?

4.   How much is Red's "normal" markup?

5.   When Andy returns to his cell from the infirmary, he finds the
     poster of Rita Hayworth and a note from Red on his bunk. What
     does the note say?

6.   For his ten-year anniversary in Shawshank, Andy is given a poster
     of Marilyn Monroe with her skirt blowing up. What film is this
     photograph from?

7.   How much money did Byron Hadley's brother leave him in his will?

8.   What two types of stone does Andy fashion the chess pieces from?

9.   What is the full name of the head "bull queer" who takes a liking
     to Andy?

10. What is the name of Brooks' bird?

11. What is Warden Norton's prophetic statement regarding Andy's Bible?

12. What does Warden Norton's first rule prohibit?

13. In what year is Andy sent to Shawshank?

14. In what city was Andy employed as the vice-president of a bank?

15. Andy hangs a poster of Racquel Welch in his cell. From what
     1966 film was this photograph taken?

HARD AS HELL

1. Who appears as the younger version of Red in the mug shots attached to his parole papers?

2. What two names are carved into the wall of Andy's cell before he attempts to carve his own?

3. How many wardens has Brooks seen come and go during his "tenure" at Shawshank?

4. What is the name of the guard that Andy sets up the college trust fund for?

5. Andy informs Hadley that the Internal Revenue Service will allow a one-time only tax-free gift to a spouse. What is the maximum amount of money the IRS will allow?

6. *The Shawshank Redemption* was filmed inside an old correctional facility located in Ohio. What is the name of this facility?

7. When he's attacked by the "sisters," Andy breaks someone's nose. What is the name of this inmate?

8. Andy, Red, Haywood, and some of the others are assigned to tar the roof of the license plate building. In what year is this?

9. Which cast member made his acting debut in *Mean Streets* (1973)?

10. What is the name of the inmate pulling infirmary duty who informs Haywood that his "winning horse" is dead?

11. What is Red's full name?

12. What two things does Red say never happened again after Hadley beat Boggs?

13. How many years does Red figure it would take a man to tunnel out of Shawshank with a rock hammer?

14. The inmates watch a film starring Rita Hayworth. What is this film?

15. What is the Mozart selection Andy plays over the loudspeaker?

QUIZ #34: CHILDREN OF THE CORN III: URBAN HARVEST (1994)

Screenplay by: Dode B. Levenson
Directed by: James D.R. Hickox
Starring: Daniel Cerny, Ron Melendez, and Jim Metzler
Dimension Films

In the third installment of everyone's least favorite horror franchise, two Gatlin youngsters are adopted after the "mysterious" disappearance of their father. (Apparently this happens all the time in Gatlin, so how mysterious could this really be?) When the two boys, Eli (Daniel Cerny) and Joshua (Ron Melendez), are adopted by a family in urban Chicago, they bring the Gatlin legacy with them. (Little brother Eli even brings a suitcase filled with ears of corn!)

If only *Children of the Corn II: The Final Sacrifice* had truly been the final sacrifice! Let's just say that this is likely the worst film in the long, horrible series of *Corn* films. (I've read reviews from online critics calling this the best film in the series, as well. Let's face it; the whole series is so poor that one can hardly differentiate between the best and the worst.) This film has no redeeming value. This is two hours of your life you can never get back. I had to watch this film to complete this book, folks, so consider it a sacrifice made for you. If you haven't seen this "film" yet, avoid it at all costs.

EASY

1. What does Eli say is "sacred"?

2. What does Joshua refer to as Eli's "other half"?

3. What does Eli say is the "surest way to a pious life"?

4. Two years before his turn as Eli in *Children of the Corn III*, Daniel Cerny had appeared as "The Kid" in a silly Charles Band-produced horror film. What is this film?

5. What is the name of the hoodlum who pulls a knife on Eli?

6. Composer Daniel Licht scored the second and third installments in the *Children of the Corn* series. In 1996, he also scored a Stephen King adaptation directed by Tom Holland. What is this film?

7. The character in the film played by James O'Sullivan shares his name with the main character from *Sleepwalkers* (1992). What is his name?

8. According to Eli, what happened to his parents?

9. Actor Michael Ensign also appears in *Titanic* (1997). What is the name of the character he plays in that film?

10. Who does Maria say are "gonna be first"?

11. Where does Eli bury his Bible?

12. What does William call a "brand-new Japanese invention"?

13. How many feature films had James D.R. Hickox directed before *Children of the Corn III*?

14. Eli's Bible has been fashioned from a real published book. What is this?

15. The year after the release of *Children of the Corn III*, cinematographer Gerry Lively worked on a comedy starring Ice Cube, Chris Tucker, and T. "Tiny" Lister, Jr. What is this film?

MEDIUM DIFFICULTY

1. Supervising producer Jim Begg served as producer on the first installment of another dismal horror franchise the year before *Children of the Corn III* was released. What is this film?

2. What is the first country for which William negotiates distribution of Eli's corn?

3. What is the name of the substitute teacher played by Kelly Nelson?

4. What is Father Nolan's first name?

5. *Children of the Corn III* is one of two shoddy horror films featuring Ron Melendez released in 1994. What is the other film?

6. What is Maria and Malcolm's surname?

7. As he dies, what does Father Nolan say must be destroyed?

8. Which cast member later appeared in *Apollo 11* (1996), *L.A. Confidential* (1997), and *The Big Brass Ring* (1999)?

9. What is the name of the social worker assigned to Eli and Joshua?

10. What is the name of the song performed by the Lifers Group which appears in the film?

11. The director of *Young, Hot 'N' Nasty Teenage Cruisers* (1977) and *My Breakfast with Blassie* (1983) appears as Derelict Man. Who is this?

12. What is William and Amanda's surname?

13. What does Eli call a "taste of home"?

14. What was the early production title of *Children of the Corn III*?

15. When Eli and Joshua arrive in Chicago, they see a man carrying a sign down the street. What does the sign read?

HARD AS HELL

1. A newspaper is shown with the headline "Four Murdered in Base-ment." What is this newspaper?

2. A newspaper is shown with the headline "Ten Farmers Missing in Strange Disappearance." What is this newspaper?

3. What is the population of Gatlin?

4. Director James D.R. Hickox's mother is the five-time Academy Award nominated editor of films such as *Lawrence of Arabia* (1962), *The Elephant Man* (1980), and *Erin Brockovich* (2000). Who is this?

5. Who is this film dedicated to?

6. What does Eli say just after killing William?

7. Prior to *Children of the Corn III*, screenwriter Dode B. Levenson's only screenwriting credit was for a 1993 film starring Darlen Vogel, Shane Fraser, and Roddy McDowell. What is this film?

8. What chapter of Genesis does Father Nolan focus on in his sermon?

9. Where is William employed?

10. How old was Joshua when he first moved to Gatlin?

11. A newspaper is shown from 1964 with a photograph of Eli on the front page. What is this newspaper?

12. What is the date of the 1964 newspaper with the picture of Eli on the front page?

13. What is the name of the character played by uncredited actor Jason Waters?

14. Associate producer Jim Begg's first production credit came on a 1961 Western directed by Lindsay Shonteff. What is this film?

15. What is the seating capacity of the bus that brings Eli and Joshua to Chicago?

QUIZ #35: THE MANGLER (1995)

Screenplay by: Stephen David Brooks, Tobe Hooper,
and Harry Alan Towers
Directed by: Tobe Hooper
Starring: Robert Englund, Ted Levine, and Daniel Matmor
New Line Cinema

Stephen King briefly went to work in an industrial laundry after graduating from the University of Maine in 1970. While working there, King observed a coworker who fell into the pressing machine, which the workers called the "mangler." The result of this accident was that King's coworker lost both hands, and the young would-be novelist wound up with an idea for a short story about an industrial ironing machine that is possessed by a demon with a taste for blood. In 1995, Tobe Hooper helmed a low budget adaptation of this story for New Line Cinema.

In a 1988 interview with Stephen J. Spignesi, Hooper alluded to the fact that he was interested in directing another King story (he had previously directed *Salem's Lot*, 1979), although he wouldn't say which one. As entertaining as King's short story "The Mangler" is, it's difficult for one to imagine Hooper carrying a torch for this project for nearly a decade; let's face it, a story featuring an industrial ironing machine as the villain is hardly the stuff cinematic dreams are made of.

EASY

1. What does Mr. Gartley say there's never enough of?

2. What does Hutton say "don't mean shit to me"?

3. *The Mangler* was director Tobe Hooper's second Stephen King adaptation. What was his first?

4. Who cuts her hand on the mangler at the beginning of the film, giving it a taste for blood?

5. What do the photographer and the undertaker have in common?

6. What is Mr. Stanner's first name?

7. What is Hutton's first name?

8. What is Mark attempting to remove when the ice box attacks him?

9. According to Mark, what is the most common ingredient in spells?

10. What does Mr. Gartley call a "bad career move"?

11. What is Adele fishing out of the mangler when it pulls her in?

12. What does Mark define as being "a kind of energy like electricity or fire"?

13. Actor Robert Englund appeared on the cult television series *V*. What was the name of his character?

14. Another accident involving the mangler causes several workers to be burned the night of Adele's death. How many people are burnt?

15. *The Mangler* marked Robert Englund's third appearance in a film directed by Tobe Hooper. What were Englund and Hooper's two previous collaborations?

MEDIUM DIFFICULTY

1. What is the brand name of the pills Hutton removes from Adele's purse?

2. What does Hutton call Mark's book on the occult?

3. Director Tobe Hooper appears as an actor in a Stephen King adaptation helmed by Mick Garris. What is this film?

4. What is the name of the industrial laundry where the "mangler" is located?

5. What is the Rikers Valley slogan?

6. What snack does the undertaker offer Hutton?

7. What does Mark liken to "controlled nuclear fission"?

8. What is the name of the child who suffocates inside the ice box?

9. What does Hutton see on the outside of the ice box, over the name of the industrial laundry?

10. What does the sign hanging near the mangler claim will "make you free"?

11. What name does Mr. Gartley encourage Lin Sue to call him?

12. Who attempts to pull Adele free from the mangler?

13. What is the name of the burn victim Hutton visits in the hospital?

14. Which cast member also appears in *Ironweed* (1987), *The Silence of the Lambs* (1991), and *Wild Wild West* (1999)?

15. Which cast member directed the films *Homeboys II: Crack City* (1989) and *Buffalo Heart* (1996)?

HARD AS HELL

1. What company manufactured the mangler?

2. In 1970, Stephen King worked in an industrial laundry located in Bangor, Maine. What was the name of the industrial laundry where King was employed?

3. Aside from cowriting the screenplay, Stephen David Brooks also performed two other duties on *The Mangler*. What were these?

4. For how many years has Hutton worked on the police force?

5. What was the date when Sherry's parents were killed?

6. What college did Mark attend?

7. What is the population of Rikers Valley?

8. What is Mark's surname?

9. To what address is the possessed ice box delivered to?

10. What is the name of the judge Hutton remarks that Mr. Gartley "owns"?

11. As Hutton tells Mark about the mangler's first victim, how far away does he say the industrial laundry is?

12. *The Mangler* won an award at the 1995 Fantafestival. In what category was this award?

13. What is the name of the dispatcher?

14. What is the surname of the delivery man with the expired drivers' license?

15. What is the name of Hutton's deceased wife?

QUIZ #36: DOLORES CLAIBORNE (1995)

Screenplay by: Tony Gilroy
Directed by: Taylor Hackford
Starring: Kathy Bates, Jennifer Jason Leigh, and Christopher Plummer
Columbia Pictures

Published in 1993, *Dolores Claiborne* is one of Stephen King's more serious attempts at mainstream fiction. The novel, told entirely in first-person narrative by its protagonist, is completely devoid of the supernatural elements so often associated with King's work. Perhaps that's why the novel received mixed reviews; while *Dolores Claiborne* is unquestionably one of the author's finest works, it wasn't what readers expected.

"Don't say that I'm stretching my range or that I've left horror behind," King said in a *USA Today* interview. "I'm just trying to find things I haven't done, to stay alive creatively."

Two years after the novel's publication, a film adaptation of *Dolores Claiborne* arrived in theaters. The Taylor Hackford-helmed film boasted a reunion of *Misery* (1990) star Kathy Bates and screenwriter William Goldman (whose contributions were uncredited), and came hot on the heels of *The Shawshank Redemption* (1994). However, despite the film's high-caliber cast and its loyalty to King's original story, it failed to capture the essence of the novel.

Los Angeles Times critic Kenneth Turan slammed, "Like a frightening situation from one of the man's own novels, no power on Earth can apparently stop the zombie-like progression of Stephen King books to the screen. Page-turners usually make for engrossing films, but with King it's been largely downhill since Brian De Palma did the electric *Carrie* in 1976. *Dolores Claiborne* is the latest King novel to make the transition, and it makes you wonder who would have bothered if the author's first name had been Irving."

EASY

1.   How much money does Vera Donovan leave Dolores in her will?

2.   What is the name of Selena's editor?

3.   Five years before her turn in *Dolores Claiborne*, actress Jennifer Jason Leigh appeared in a film directed by *The Shawshank Redemption* helmer Frank Darabont. What is this film?

4.   How much is Dolores paid to "touch up the house once a week" in the winter?

5.   A legendary screenwriter performed uncredited rewrites on Tony Gilroy's script. Who is this?

6.   What's the furthest Dolores has ever been from Little Tall Island?

7.   *Dolores Claiborne* was the second Taylor Hackford film written by Tony Gilroy. What was the first?

8.   *Dolores Claiborne* marked actress Kathy Bates' third appearance in a Stephen King adaptation. What are the other two King films she had appeared in previously?

9.   How many years has it been since Selena's last trip to Little Tall Island?

10.   The playwright responsible for *Pounding Nails Into the Floor With*

My Head, Sex, Drugs, Rock & Roll, and *Suburbia* appears as an actor in this film. Who is this?

11. What does Dolores dub "the only thing left that's important"?

12. Who warned Joe St. George that Dolores would "let (herself) go"?

13. What does Selena's editor say the difference between "terrific" and "wonderful" is?

14. How much of Selena's college money did Joe actually spend?

15. What does Vera say happens every day?

MEDIUM DIFFICULTY

1. What college did Selena attend?

2. How many applicants are there for the housekeeping position at Vera Donovan's?

3. Who does Joe say are always joking about what a "looker" Dolores is?

4. According to Vera, what can be the "only thing a woman has to hold on to"?

5. What does Vera insist her toilets be scrubbed with?

6. *Dolores Claiborne* features actor Bob Gunton's second appearance in a Stephen King adaptation in as many years. What King adaptation did Gunton appear in the year before *Dolores Claiborne* was released?

7. How long does Vera Donovan want every window in the house open each day?

8. What grade did Selena skip?

9. How long does it take Selena to track down the cardiologist who won't go "on the record"?

10. What is the name of the prison where Dolores says Joe will be sent for child molestation?

11. How old was Selena the first time she met Detective John Mackey?

12. How many years apart are the deaths of Joe St. John and Vera Donovan?

13. Dolores framed a picture of Selena with a famous person. Who is this?

14. Which cast member attended Ringling Bros. Clown College before becoming an actor?

15. How long does the eclipse last?

HARD AS HELL

1. How much is Selena's college fund before Joe withdraws it?

2. In what city is Vera's winter home located?

3. What is the name of Vera Donovan's husband?

4. In what city does Selena say she must be the following Monday?

5. What is the name of the hotel where Dolores went to work at age thirteen?

6. How much is Dolores paid per week to clean Vera Donovan's home in the summer?

7. How long did it take Dolores to earn the money Joe stole?

8. How many homicides has John Mackey closed in his thirty-year career?

9. What is the name of the ferry to Little Tall Island?

10. From where was Vera's husband traveling when he was killed?

11. How many years before her death was Vera's will prepared?

12. Selena learns that her mother is a suspect from a newspaper clipping faxed to her. From what newspaper is the clipping?

13. How many clothes pins does Vera insist Dolores use in hanging each sheet?

14. In a scene cut from the film, what does Dolores break to pieces after Joe's death?

15. How many years did Dolores work for Vera?

QUIZ #37: THE LANGOLIERS (1995)

Screenplay by: Tom Holland
Directed by: Tom Holland
Starring: Patricia Wettig, Dean Stockwell, and David Morse
Laurel Entertainment

Sometimes films made for television get a bad rap because of those count-less soon-to-be-on-The-Lifetime-Channel "films" featuring the likes of Meredith Baxter Birney or Richard Crenna. Certainly now-classic tele-films such as *Brian's Song* (1971) and *Duel* (1971) rise above such fare. *The Stand* (1994) and *Stephen King's The Shining* (1997)—both directed by Mick Garris—are examples of superb telefilms crafted from King's writ-ing. Well, simply put, *The Langoliers* is not one of these standout telefilms; although not as bad as *The Tommyknockers* (1993), it's close. The special effects are poor, the acting is weak, and the screenplay is even weaker.

"It was okay," King said of *The Langoliers*. "I wasn't crazy about it. That one was more of a TV thing." However, director Tom Holland and producer Richard Rubinstein would redeem themselves the following year with the much better King adaptation, *Thinner* (1996).

EASY

1.   What is the destination of the plane when its passengers disappear?

2.   What is said to be Bob Jenkins' "bread and butter"?

3. What is the name of the aunt who wanted to send Bethany to rehab?

4. *The Langoliers* was actor Frankie Faison's second venture into the world of Stephen King. What was the first King adaptation Faison starred in?

5. What is Captain Engle's first name?

6. Who appears briefly as Harker?

7. How many years does Laurel say it's been since her last vacation?

8. What is the flight number of the plane which slips through the rip in time?

9. What is the name of the man Laurel was flying to meet?

10. Who does Craig Toomy beg to make the Langoliers go away?

11. What is the name of the fictitious hold Nick Hopewell promises to put on Toomy if he refuses to cooperate?

12. Actress Patricia Wettig has won two Emmys for her performance on a popular television drama. What is this series?

13. What were the flight's survivors doing when the rest of the passengers disappeared?

14. What musical instrument does Albert Kaussner play?

15.. *Night of the Living Dead* (1968) alum S. William Hinzman appears in a cameo role. The year before *The Langoliers* aired, Hinzman wrote and directed a horror film. What is this?

MEDIUM DIFFICULTY

1. *The Langoliers* was the second Stephen King adaptation to feature director Tom Holland as an actor. What was the first?

2.   What is the name of Captain Engle's ex-wife?

3.   Which cast member also appears in ...*And Justice for All* (1979), *The Amityville Horror* (1979), and *JFK* (1991)?

4.   The plane is rerouted to an airport in Maine. What is the name of this airport?

5.   What does Roger Toomy say the letter "B" stands for?

6.   Actor Dean Stockwell wrote and co-directed a 1982 film featuring Neil Young, Dennis Hopper, Sally Kirkland, and rock group Devo. A young Kevin Costner also served as stage manager on this project. What is this film?

7.   *The Langoliers* was one of three Stephen King adaptations to debut in 1995. What are the other two films?

8.   The name of a composer is printed on Albert's shirt. Who is this?

9.   What is Bob Jenkins' occupation?

10.   *The Langoliers* was nominated for an Emmy in 1995. In what category was the telefilm nominated?

11.   What are the chances that Dinah's vision will be at least partially restored by her impending operation?

12.   Dinah says Laurel Stevenson's voice sounds just like her teacher at the blind school. What is the name of this teacher?

13.   Director Tom Holland wrote and helmed a second King adaptation the year after *The Langoliers* first aired. What is this film?

14.   What grade does Laurel Stevenson teach?

15.   What desert is the Aurora Borealis said to be over?

HARD AS HELL

1. What is the name of the Irish Republican Army financier Nick has been assigned to kill?

2. Three airline pilots served as technical advisors for Stephen King while he was writing the novella this film is based upon. What are their names?

3. What is the minimum take-off speed of the survivors' plane?

4. When first asked what he does for a living, what title does Nick Hopewell offer?

5. What is the name of Dinah's aunt?

6. What do the plane's passengers notice as being different in the Maine airport from inside the plane?

7. At what time did all the clocks in Bangor stop?

8. What is the name of the fictitious airline the passengers are flying on?

9. What is the name of the character played by Stephen King?

10. In "A Note on *The Langoliers*," Stephen King explains that the idea for this novella came from a mental image. What was this?

11. Where was Toomy's nine a.m. meeting to have been held?

12. How much of his company's money did Craig Toomy intentionally lose?

13. What is the name of the school where Albert is enrolled?

14. The same year as his turn in *The Langoliers*, actor David Morse appeared alongside *The Shining's* (1980) Jack Nicholson and Piper Laurie of *Carrie* (1976) in another film. What is this film?

15. How much does Craig Toomy threaten to sue Captain Engle and the airline for?

QUIZ #38: THINNER (1996)

Screenplay by: Michael McDowell and Tom Holland
Directed by: Tom Holland
Starring: Robert John Burke, Joe Mantegna, and Lucinda Jenney
Paramount Pictures

This 1984 "Richard Bachman" novel was optioned long before anyone knew it had actually been written by Stephen King. Interestingly (and ironically, given King's reasoning for using the Bachman pseudonym), the film's alternate title is *Stephen King's Thinner*. (Had King not been found out, it is unlikely the film would have been titled *Richard Bachman's Thinner*.)

Director Tom Holland sees *Thinner* as a morality play. "The film is about moral culpability," Holland said. "It's about a man who refuses to accept responsibility for his actions and finally ends up eating, both figuratively and literally, his own just desserts. This story demonstrates that it's dangerous to blur the edges between wrong and right. Although Billy is essentially a nice guy, his refusal to pay for his mistake causes his body to become his enemy. His horrible situation leads him on a desperate race against time."

After King saw a completed version of the film and voiced his disappointment, Holland and company reshot much of the film and released it later in the year. However, the film was not well received. As author George Beahm observes in *Stephen King from A to Z*, "The result: A film that tried to please everyone... and pleased very few people in the end."

EASY

1. What is the name of the pharmacist played by Stephen King?

2. Kirk jokingly offers to pay Billy to run over Cary Rossington. How much does he offer to pay?

3. What does Hopley testify that Billy was "as sober as"?

4. Actor Josh Holland appears in the film. What is his relation to director Tom Holland?

5. Who is Heide Halleck having an affair with?

6. At the beginning of the film, Billy weighs 300 pounds. How much does he tell his wife, Heidi, he weighs?

7. *Thinner* was the second Stephen King film that screenwriter Michael McDowell worked on. What was the first?

8. What does Richie Ginelli poison the gypsies' dogs with?

9. What does Tadzu Lempke say "ain't about bringing back the dead"?

10. When Tadzu Lempke touched Cary Rossington, what did he say?

11. Who is the "mook" Ginelli hires to watch the gypsy camp?

12. What does Hopley ask Billy to do when he finds the gypsy king?

13. What is the name of the curse Billy threatens to put on the gypsies?

14. Ginelli throws liquid into Gina Lempke's face, telling her it's acid. What is this really?

15. In Billy's dream, Tadzu Lempke guesses his weight. What is it?

MEDIUM DIFFICULTY

1. Who does Max Duganfield testify ordered a hit on him three years prior?

2. Where do the gypsies go each year "at the end of the season"?

3. What does Ginelli say he tends to believe?

4. According to Tadzu Lempke, where will the curse be when he dies?

5. *Thinner* was the second Stephen King adaptation directed by Tom Holland. What was the first?

6. As Billy is leaving Hopley's home, he hears a sound. What is this?

7. What does Heidi say rapid weight loss is an early warning sign of?

8. Who provides Billy information at Quigley Realty?

9. Ginelli leaves a note on the gypsies' dog pen. What does it say?

10. What is Richard Ginelli's nickname?

11. How much is the reward that Heidi and Mike Houston put up for Billy?

12. Under what pseudonym does Ginelli pose as an FBI agent?

13. According to Billy, what does Kirk Benchley prove again?

14. How long does it take for Billy to lose the first forty pounds after having the curse put on him?

15. *Thinner* was the seventh Stephen King adaptation produced by Richard P. Rubinstein. What was the first film Rubinstein produced which featured King as an actor?

HARD AS HELL

1. Under what working title was the novel *Thinner* written?

2. What are the three things Cary Rossington says gypsies bring with them?

3. What is the name of the elderly woman Billy runs over with his car?

4. Director Tom Holland appears as an actor in two Stephen King adaptations. What are these?

5. What is Chief Hopley's first name?

6. What time does the Seven Seas Lounge and Bar open for business?

7. Who was the original novel by "Richard Bachman" dedicated to?

8. How old is Tadzu Lempke?

9. What is the name of the clinic Mike Houston sends Billy to?

10. What is the name of Cary Rossington's wife?

11. What is the name of Billy's tailor?

12. What is the nickname Billy uses for Mike Houston which Heidi hates?

13. While the gypsies are staying in Fairview, whose farm do they rent?

14. Where is Cary Rossington staying in Minnesota?

15. In what year did Tadzu Lempke enter the United States?

QUIZ #39: SOMETIMES THEY COME BACK...AGAIN (1996)

Screenplay by: Adam Grossman and Guy Riedel
Directed by: Adam Grossman
Starring: Michael Gross, Alexis Arquette, and Hilary Swank
Trimark Pictures

Although the first *Sometimes They Come Back* (1990) was effective, things began getting out of hand when the producers decided to make a sequel. Following in the footsteps of the *Children of the Corn* series, this film has little to do with the first installment or King's short story. If anything, this sequel is a rehash of the first film, with completely new characters and a new set of baddies circa 1955.

One *Cavalcade of Schlock* reviewer suggests that the film is best viewed when intoxicated (never a good prerequisite for a film); said reviewer goes on to observe: "I don't know what would possess someone to greenlight a sequel to an obscure TV movie based on a relatively obscure story by an author who's had, by my count, no less than 13 of his short stories filmed. Well, maybe 12 if you agree that *The Lawnmower Man* should've had King's name removed, and maybe 14 if you think that King should sue Joe Dante for *Small Soldiers'* shameless 'Battleground' theft... I dunno, guys, there's enough weird, goofy shit going on here to keep me amused for ninety-seven minutes, but I'd hardly say you should put this one your must-see list."

EASY

1. What is unusual regarding Milton Subotsky's co-producer credit on *Sometimes They Come Back...Again*?

2. What cartoon character is Steve obsessed with?

3. What must be eaten to "assume the power of the beast"?

4. Alexis Arquette appeared in another sequel to a Stephen King adaptation in 1998. What is this film?

5. What is the alternate title for *Sometimes They Come Back...Again*?

6. What is in the package delivered to Jon?

7. What does Maria find in Tony Reno's jacket pocket?

8. What is the significance of the watch Tony gives Michelle?

9. What is the name of the minister Jon spoke with after the death of his sister?

10. What does Jon say pigs are cleaner than?

11. Maria says she has two words for Jules. What are these?

12. What is Steve's surname?

13. What is Jon's profession?

14. Who is the first of his minions that Tony brings back from Hell?

15. Actress Hilary Swank later won a Best Actress Oscar for her role in a 1999 film. What is this film?

MEDIUM DIFFICULTY

1. Jon's mother is killed when she falls on a small statue of an animal. What is this animal?

2.   What is Maria's surname?

3.   Tony says of the Tarot cards, "It's the one on the top you need to watch for." What is this card?

4.   Who informs Michelle that Tony is "not like other people"?

5.   What are Vinnie's first words after he's brought back by Tony?

6.   What is Lisa's age at the time of her death?

7.   What is the name of the pig that belonged to Jon's mother?

8.   *Sometimes They Come Back...Again* was the second Stephen King-related film in which actor William Morgan Sheppard played a priest. What was the first?

9.   What does Tony say as he picks up Steve's severed hand?

10. A book written by Stephen King is visible beneath the diary Jon finds. What is this book?

11. What does Maria find lying beside Steve's lawnmower?

12. How often did Jules and Maria clean house for Jon's mother?

13. What is the name of the town in which this film takes place?

14. What does B.F.P. stand for?

15. Which cast member also appears in *Son in Law* (1993), *The Sandlot* (1993), and *Johnny Mysto: Boy Wizard* (1996)?

HARD AS HELL

1.   At what time does Steve mow the lawn, waking Jon?

2.   What number does Tony play repeatedly on the jukebox?

3.   What is Lisa's nickname for Jon?

4.   What does Archer say is "quickly reignited"?

5.   *Sometimes They Come Back...Again* producer Guy Riedel also produced a Marilyn Monroe biopic released in 1996. What is this film?

6.   Who does Archer say was the last man to break the Sabbath?

7.   Where does Jon find the bicycle that reminds him of his sister's death?

8.   How many volts of electricity does Steve say the gloves he gives Jon will protect him from?

9.   Jon visits the morgue of the local newspaper in search of answers. What is the name of the newspaper?

10.   How did Jon's wife die?

11.   What is the name of Jon's mother?

12.   From what did Jon's father die?

13.   What is the name of the diner where Michelle meets Tony?

14.   Who is found dead in the kitchen during Michelle's birthday party?

15.   *Sometimes They Come Back...Again was* one of two films released in 1996 featuring both Michael Gross and Hilary Swank. What is the other film?

QUIZ #40: CHILDREN OF THE CORN IV: THE GATHERING (1996)

Screenplay by: Stephen Berger and Greg Spence
Directed by: Greg Spence
Starring: Naomi Watts, Jamie Renee Smith, and Karen Black
Dimension Films

In this fourth installment, a small town is victimized after its children become feverish and transform into the evil minions of a dark minister returned from the dead to find a young child similar to himself. This film is
mildly entertaining if you can shut off your brain for an hour-and-a-half,
but it's not frightening as it relies on the same proven formula utilized in
the first three films in the series, and it has little to do with King's original
short story, "Children of the Corn."

A *Night of the Creeps* review written by Eagle Te says it all: "*Children
of the Corn IV* damn near falls completely on its face as for the major-
ity of the film you will find yourself bored senseless. There simply isn't
enough action or stupid dialogue...to hold your attention for very long."
So is *Children of the Corn IV* completely without merit? As any cineaste
will tell you, no film is without merit. However, the *Children of the Corn*
franchise may make you reconsider this idealistic view.

EASY

1.   According to James, what is Charles Manson's favorite flavor of ice cream?

2.   What is the name of the school where Mary Anne has been hired as nurse?

3.   When Grace sees her mother's rosary, what does she remind her?

4.   Who murders Doc Larson?

5.   What does Doc advise Grace not to allow her mother to hear?

6.   *Children of the Corn IV* was one of two films screenwriter Stephen Berger saw produced in 1996. The other was a telefilm directed by Peter Geiger. What is this film?

7.   Mary Ann makes a reference to a 1973 horror film when she says she doesn¹t want to be in charge when the children's "heads start spinning and they start hurling pea soup." What is this film?

8.   What is the name of the clinic where Grace works with Doc Larson?

9.   Who is Margaret's real mother?

10.   Just before Mary Ann is finished off, her hands are pinned to the door. What are they pinned down with?

11.   After the "wicked boy preacher" was burned, where were his bones and ashes placed?

12.   *Children of the Corn IV* was one of two films featuring actor Brent Jennings released in 1996. In the other film, Jennings appears alongside Delroy Lindo, Mykelti Williamson, and Blair Underwood. What is this film?

13.   How does Doc Larson attempt to break the children's fevers?

14. What does June say she can never remember about her nightmares?

15. In what county does this story take place?

MEDIUM DIFFICULTY

1. James brags about owning the entire set of serial killers trading cards. According to James, how many cards are in the set?

2. Who does Mary Ann say may be better help than the toxicology team?

3. Actress Charlize Theron makes an early uncredited appearance in *Children of the Corn IV.* Three years after the release of this film, Theron and screenwriter Stephen Berger would appear in a film together. What is this film?

4. According to Jane Nock, what was the strange thing about the "amazing boy preacher"?

5. Actress Karen Black saw her first screenplay produced the same year *Children of the Corn IV* was released. What is this film?

6. Who is the "like child" the evil preacher has returned for?

7. Who do the McLellan twins claim to be?

8. Eleven years before he served as cinematographer on *Children of the Corn IV*, Dean Lent made his directorial debut on a film which he cowrote and co-directed with Allison Anders and Kurt Voss. This film was nominated for an Independent Spirit Award for Best First Feature. What is this film?

9. What are the hours Doc Larsen's office is open Monday through Friday?

10. Doc Larsen says the problem with Jane isn't that she won't leave the house. What is the problem?

11. The year *Children of the Corn IV* was released, actress Naomi Watts also appeared in a film directed by George Hickenlooper which also features *Thinner* (1996) actor Joe Mantegna and J.T. Walsh of *Needful Things* (1993). What is this film?

12. What is the name of the "boy preacher" who commands the children?

13. After the death of Sheriff Biggs, where does Donald Atkins hide out?

14. What does Doc Larsen say makes viruses "such a fun date"?

15. *Children of the Corn IV* was one of two films edited by Christopher Cibelli in 1996. The other film features *The Langoliers* (1995) actor Dean Stockwell and Harry Dean Stanton of *The Green Mile* (1999). What is this film?

HARD AS HELL

1. Actor Brandon Kleyla and makeup effects supervisor Roy Knyrim reunited on another film two years after the release of *Children of the Corn IV*. This film was nominated for three Academy Awards, winning one. What is this film?

2. Two years after the release of *Children of the Corn IV*, helmer Greg Spence directed his second film, which featured *The Dead Zone* (1983) actor Christopher Walken. What is this film?

3. What does Donald Atkins use to spike the shotgun shells with?

4. Actor William Prael makes an appearance as Concerned Father. Three years later, Prael turned up in *Children of the Corn 666: Isaac's Return* (1999) playing another character. What is the name of the character he plays?

5.   What are the names of the real-life twins who appear as Charlie and Scott McLellan?

6.   At the end of the film, what does James see which indicates that the terror may not be over?

7.   *Children of the Corn IV* is one of three films featuring Charlize Theron released in 1996. What are the other two films?

8.   What do Grace and Donald Atkins find scrawled in blood on a wall inside the clinic?

9.   What does James say Charles Manson's astrological sign is?

10. Composer David C. Williams scored two films released in 1996. One is *Children of the Corn IV*. The other stars Russell Crowe, Helen Slater, and Michael Lerner. What is this film?

11. Marcus tosses a burlap bag to Sheriff Biggs. What's inside the bag?

12. Which cast member made their acting debut in *To Kill a Mockingbird* (1962)?

13. On what date was June Rhodes born?

14. Sandra Atkins is slain while packing for her family's relocation. Where were the Atkins planning to move?

15. When Sandra Atkins calls the television an "idiot box," her husband, Donald, jokes that it's not an idiot box when her favorite show is on. What show is it?

QUIZ #41: STEPHEN KING'S THE SHINING (1997)

Screenplay by: Stephen King
Directed by: Mick Garris
Starring: Rebecca De Mornay, Steven Weber, and Melvin Van Peebles
Warner Bros.

Traditionally network television is where horror has gone to die. Because of the medium's many constraints, it has long been considered impossible to craft an effective horror film for the small screen. However, *Stephen King's The Shining*—the most frightening thing ever conceived for television (with the possible exception of Steven Bochco's shortlived musical drama *Cop Rock*)—proves that effective horror can be achieved and tension can be maintained despite those annoying commercial breaks every twenty minutes.

With this project, director Mick Garris and screenwriter King had a lot to live up to. Stanley Kubrick's original 1980 adaptation of *The Shining*, which King had spent more than fifteen years criticizing, was now considered a classic in many circles, as well as a bonafide staple in American popular culture. ("Herrrrre's Johnnnny!") But Garris and King's retelling succeeded admirably. This was achieved in large part due to the filmmakers' vow to avoid comparisons between the two films. Where Kubrick's film was heavy on style, this second adaptation focused on substance. Besides its being much more faithful to King's novel, this version of *The Shining* shines just a little brighter because the miniseries format afforded Garris the chance to depict Jack Torrance's descent into madness as being a more gradual one. (In Kubrick's version, there is no transformation; Torrance simply becomes insane in a span of minutes.) The miniseries also features King's strongest effort as a screenwriter to date.

EASY

1. What director makes a cameo appearance as "Gas Station Howie"?

2. According to Stuart Ullman, who invented Denver Croquet?

3. Stephen King's bandleader shares his name with a character from another King adaptation played by Miko Hughes. What is this film?

4. What is the significance of January fifth?

5. The uncredited actor who voices Jack Torrance's father appears prominently in the Stephen King adaptations *The Stand* (1994) and *Night Flier* (1997). Who is this?

6. What is the name of the children's book Danny is shown reading?

7. According to Jack, what does love mean never having to say?

8. What Wilson Pickett tune plays on the jukebox as Dick comes to the realization that Danny is in danger?

9. Wendy discovers a party mask, panties, and confetti. Where does she find these things?

10. Frank Darabont, the director of *The Shawshank Redemption* (1994), appears in a cameo role as Dr. Daniel Edwards. Director Mick Garris and Darabont share a screenwriting credit on a 1989 movie helmed by Chris Walas. What is this film?

11. What type of dinner does Wendy say is her specialty?

12   What does Dick say he will cook the "best ever" in St. Pete?

13.   Danny remembers an incident when he became excited during a basketball game he attended with his father. What happened?

14.   The woman in room 217 is played by the wife of someone closely involved with the production of this film. Who is this?

15.   What did Dick Halloranns mother believe "keeps us young"?

MEDIUM DIFFICULTY

1.   What is the name of the debate student Jack assaulted in Vermont?

2.   What does the plaque beside Jack's typewriter remind him?

3.   The spirits of the hotel restrain Wendy momentarily as the topiary animals close in on Danny. In what room is Wendy locked?

4.   *Stephen King's The Shining* is the second film to feature appearances by both Pat Hingle and Stephen King. What was the first film in which Hingle and King appeared together?

5.   In what room of the Overlook Hotel is the bar located?

6.   Melvin Van Peebles appears in the film as Dick Hallorann. In 1971, Van Peebles directed a film—his third—that is often credited with ushering in the "black film revolution" of the Seventies. What is this film?

7.   The year *Stephen King's The Shining* made its debut, actor Elliott Gould also made an appearance as a loan shark in a film starring Harvey Keitel. What is this film?

8.   In Stanley Kubrick's 1980 adaptation of the *The Shining*, Jack Torrance peers through the splintered hole in the door and says, "Here's Johnny!" This line is not used in the remake. In this version, what does Jack say when he looks through the door at Wendy?

9.   When Jack looks in the medicine cabinet in room 217, he finds a single item inside. What is this?

10.   The screenwriter who makes a cameo as "Second Ghost in Playhouse" is the son of a legendary filmmaker. Who is this?

11.   *Stephen King's The Shining* is one of two made-for-television King adaptations directed by Mick Garris which debuted in 1997. What is the other film?

12.   In 1997, *Stephen King's The Shining* was nominated for three Emmys, winning two. In what category did the film lose?

13.   What does Wendy dub the "ugliest thing in the universe"?

14.   What is the first telepathic statement Dick makes to Danny?

15.   What does Jack call "an old stew bum trick"?

HARD AS HELL

1.   Dick calls Howie an "M.F.A." What does this mean?

2.   What is the number of the flight to Denver that Dick misses?

3.   In what state was the cabin Wendy stayed in as a child?

4.   In real life, actor Melvin Van Peebles sports a tattoo on his derriere which reads "*Ne Bessie.*" What is the translation of this Bambouran phrase?

5.   Actress Rebecca De Mornay made her directorial debut in June 1995 on a popular cable television series. The title of the episode, which also showcased De Mornay's acting talents, was titled "The Conversion." What is this series?

6.   On what date do the topiary animals come to life around Danny?

7. At the conclusion of the miniseries we learn that the Overlook Hotel is being rebuilt. What is the name of the company behind its reconstruction?

8. Jack describes Wendy as personifying what he calls "The Three B's." What are these?

9. This miniseries was filmed at the Stanley Hotel in Estes Park, Colorado. What is the significance of this hotel?

10. What is the name of Jack's father?

11. What is the name of the apartment complex where the Torrances reside before spending the winter in the Overlook Hotel?

12. Jack finds a note from "the management" which reads: "Mr. T, if you desert your post, you will not be allowed back." Where does he find this note?

13. On what date is Jack attacked by wasps?

14. Who were the four United States Presidents who stayed at the Overlook Hotel?

15. How many gallons of red eye chili are left in the kitchen for the Torrances?

QUIZ #42: QUICKSILVER HIGHWAY (1997)

Screenplay by: Mick Garris
Directed by: Mick Garris
Starring: Christopher Lloyd, Matt Frewer, and Raphael Sbarge
National Studios

In 1996, Stephen King explained the concept behind *Quicksilver Highway* to *Fangoria* journalist Linda Marotta. "'The Chattery Teeth' is going to be part of what they call a movie for television but is really something different that Mick Garris is doing," the novelist said. "It's a kind of pilot for a series he'd like to put together where there would be two episodes every week with the same cast of actors, but they'd be different stories."

After long being touted as the kings of the horror genre, Stephen King and Clive Barker's works come together gloriously in this television anthology narrated by Christopher Lloyd. While there are some inherent weaknesses in *Quicksilver Highway* which come from the original source material ("The Body Politic" and "The Chattery Teeth" can hardly be called either King or Barker's best work), the script and direction are handled deftly by Garris, who manages to achieve the rarest of rare here—the good anthology film—despite the limitations of the medium he was working in.

Sadly, a series based on Garris' concept has yet to be seen, but *Quicksilver Highway* delivers the goods. King expert George Beahm observes: "[T]his pairing of Barker and King works because it gives both stories room to breathe, to develop. It shows that the material can effectively be done on television, which leads to the question: Why even bother to do an anthology-style film for the big screen?"

EASY

1. *The Quicksilver Highway* segment "The Chattery Teeth" was one of two 1997 Stephen King adaptations directed by Mick Garris. What is the other film?

2. What is the audio book Bill listens to while driving?

3. What is Bill's surname?

4. What is the event Bill must get home for?

5. What is the name of the candle made from the pickled hand of a human?

6. After the newlyweds' car breaks down, what is the only thing they have to eat?

7. Who makes a cameo as the anesthesiologist who asks, "What did I ever do to you?"

8. In "The Body Politic," what do Charlie the pickpocket and Dr. George have in common?

9. How much does Bill pay for the chattery teeth?

10. The composer who scored the film was the lead singer for the band Devo. Who is this?

11. What does the hitchhiker say he's "got no use for"?

12. Who makes a cameo as the surgical assistant who asks, "Late night last night, Dr. George?"

13. In what city does Bill reside?

14.   How long is Bill in a neck brace after the accident?

15.   This *Quicksilver Highway* executive producer directed *Predator* (1987), *Die Hard* (1988), and *Last Action Hero* (1993). Who is this?

MEDIUM DIFFICULTY

1.   The scene in which Dr. George battles his hand resembles a similar scene in a 1987 film directed by Sam Raimi featuring Bruce Campbell. What is this film?

2.   What three words does Bill insist are not his name?

3.   What is the name of the store where Bill purchases the chattery teeth?

4.   What nickname do both Kerry and Bill use for their wives?

5.   What is the name of Scooter's wife?

6.   What is the name of the truck stop where Bill plans to drop off the hitchhiker?

7.   What does Quicksilver say one must be either "blind or a fool" if they cannot see?

8.   What actor appears as Dr. George's therapist?

9.   What does Bill sell for a living?

10.   In 1998, *Quicksilver Highway* was nominated for an International Fantasy Film Award. In what category was this nomination?

11.   The actress who appears as Dr. George's wife is married to someone else involved with the production. Who is this?

12.   In 2001, cinematographer Shelly Johnson was nominated for his work on a television series produced by director Mick Garris. What is this series?

13. What is Olivia and Kerry's surname?

14. What is Quicksilver's first name?

15. Editor Norman Hollyn served as an apprentice on a 1976 film edited by Alan Heim which was nominated for ten Academy Awards. What is this film?

HARD AS HELL

1. What does Quicksilver call the "powerful little voice" that whispers in your ear?

2. What is the name of Bill's son?

3. What is the name of Dr. George's wife?

4. What is the name of the amusement park where Quicksilver entertains Charlie?

5. What is the name of the "bulletproof girl"?

6. What is the apartment number of the woman who cuts off her nose at the end of "The Body Politic"?

7. What brand of cigarettes does the hitchhiker purchase?

8. What was the original price of the chattery teeth?

9. What is the name of Bill's wife?

10. What is the name of Dr. George's therapist?

11. What is Harriet DaVinci's age?

12. Which of Dr. George's hands "must wield the weapon"?

13. What phrase is written in blood on the hospital floor in "The Body Politic"?

14. How many facelifts has Harriet DaVinci had?

15. What is the name of the highway patrolman who said animals "worked (the hitchhiker) over pretty well"?

QUIZ #43: THE NIGHT FLIER (1997)

Screenplay by: Mark Pavia and Jack O'Donnell
Directed by: Mark Pavia
Starring: Miguel Ferrer, Julie Entwisle, and Dan Monahan
New Amsterdam Entertainment Inc.

Before the cameras began rolling on *The Night Flier*, Stephen King called screenwriters Mark Pavia and Jack O'Donnell "great guys," raving "they did a great screenplay." But, when the modestly-budgeted flick was set to debut on cable, the film looked to be just another shoddy adaptation of a King short story. However, *The Night Flier* was so popular that New Line Cinema purchased the distribution rights and placed the film in theaters the following year.

The Night Flier is easily one of the finest King adaptations to date. Pavia's film debut is an impressive one and although the film begins to unravel a bit in the third act, it still stands above most adaptations of King's horror works—especially those of his short stories, which often tend to feel padded. Journeyman actor Miguel Ferrer shines in the lead role as despicable tabloid journalist Richard Dees.

"One of the great things about reviewing overlooked cult films is that occasionally, instead of panning a movie, you get to uncover a worthy gem," writes *DVD Cult* critic Aaron Miller. "*The Night Flier* is by no means perfect, and it's not the greatest King adaptation ever, but it has a lot to offer in terms of characters, mystery, and horror. Miguel Ferrer's performance must be seen to be believed."

EASY

1. What is the name of the tabloid Richard Dees writes for?

2. One tabloid headline reads: "Springhill Jack Strikes Again!" This is a reference to another work by author Stephen King. What is this?

3. One tabloid headline reads: "Killer Diet: Gypsy's Curse Flayed Fat Lawyer's Flesh!" This is a reference to another work by King. What is this?

4. Ezra Hannon says he noticed something strange beneath the Night Flier's luggage bay. What was this?

5. *The Night Flier* was one of two Stephen King adaptations released in 1997 featuring actor Miguel Ferrer. Ferrer's appearance is uncredited in the other film. What is this film?

6. Richard Dees calls Katherine "Jimmy." Who is this a reference to?

7. Richard Dees predicts the Night Flier will rank "right up there" with three serial killers. Who are these?

8. One tabloid headline reads: "Headless Lamaze Leads to Successful Birth!" This is a reference to another work by King. What is this?

9. What is the name of the funeral parlor where Dees photographs Buck Kendall's corpse?

10. Over what age does Dees' editor advise him to keep photographed victims?

11. One tabloid headline reads: "Naked Demons Levelled My Lawn!" This is a reference to another work by King. What is this?

12. One tabloid headline reads: "Kiddie Cultists in Kansas Worship Creepy Voodoo God!" This is a reference to another work by King. What is this?

13. According to Claire Bowie, from where did the Night Flier travel to Cumberland County Airport?

14. What message does Dees find scrawled in blood on his motel room window?

15. One tabloid headline reads: "Satanic Shopkeeper Sells Gory Goodies!" This is a reference to another work by King. What is this?

MEDIUM DIFFICULTY

1. At the scene of the Night Flier's massacre inside the airport in Wilmington, Dees pulls something from the mouth of a dead man. What is this?

2. Who does Dees pose as when interviewing the Duffry, Maryland sheriff?

3. Stephen King's short story "The Night Flier" features character Richard Dees' second appearance in a King tale. In what King work did Dees first appear?

4. Actress Julie Entwisle would appear in another Mark Pavia-directed horror film co-written by Pavia and Jack O'Donnell in 2000. What is this film?

5. Three years after the release of *The Night Flier*, producer Neal Stevens made his directorial debut with a film produced by *The Dead Next Door* (1988) helmer J.R. Bookwalter. What is this film?

6. What message does Dees find scrawled on the napkin under his drink?

7. What is the name of the beautician Dees questions about Ellen Sarch?

8. At the time of his death, how old is Claire Bowie?

9. What is Richard Dees' journalistic philosophy?

10. What model is the Night Flier's plane?

11. What is the article Katherine describes as being "really tough"?

12. Who is the first person the Night Flier murders in the film?

13. Stephen King's short story, "The Night Flier," first appeared in a collection of stories edited by Douglas E. Winter. What is the title of this book?

14. In 1999, *The Night Flier* was nominated for a Saturn Award by the Academy of Science Fiction, Fantasy & Horror Films. In what category was the film nominated?

15. Where does Dees land after discovering that the Duffrey airstrip is closed?

HARD AS HELL

1. Katherine receives her first byline because of Dees' downfall. What is the headline of this story?

2. What is the tail number on the Night Flier's plane?

3. The Night Flier goes by the name Dwight Renfield. "Renfield" was a character in Bram Stoker's novel, *Dracula*. Why did the killer adopt the name "Dwight"?

4. What is the population of Duffrey, Maryland?

5. What is Katherine's surname?

6. *The Night Flier* was the seventh Stephen King film on which Mitch Galin served as a producer. What are the previous six films?

7. Dees and Katherine stay at the same motel in Duffrey. What is the name of this motel?

8. Who is Richard Dees' editor?

9. Richard P. Rubinstein is a name familiar to fans of King's films. Laurel Entertainment, which Rubinstein founded with George

Romero, made a number of King adaptations, and Rubinstein has served as producer on films ranging from *Creepshow* (1982) to *Thinner*. What was the first Rubinstein-produced film to feature Stephen King as an actor?

10.   What is the name of the reporter whose vacancy at the tabloid was filled by Katherine?

11.   What was Claire Bowie's middle name?

12.   Dees says he needs only three things in life. What are these?

13.   Robert Kurtzman served as special makeup effects supervisor on *The Night Flier*. The same year, Kurtzman directed his second film. What is this film?

14.   What is the name of Ezra Hannon's wife?

15.   What does Renfield say intrigues him about Dees?

QUIZ #44: TRUCKS (1997)

Screenplay by: Brian Taggert
Directed by: Chris Thomson
Starring: Timothy Busfield, Brendan Fletcher, and Brenda Bakke
Credo Entertainment Group

When Stephen King made his directorial debut with *Maximum Over-drive* in 1986, many critics remarked that the film could not possibly have been worse. Well, apparently the folks at Credo Entertainment set out to prove that statement wrong with this second adaptation of King's short story "Trucks." This uneventful adaptation debuted on USA Network in late October, 1997.

"King's version of his story may have been dumb, but it packed in a lot more entertainment than this passable fare that has too many poor attempts at humor," wrote a *Video Graveyard* reviewer. *Apollo Leisure Guide* critic Brian Webster calls the film a "highly-effective sedative" that is "dull, dull, dull, with little to keep us watching."

Maybe *Maximum Overdrive* wasn't so bad after all, huh?

EASY

1. Stephen King's short story "Trucks" was one of two King works adapted for the second time in 1997. Both remakes debuted on network television. What is the other film?

2. How many years has it been since the death of Ray's wife?

3. Who does Bob say he doesn't take orders from?

4. According to George, who gave him the .22 pistol he fires?

5. For how many years was Thad stationed at Area 51?

6. What does George credit with keeping him alive in Korea?

7. Jack and George learn that they were at the same place in 1968. Where was this?

8. Who breaks a bottle over Pete's head?

9. For how many years has Thad been retired from the military?

10. What city did Ray and Logan live in before relocating to Lunar?

11. Where does Hope say she was living when aliens were sighted 17 years before?

12. When Abby runs to answer the ringing telephone, which character saves her, dying in her place?

13. What was Hope's occupation before she was married?

14. Where does Jack say there is always "a lot of psychic energy"?

15. In what country was *Trucks* filmed?

MEDIUM DIFFICULTY

1. Three years after the release of *Trucks*, actor Brendan Fletcher made his directorial debut with a short film. This film was awarded the Australian Film Institute's award for Best Short Fiction Film. What is this film?

2. What cabin does Ray assign the Yeagers?

3. What was George's occupation after his military discharge?

4. Producer Jerry Leider has been nominated for two Razzie Awards. His first nomination, for Worst Picture, came in 1981 for *The Jazz Singer* (1980). In 1996, Leider was nominated for Worst Remake or Sequel. He shared this dubious honor with co-producer Robert Shapiro. For what film did the duo receive this nomination?

5. Jack speaks of a recent comet shower. How long has it been since that shower?

6. At the opening of the film a truck drives through an auto salvage office. What is the name of this business?

7. *Trucks* was one of two films released in 1997 featuring both Jay Brazeau and Brendan Fletcher. What is the other film?

8. How many characters in this film appeared in King's original short story?

9. What is Phil Yeager's occupation?

10. What happened long ago on the site where Lunar was established?

11. What does Ray say that George came to Lunar to do?

12. The same year *Trucks* debuted on network television, actress Brenda Bakke also appeared as a character named Lana Turner in a film nominated for nine Academy Awards. What is this film?

13. What does the acronym SETI mean?

14. What does Jack advise Abby to do when she feels stressed?

15. Abby says that she believes turquoise and silver should either be worn separately or what?

HARD AS HELL

1. What is the name of Hope's business?

2. On what short-lived science fiction series did screenwriter Brian Taggert serve as executive script consultant in the mid-1980s?

3. How long did Thad spend in the Gulf War?

4. What is the motto of Westway Refrigerated?

5. What is the final destination of the bus Hope meets in Bridgeton?

6. What is "BC972"?

7. A year after directing *Trucks*, Chris Thomson helmed a made-for-television film about a town attacked by meteors. This film starred Tom Wopat. What is this film?

8. What is the name of the independently-financed group which replaced SETI?

9. What is Jack's occupation?

10. At Ray's, the special of the day is green pea soup. How much is a bowl of this soup?

11. In 1991, screenwriter Brian Taggert cowrote a horrendous sequel to a classic horror film. This sequel stars Faye Grant, Michael Woods, and Michael Lerner. What is this film?

12. In what branch of the military did Thad serve?

13. In what city do Thad and Abby currently reside?

14. Actor Timothy Busfield is the cofounder of the B Street Theatre troupe. In what city is this located?

15. The vehicles speak with the humans by Morse code in King's short story. What is the message they send?

QUIZ #45: CHILDREN OF THE CORN V: FIELDS OF TERROR (1998)

Screenplay by: Ethan Wiley
Directed by: Ethan Wiley
Starring: Stacy Galina, Alexis Arquette, and Ahmet Zappa
Blue Rider Pictures

This fifth installment finds a group of big city teens on vacation in…Gatlin, Nebraska. (Since it's such a popular tourist spot, you almost wonder why it took three years for anyone to realize all the adults were dead.) Aside from a few unintentional laughs, a decent turn by Alexis Arquette, the stunning beauty of actress Eva Mendes, and return performances from screen icons David Carradine and Fred Williamson, *Children of the Corn V: Fields of Terror* offers nothing new or the least bit entertaining.

"It's more corn-worshipping murderous tyke madness as some friends get caught in a small town and fall victim to another gaggle of scythe-wielding young 'uns," laments *Video Graveyard* critic Chris Hartley of the film's plot. "Unwarranted fifth entry in the surprisingly long-running series starts off okay, but eventually succumbs to a dumb script and a ridiculous finale that piles on the gore. A few scattered moments (such as the first few deaths) are all right, but they bring nothing new to this series. Hopefully it'll end with this poor entry."

No such luck.

EASY

1. Angela Jones and Alexis Arquette appeared together previously in a 1994 film directed by Quentin Tarantino that also references fellow cast member David Carradine. What is this film?

2. Which of the travelers is hypoglycemic?

3. What three things does Luke Enright say he has provided for each of the children?

4. Actor Ahmet Zappa's brother, Dweezil Zappa, appears in a Stephen King adaptation. What is this film?

5. *Children of the Corn V: Fields of Terror* was the second horror sequel directed by Ethan Wiley. What was the first?

6. What is said to be the "age of sin"?

7. Who does Jacob say he did not want to be like?

8. On what charge does the sheriff attempt to arrest Luke Enright?

9. What does Ezekiel instruct an underling to do to ensure that Jacob's screams cannot be heard?

10. A 17-year-old is sacrificed in Jacob's place. Who is this?

11. Who is Jacob's sister?

12. Why does Greg suggest that Tyrus become a cannibal?

13. After stabbing Jacob, what does Ezekiel say will be his "sole purpose"?

14. Before becoming an actor, Fred Williamson was a professional football player. What three National Football League teams did Williamson play for?

15. In 1983 and 1984, director Ethan Wiley served as creature technician on one film produced by George Lucas and another produced by Steven Spielberg. What are these two films?

MEDIUM DIFFICULTY

1.   Actor Fred Williamson appeared in three films directed by *A Return to Salem's Lot* (1987) helmer Larry Cohen. What are these?

2.   What recipe does Greg joke about finding in Jacob's book?

3.   What is the name of the child that Greg calls "Stretch"?

4.   Paul Rabjohns, who scored *Children of the Corn V: Fields of Terror*, served as music editor on a 1997 film which was nominated for nine Oscars. What is this film?

5.   What part of Allison's body is injured by a chainsaw?

6.   What does Ezekiel say "we all have"?

7.   *Children of the Corn V: Fields of Terror* was one of two horrible horror sequels featuring Alexis Arquette in 1998. What is the other film?

8.   What does Greg say he thought he would find at the end of the world?

9.   Who is said to be "like Howard Hughes, only without the money"?

10.   What 1981 film did actor David Carradine write, direct, produce, edit, and appear in?

11.   What is the brand of canned pork product Greg enthuses about sarcastically?

12.   How old was Allison's brother when he ran away from home?

13.   In 2000, actress Eva Mendes appeared in a horror film directed by *Apt Pupil* (1998) editor and composer John Ottman. What is this film?

14.   Who invites Kir to let He Who Walks Beyond the Rows "show you the way"?

15.   A local mistakenly refers to He Who Walks Beyond the Rows by the wrong name. What name does he say?

HARD AS HELL

1. What are the names of the blow-up doll toting adventure-seekers who are hacked into pieces in the cornfield?

2. Who appears in a cameo as a bartender?

3. What is the name of the bus line that passes through town twice a day?

4. What is the title of the book Jacob gives Allison?

5. Actor Fred Williamson is also an accomplished director who has helmed many films. What was the first film Williamson directed?

6. A blow-up doll is hung on a road sign at the beginning of the film. What is the name of the town on the sign?

7. What is the name of the sheriff played by Fred Williamson?

8. What is the name of the girl carrying Jacob's child?

9. The bus stops at the highway junction twice a day. At what times does it stop?

10. The ashes of Kir's deceased boyfriend are spilled. What was the name of her boyfriend?

11. What does Allison drop into the silo fire?

12. The actress who appears as "Drill Girl" is the sister of someone else involved with this film. Who is this?

13. What is the name of the firm which provided makeup effects for the film?

14. Who performs the song "Suffer," which appears in the film?

15. In 1987, cinematographer David Lewis directed a comedy special featuring a well-known stand-up comic. Who is this?

QUIZ #46: APT PUPIL (1998)

Screenplay by: Brandon Boyce
Directed by: Bryan Singer
Starring: Brad Renfro, Ian McKellen, and Joshua Jackson
Paramount Pictures

Apt Pupil first went before cameras in 1987. However, the film soon stalled (and stalled again after that) due to financial woes, the deaths of actors, and other assorted problems. A decade later, producer Don Murphy and helmer Bryan Singer—both fans of Stephen King's novella—revived the project. Here, the story's ending was altered with King's consent (the novelist had final script approval); where the novella closes with Todd Bowden following in his mentor's evil footsteps, the film finishes with a more subtle ending which is, in some ways, much darker.

"I found that to get to a place where Brad Renfro could be on a freeway overpass firing a rifle at cars, I thought you had to take the journey the book takes you on, which was multiple murder," Singer explains. "They both become serial killers. I felt that in book form, it was kind of fun. I thought it was a wild romp, but in a movie, it would be a little exploitive, repetitive, and a bit corny. In dealing with the holocaust as an element in the story, it didn't feel right to go there. I felt it was much more chilling to show the beginning of that journey—the potential for Todd to become that type of creature, or even a different type of creature that's equally dangerous. He was an upper middle-class kid with good grades. He could even become President of the United States. No one knows what secrets he holds and just what he's capable of."

While the movie was not a box-office success, it received largely favorable criticism. *Phantasmagoria* reviewer Kevin Quigley praised *Apt Pupil* as "one of the better films to be made out of a Stephen King story, worthy and chilling."

EASY

1.   Ian McKellen received a Best Actor Academy Award nomination for his turn in another film released the same year as *Apt Pupil*. What is this film?

2.   What is the name of the guidance counselor played by David Schwimmer?

3.   Which cast member also appeared in *The Thin Red Line* and *Fallen* in 1998?

4.   What beverage does Todd request during his first visit to Dussander's house?

5.   Who appears in a cameo as "Doctor"?

6.   Ian McKellen and director Bryan Singer reunited on a film released in 2000. What is this film?

7.   What does Dussander say the homeless man smells like?

8.   In what year does *Apt Pupil's* story begin?

9.   What does Todd say he dusted for Dussander's fingerprints?

10.   Dussander hides under the cover of a pseudonym. What is this?

11.   Editor and composer John Ottman would make his directorial debut on a film released two years after *Apt Pupil*. What is this film?

12. What is the name of Todd's father?

13. What event does Dussander say he was forging documents before?

14. Todd occasionally rides to school with a friend. What is the name of this friend?

15. *Apt Pupil* received two Saturn Awards in 1999. In what categories were these two victories?

MEDIUM DIFFICULTY

1. *Apt Pupil* went into production and was stalled a number of times before producers Jane Hamsher and Don Murphy became involved. Who was the first actor cast as Todd Bowden in 1987?

2. What does Dussander call a "privilege of boys"?

3. *Apt Pupil* was produced by director Bryan Singer's Bad Hat Harry Productions. The name of Singer's production company references a line from a 1975 horror film. What is this?

4. What year does Todd graduate high school?

5. What is the name of Todd's mother?

6. Producer Jane Hamsher wrote a memoir about her experiences working with director Oliver Stone on *Natural Born Killers* (1994). What is the title of this book?

7. According to fliers posted in the neighborhood, what is the name of the cat Dussander kills?

8. What does Todd use to beat the dying homeless man to death?

9. What is the name of Todd's grandfather?

10. What is the name of the girl Todd dates in the film?

11. Editor and composer John Ottman had already worked on three films directed by Bryan Singer before their collaboration on *Apt Pupil*. What are these three films?

12. Who was the first director attached to *Apt Pupil* in 1987?

13. Dussander watches an episode from an old television series in which a tiny man is stalked by a huge cat. What is this series?

14. What is the name of the high school Todd attends?

15. Prior to *Apt Pupil*, screenwriter Brandon Boyce appeared as an actor in two films directed by Bryan Singer. What are these?

HARD AS HELL

1. What is the name of the Israeli professor who visits Dussander in the hospital?

2. What is the date of the *True War* magazine Todd reads?

3. What is Todd's high school mascot?

4. What does a sign posted in the hallway of Todd's school dare students to be?

5. What is the name of the Jewish patient who recognizes Dussander in the hospital?

6. What is Todd's baseball jersey number?

7. In what year does Todd say Dussander was spotted in West Berlin?

8. In what months did Dussander serve at Auschwitz?

9. What is the name of the costume company Todd purchases the replica Nazi uniform from?

10. What is the name of the store where Dussander purchases his liquor?

11. On what day of the week does Todd present Dussander with his "gift"?

12. What is the name of the book written by David Kahn that Todd reads about the Nazis?

13. What does Dussander tell Todd's family kept him out of combat?

14. In what year does Dussander claim he became an American citizen?

15. Dussander tells Todd of an incident when the poison gas didn't work and he was forced to send in gunmen to kill the prisoners. How many gunmen did he send in?

QUIZ #47: SOMETIMES THEY COME BACK...FOR MORE (1998)

Screenplay by: Adam Grossman and Darryl Sollerh
Directed by: Daniel Zelik Berk
Starring: Clayton Rohner, Faith Ford, and Max Perlich
Trimark Pictures

With this third installment, *Sometimes They Come Back* threatens to topple *Children of the Corn* as the premier franchise of bastardized King-inspired straight-to-video movies; sadly, *Sometimes They Come Back...For More* has less to do with King's original short story than the *Corn* films. For what it's worth, the film is mildly entertaining and much more sleek than the two films which precede it, if not as good. The flick also benefits from superb casting as charismatic actor Clayton Rohner appears in the lead. However, in the end, Rohner's considerable charm and the film's lavish (for a straight-to-vid "B" movie) sets cannot save it from itself. A horrendous screenplay and lackluster direction make *Sometimes They Come Back...For More* a one-time viewing.

Let's just hope they don't come back...anymore.

EASY

1.   What is the name of the "illegal mining operation courtesy of the Pentagon"?

2.   Which cast member appears in music videos by Young MC, The Pharcyde, and Luscious Jackson?

3.   Special effects coordinator Frank Ceglia provided the effects for a 1992 Stephen King "adaptation" which King successfully sued to have his name removed from because the film bore no resemblance to his original work. What is this film?

4.   Who is Cage's half brother?

5.   Who observes that the "apple doesn't fall far from the tree"?

6.   What was Mary's occupation in the war?

7.   Actress Faith Ford received Golden Globe nominations in 1991 and 1992 for her work on a popular television series. What is this series?

8.   What was Robert Reynolds' occupation?

9.   What is Shebanski's rank?

10. On what short-lived television series did Clayton Rohner appear as agent Chandler Smythe?

11. What is Cage's first name?

12. When Cage instructs him to "keep going toward the light, Carol Ann," what horror film is being misquoted?

13. What design is imprinted on the foreheads of the undead?

14. Actress Chase Masterson appeared as a regular on *Star Trek: Deep Space Nine* for four years. What is the name of the character she played?

15. What is Major O'Grady's first name?

MEDIUM DIFFICULTY

1. Actor Damian Chapa directed a film which was released the same year as *Sometimes They Come Back...For More*. This film stars Natasha Henstridge, Stephen Duerr, and Chapa himself. What is this film?

2. What does Shebanski call "toast"?

3. What does Cage use to impale Schilling?

4. The name "Jon Porter" is scrawled on a map in Schilling's room. What film is this a reference to?

5. Actor Max Perlich appeared on the television series *Homicide: Life on the Street* from 1995 to 1997. What is the name of the character Perlich played?

6. What is the deepest level of the mine?

7. What does Cage find on Schilling's desk?

8. Major O'Grady says there are "only two questions" which need answered. What are these?

9. Which cast member appeared as a recurring character on *Melrose Place*?

10. Which cast member appeared in a different role in the film's predecessor, *Sometimes They Come Back...Again* (1996)?

11. What is the name of the medical officer assigned to the ice station?

12. The name "Jim Norman" is scrawled on the map next to the location Bangor, Maine. What film is this a reference to?

13. Screenwriter Adam Grossman made his directorial debut in 1996 with a Stephen King-related film. What is this film?

14. What is Schilling's first name?

15. What does Schilling say will happen if he returns to Hell?

HARD AS HELL

1.   Who appears in a cameo role as "Soldier in Bar"?

2.   What are the film's two alternate titles?

3.   Prior to directing *Sometimes They Come Back...For More*, Daniel Zelik Berk produced a 1996 film directed by *Firestarter* (1984) helmer Mark L. Lester. What is this film?

4.   A film directed by screenwriter Adam Grossman was released the same year as *Sometimes They Come Back...For More*. This film was executive produced by Wes Craven. What is this film?

5.   The inscription on the ring says, "To Mary." What year is inscribed on the ring?

6.   What does Shebanski say the "guy in charge of power" is doing just down the hall?

7.   Schilling tells Cage that he was "brought to this planet for one purpose." What is this?

8.   What is the title of the book Cage finds in Schilling's room?

9.   Why does Cage reason that Shebanski might have hidden Baines' body?

10.   What is Robert Reynolds' rank?

11.   What is Shebanski's first name?

12.   After how many hours does "standard operating procedure" dictate that backup should be sent after Cage and O'Grady?

13.   Who served as both line producer and second unit director on this film?

14.   What is the "joy" Schilling encourages Cage to experience?

15.   What does Schilling say only weaklings and fools believe in?

QUIZ #48: STORM OF THE CENTURY (1999)

Screenplay by: Stephen King
Directed by: Craig R. Baxley
Starring: Timothy Daly, Colm Feore, and Debrah Farentino
Greengrass Productions

Stephen King's second story written expressly for film (and the first expressly for television) is the tale of an ancient evil which arrives on Little Tall Island simultaneously with the much-ballyhooed "storm of the century."

"It's about the biggest snowstorm I could imagine," said King, who also served as executive producer with Emmy Award-winner Mark Carliner. That meant taking some of the storm effects of *The Shining* and taking them to the fifth or sixth power. "We've met the challenge by using the most amazing sets. This is a very expensive project and all of the money is going to be up on the screen. I like the idea of using a storm in this story because the forces of nature are so huge. Because we are human, and because we tend to personalize things, I think we always see huge storms as a metaphor for the storms that go on in our emotions; the constant battle between our desires and what we believe is right. So I thought, wouldn't it be great to take a big storm—the macrocosm— and then take a little storm, which is this evil being, Andre Linoge, who shows up in Little Tall Island, and combine them."

EASY

1. *Storm of the Century* is the second King film which takes place on Little Tall Island. What was the first film?

2. Linoge says the people of another island "knew how to keep a secret." What island is this?

3. Which cast member also appears in *Face/Off* (1997), *City of Angels* (1998), and *Pearl Harbor* (2001)?

4. Timothy Daly's character asks, "Do you see Superman around here?" What is the significance of this?

5. Who appears in an uncredited cameo as a lawyer urging, "Get what's coming to you"?

6. What is the name of the seafood wholesaler Linoge says has "got the marijuana business to fall back on"?

7. What year did the "storm of the century" occur?

8. Senior producer Tom Brodek produced and appeared as an actor in a 1985 film starring Jeff Goldblum and Ed Begley, Jr. What is this film?

9. Cat Withers reads *The Little Puppy* to the children. This book is also referred to in a novel by Stephen King. What is this novel?

10. What NBA team does Davey Hopewell dream of playing for?

11. On what television sitcom did actor Timothy Daly and Steven Weber of *Stephen King's The Shining* (1997) appear as brothers?

12. *Storm of the Century* is one of two King films released in 1999 featuring actor Jeffrey DeMunn. What is the other film?

13. Composer Gary Chang, who scored *Storm of the Century*, composed a score which was ultimately rejected for a 1993 film

directed by John Badham. This film stars Bridget Fonda, Gabriel Byrne, and Dermot Mulroney. What is this film?

14.   The handle of Linoge's cane features the head of an animal. What is this animal?

15.   What is the name of Molly Anderson's daycare?

MEDIUM DIFFICULTY

1.   Who is the first person on Little Tall Island to come into contact with Andre Linoge?

2.   What is discovered written in lipstick on the women's restroom mirrors inside the Town Hall?

3.   What is the name of the Mark Twain story Stephen King says his "small town tales," such as *Storm of the Century*, are indebted to?

4.   Who is the town manager?

5.   In February 1999, ABC producers caught flak from meteorologists and television analysts alike for a *Storm of the Century* promotion. What was this?

6.   What does Linoge say "Hell is all about"?

7.   What is the name of Alton Hatcher's daughter?

8.   *Storm of the Century* was the second Stephen King film on which David Connell served as cinematographer. What was the first?

9.   Director Craig R. Baxley served as second unit director on a 1981 film which garnered twelve Academy Award nominations. What is this film?

10.   What is the name of the real estate company where Robbie Beals is employed?

11.   In what subject does Linoge say Mike Anderson nearly received a "D"?

12.   Who was the father of Cat Withers' aborted child?

13.   Stephen King says his idea for *Storm of the Century* began with a single image. What was this?

14.   Before films are scored, they are often given temporary tracks of already-existing music, called "temp tracks." Much of the temp track for *Storm of the Century* came from the soundtrack of a Stephen King adaptation. What is this film?

15.   *Storm of the Century* was the third King story to take place on Little Tall Island. The first to feature the location was a short story. What is this story?

HARD AS HELL

1.   Where did the townsfolk gather during the "storm of '27"?

2.   What is the name of Kirk Freeman's sister?

3.   What is the name of Angela Carver's son?

4.   In what city was Robbie Beals when his mother died?

5.   *Storm of the Century* was nominated for two Saturn Awards in 2000, winning one in the category "Best Single Genre Television Presentation." In what category did the film lose?

6.   In the introduction, how many years does Mike Anderson say it's been since the "storm of the century"?

7.   What is the name of Alton Hatcher's wife?

8.   In her fourth film role, Kristin Baxley appears as Annie Huston. How many of the four films Baxley appears in were not directed by her husband, Craig R. Baxley?

9.   In what town does the one-eyed kid with the lisp which Jack Carver, Lucien Fournier, and Alex Haber assaulted now reside?

10.   Volumes one and two of a videocassette series are advertised in the film for $19.95 apiece. What is the name of this morbid video series?

11.   Stephen King was one of two executive producers on *Storm of the Century*. Who was the other executive producer?

12.   What is the name of the child who says he once fed a monkey at the Bangor fair?

13.   How much is Mike Anderson paid each year to be constable of Little Tall Island?

14.   Filmmaker Craig R. Baxley's directing career began with episodes of a popular '80s television series. What is this series?

15.   What is the telephone number advertised for the law firm of Mcintosh and Redding?

QUIZ #49: THE RAGE: CARRIE 2 (1999)

Screenplay by: Rafael Moreu
Directed by: Katt Shea
Starring: Emily Bergl, Jason London, and Dylan Bruno
United Artists

You have to ask yourself just who the "genius" at United Artists was that first cooked up the idea for this turkey. From the very start, *The Rage: Carrie 2* had all the ingredients for disaster; the film has very little to do with the original *Carrie* (1976), connected only by a half sister who is twenty-three years younger than Carrie White, and lacks the three things that made the first film effective: director Brian De Palma, screenwriter Lawrence Cohen, and, of course, a story by Stephen King. Instead, this film offers up (then and still) unproven actors, writer, and director. This film typifies the laziest of sequels in that it is merely a rehash of the original with lesser talents, a method which has served the *Children of the Corn* (1985) franchise well.

Orlando Weekly film critic Brad Haynes explains: "[Director Katt] Shea, unfortunately, brings no style to *Carrie 2*. Unimaginative duplications plague the entire production, especially the ending, which is virtually verbatim. And visually, Shea's computer-graphic-enhanced finale doesn't even come close to De Palma's shriek-inducing dream sequence. An example of formulaic filmmaking and lost potential, *The Rage: Carrie 2* is neither scary nor suspenseful..."

EASY

1. What does Tracy paint on the side of Jesse's vehicle?

2. What type of flowers does Rachel suggest that Jesse show up on her doorstep carrying?

3. The first director assigned to *The Rage: Carrie 2* quit after two weeks of shooting because of creative differences. Who was this?

4. Carrie White and Rachel Lang were fathered by the same man. What is his name?

5. An alternate (and, as unbelievable as it may be, worse) ending of the film exists. Instead of exploding into a million pieces, something shoots out of Rachel's mouth. What is this?

6. What is the name of Eric Stark's father?

7. What is the name of the nosy salesclerk who follows Rachel around the department store?

8. What is the alternate title for *The Rage: Carrie 2*?

9. What occupation does Jesse predict for himself if he doesn't land a football scholarship?

10. What is the name of Rachel's pet beagle?

11. Which cast member appears in the Aerosmith video "Amazing"?

12. What did director Katt Shea include in *The Rage: Carrie 2* which she feared would give critics ammunition to blast her film?

13. What does Rachel say she's not sure she believes in?

14. Zachery Ty Bryan finished an eight-year stint on a popular sitcom the year *The Rage: Carrie 2* was released. What is this sitcom?

15. What cargo is the truck that hits Rachel's dog carrying?

MEDIUM DIFFICULTY

1. *The Rage: Carrie 2* was screenwriter Rafael Moreu's second pro-
    duced script. What was the first?

2. How much do Rachel's stepparents earn per month for keeping her?

3. What is the name of the college Jesse attends?

4. Which cast member was a National Forensics League national
    champion in Poetry Reading in 1993?

5. What is the name of Jesse's "Melrose Place Super Bitch" girlfriend?

6. While discussing her non-conformity with Jesse, Rachel references
    a song by R.E.M. What is this song?

7. Why does Monica Jones suggest that Jesse should receive more
    points for sleeping with Rachel?

8. Coach Walsh orders Mark to drop his shorts so he can inspect
    him. What does the coach say he's looking for?

9. What is the name of Rachel's mother?

10. Cinematographer Don Morgan worked on a film released in 1997
    that was directed by Sidney J. Furie and stars Lorenzo Lamas and
    Gary Busey. What is the significance of this film regarding *The
    Rage: Carrie 2*?

11. In a shot cut from the final film, Rachel kicks something while
    walking through the rubble from the burned down high school.
    What does she kick?

12. How much money does Mark first offer Rachel for Lisa's photographs?

13. What is the name of the nonexistent man Rachel's mother waves to?

14. Who appears in a cameo role as the assistant district attorney?

15. What did Rachel's mother tell her was the name of her father?

HARD AS HELL

1. Director Katt Shea landed her first acting gig in a 1982 film starring Dennis Drake, Steven Holt, and Peter Brady Reardon. What is this film?

2. In 2000, *The Rage: Carrie 2* was nominated for a Saturn Award. In what category was this nomination?

3   At what time does the high school recognize a moment of silence for Lisa?

4. What is the name of the institution where Rachel's mother resides?

5. What is the surname of the sheriff who confronts Eric?

6. Director Katt Shea hired cinematographer Donald Morgan based on the mistaken belief that he had worked on one of her favorite films. What is this film?

7. What is the name of Monica Jones' boyfriend?

8. What is the name of the band Jesse says he loves?

9. What is Rachel's address?

10. Who was the first girl Jesse had sex with after beginning the contest?

11. What is the occupation of Eric's father?

12. What is the name of Rachel's stepfather?

13. The burned down high school is actually the remnants of a real-life factory that had burned down. What type of factory was this?

14. What is the name of the photo mat where Rachel works?

15. How many points does Jesse receive for sleeping with Rachel?

QUIZ #50: CHILDREN OF THE CORN 666: ISAAC'S RETURN (1999)

Screenplay by: John Franklin and Tim Silka
Directed by: Kari Skogland
Starring: Natalie Ramsey, John Franklin, and Paul Popowich
Dimension Films

In the sixth nonsensical installment in the *Children of the Corn* franchise, the filmmakers opt to return the to series' roots and reintroduce the character Isaac, who appeared in the first *Corn* film. Luckily, Isaac is a dwarf, so the children don't seem to mind that he's well past the age of eighteen (the age when a child enters maturity and must be killed in Gatlin).

As can be expected, *Children of the Corn 666: Isaac's Return* was not a critical darling. *Apollo Movie Guide* critic Ryan Bracknell says, "They're back, but why? After watching the sixth and hopefully final chapter in the *Children of the Corn* series, I can assure you there's not much to look forward to in Isaac's return... The plot relies far too much on the previous *Children of the Corn* films for this movie to stand on its own." *Movie Report* film critic Michael Dequina echoes that sentiment in his review: "I had not seen a single *Children of the Corn* film before watching the newest straight-to-tape installment, and after seeing *666*, I have no desire to catch up on the back story. Anyway, there's really not much of a story to begin with in *Isaac's Return*... [The film] runs a scant seventy-eight minutes, but it feels at least twice as long; there's nothing interesting, let alone scary or exciting in this cheapie. Even the acting, while bad, isn't quite bad enough to be laughable."

EASY

1. How many miles outside Gatlin is Hannah when she picks up Zachariah Johnson?

2. Who does Dr. Michaels say would be in jail were it not for "creative paperwork"?

3. Who does Gabriel demand "On your knees, bitch"?

4. What is the name of the Gatlin sheriff?

5. What is Rachel's surname?

6. What is Hannah's surname?

7. Nancy Allen also appears in *Carrie* (1976). What role does she play in that film?

8. What does Jesse advise Hannah would be a "good way to make friends"?

9. Who was Isaac's first born child?

10. What holiday does Hannah's birthday coincide with?

11. Who does Dr. Michaels call the "medical miracle"?

12. What does Cora advise Hannah to embrace?

13. What does Rachel say is the only power Isaac possesses?

14. Who is Matt's father?

15. Which cast member did the *New York Times* once dub the "finest classical American actor since John Barrymore"?

MEDIUM DIFFICULTY

1. In 1997, director Kari Skogland helmed a film about characters named Lucas, Goldman, and Mamet. What is this film?

2. What name does Zachariah Johnson suggest should Hannah have a child?

3. What does Isaac say Hannah's visions are "born of"?

4. What is the name of the Gatlin County Hospital patient who attempts to smother Isaac?

5. What does Hannah say she forgot to do between "breaking and entering and being stalked"?

6. Which cast member once spent nine months in an English jail when charged with smuggling cocaine?

7. What word does Gabriel say, causing Cora to shoot herself?

8. Who does Gabriel warn, "You are so dead"?

9. Actress Natalie Ramsey started her career as a regular on *Days of Our Lives*. What character did she play?

10. What does Isaac say Hannah cannot escape?

11. What is Dr. Michaels' response when he's warned that smoking will kill him?

12. Which actor appears in both *Children of the Corn* (1984) and *Children of the Corn 666: Isaac's Return*?

13. What message is written in blood in the bathroom of Hannah's motel room?

14. What does Rachel call "repulsive"?

15. Who does Isaac instruct to "father the child who shall lead us all"?

HARD AS HELL

1. Which cast member appears in *Children of Corn IV: The Gathering* (1996) as "Concerned Father" and in *Children of the Corn 666: Isaac's Return* as "Jake"?

2. Paul Popowich played a recurring character on *Beverly Hills, 90210* in 1998. What was the name of his character?

3. What is the name of the fictitious game show Gabriel welcomes viewers to before he impales Isaac?

4. Hannah proposes a title for an episode of *The Jerry Springer Show* she could appear on. What is this?

5. Associate producer Craig Nicholls also worked on *Children of the Corn V: Fields of Terror* (1998). What was his role on that project?

6. What year did "Baby Colby" supposedly die?

7. What room in the motel does Hannah stay in?

8. How long was Isaac in a coma?

9. Cinematographer Richard Clabaugh made his directorial debut in 2000 with another horror film. What is this film?

10. Which direction is Hemingford from Gatlin?

11. Who does Isaac say had visions of a perfect world?

12. Where are the extra towels in Hannah's motel room located?

13. Producer Bill Berry directed a 1976 blaxploitation film starring Roy Jefferson and Mike Thomas. What is this film?

14. In what nearby city is the Hilton located?

15. What ornament hangs from Hannah's rearview mirror?

QUIZ #51: THE GREEN MILE (1999)

Screenplay by: Frank Darabont
Directed by: Frank Darabont
Starring: Tom Hanks, David Morse, and Bonnie Hunt
Warner Bros.

After reading the first chapter ("The Two Dead Girls") of Stephen King's serialized novel *The Green Mile*, screenwriter/director Frank Darabont agreed to adapt the story to screen. Having already made *The Shawshank Redemption* (1994), Darabont jokingly called himself the master of the world's smallest genre: the Stephen King prison drama.

"I had no intention of (making another prison film)," Darabont says. "You know, your best-laid plans are thwarted by fortune, because Steve dreamed up this fantastically good story. It did give me pause when I heard the word 'prison' drop out of his mouth. I thought, 'Oh, criminy. Not again. I can't do that twice.' But then I thought, 'That's a stupid reason to avoid making a film of a story that I thought was really great.'"

Darabont performed the same magic with *The Green Mile* that he did on *The Shawshank Redemption*, which are easily two of the finest King adaptations to date. Darabont also received Oscar nominations for Best Screenplay and Best Picture, just as he had with *Shawshank*. (Sadly, even with eleven Academy Award nominations the two films received no Oscars.)

EASY

1. By what nickname do the guards refer to the electric chair?

2. According to Brutal, adult admission upon entrance of Mouseville is ten cents. How much is admission for children?

3. A prison plumber is dressed as a V.I.P. for Del and Mr. Jingles' show. What is this man's name?

4. What is Brutal's real name?

5. A friend of actor Michael Clark Duncan suggested that he audition for the role of John Coffey, saying, "Michael, I'm telling you right now: You are John Coffey. ... You could be this guy; I know you'd be perfect for this part." Who was this?

6. How old was Arlen Bitterbuck when he was married?

7. Del sings, "Percy Wetmore, do a dance..." What is the next line of his song?

8. What does William Wharton's tattoo say?

9. *The Green Mile* was the third film featuring both Tom Hanks and Gary Sinise. What two films had Hanks and Sinise already appeared together in?

10. What cell block is death row?

11. What is the name of the prison where Paul Edgecomb is employed?

12. What is the name of Warden Hal Moores' wife?

13. The name of the character played by Barry Pepper is quite similar to the name of the journeyman actor who appears as Toot-Toot. What are these two names?

14. What are the names of the "two dead girls"?

15. *The Green Mile* was actor William Sadler's second appearance in a film directed by Frank Darabont. (*The Shawshank Redemption* was the other.) However, in 1991 Sadler appeared in a telefilm written by Darabont and co-directed by Tom Holland, the director of *The Langoliers* (1995) and *Thinner* (1996). What is this film?

MEDIUM DIFFICULTY

1. What does the sign outside Trapingus Parish advise?

2. Who suggests a cigar box with cotton batting for Mr. Jingles' bed?

3. What does William Wharton pay Toot-Toot for the Moon Pie he spits in Brutal's face?

4. *The Green Mile* was David Morse's second appearance in a Stephen King adaptation. What was the King film the actor had previously appeared in?

5. According to Brutal and Paul, where is Mouseville located?

6. Before collaborating on *The Green Mile*, director Frank Darabont performed uncredited rewrites for a film featuring actors Tom Hanks and Barry Pepper. What is this film?

7. During executions on "The Green Mile," who throws the switch?

8. In *The Green Mile*, David Morse plays a guard on death row. The following year, Morse appeared in a film in which his character is responsible for a woman being sent to death row. What is this film?

9. What does Brutal say "can follow a man around for a long, long time"?

10. Who shaves Arlen Bitterbuck's head before his execution?

11. In what year does John Coffey arrive at the prison?

12. While watching a movie featuring Fred Astaire and Ginger Rogers, Paul becomes overwhelmed with memories. What is this film?

13. How many people did William Wharton murder during the holdup which landed him in prison?

14. The year before his appearance in *The Green Mile*, Brian Libby played a prison guard in a telefilm co-written by Darabont. What is this film?

15. What is the name of the state hospital where Percy has applied?

HARD AS HELL

1. The nursing home residents briefly watch *The Jerry Springer Show*. What is the title of the episode they watch?

2. What does Hal Moores say his wife's brain tumor is the size of?

3. In Stephen King's original serial novel, what year did the events in the prison take place?

4. Who served as composer on both *The Shawshank Redemption* and *The Green Mile*?

5. What is the name of the doctor Paul plans to visit for urinary infection before being "helped" by John Coffey?

6. In researching the role of William Wharton, actor Sam Rockwell read a number of books and spoke with real prison inmates. The book Rockwell noted as being the most helpful was written by Jack Henry Abbott and details a convicted killer's twenty-five-year stint in prison. What is the title of this book?

7. While rehearsing for Arlen Bitterbuck's execution, Toot-Toot jokes that he would like an actress to sit on his face. Who is this?

8.   *The Green Mile* was actor Harry Dean Stanton's second appearance in a Stephen King adaptation. What was the first King-inspired film in which he appeared?

9.   Tom Hanks made his directorial debut on a television series which Frank Darabont occasionally wrote for. What is this series?

10. *The Green Mile* was nominated for four Academy Awards in 2000. In what categories were these nominations?

11. What is the date of Arlen Bitterbuck's execution?

12. Director Frank Darabont broke into the film industry as a production assistant on a 1981 horror film. What is this film?

13. After reading the first installment of the serial novel, *The Green Mile*, director Frank Darabont immediately flew to Colorado to talk with King. Why was King in Colorado?

14. In what state does *The Green Mile* take place?

15. After viewing an early working print of *The Green Mile* in early 1999, novelist King had only one criticism. What was this?

QUIZ #52: HEARTS IN ATLANTIS (2001)

Screenplay by: William Goldman
Directed by: Scott Hicks
Starring: Anthony Hopkins, Anton Yelchin, and David Morse
Warner Bros.

Stephen King has called *Hearts in Atlantis* one of the better adaptations of his work. However, fans of King's book may find themselves disappointed by the filmmakers' decision to remove the supernatural element contained in the original collection. "[Screenwriter] Bill Goldman made the choice to just focus on the first of the stories and bookended one of the last stories and pretty much forgot about the rest, because it was too diverse to be part of a coherent narrative," explains director Scott Hicks. "In the novel, the 'low men' are actually aliens, and Ted might be an alien. I decided to remove all that and focus on the human story because I found that much more interesting."

Unfortunately, the film itself isn't all that interesting. Despite fine performances from Anthony Hopkins and newcomer Anton Yelchin, Hicks' direction coupled with the saccharine-sweet schmaltz of Goldman's script leaves *Hearts in Atlantis* limp. *Salon* critic Andrew O'Hehir observes, "You come out of the theater with nothing more specific than half-pleasant memories of baseball gloves, Ferris wheels, and vintage automobiles. I've had naps that were more exciting."

EASY

1. What is the name of Carol's daughter?

2. What parcel delivery service brings Sully's baseball glove to Bobby's house?

3. What is Carol's surname?

4. The barmaid at The Corner Pocket gives Bobby a photograph of a man. Who is this?

5. What does Ted tell Carol to bite down on while he relocates her shoulder?

6. Why does Bobby's mother say she distrusts Ted the first time she sees him?

7. What beverage does Ted keep in his refrigerator?

8. What does Bobby say people "always believe will stay the same"?

9. An instrumental performed by Santo and Johnny appears in the film. It is also Charles Brady's favorite tune in *Sleepwalkers* (1992). What is the title of this song?

10. Who does Ted say was the "greatest football player who ever lived"?

11. Ted explains that he would be among the ten most wanted fugitives if there were Library Police. This is a nod to another Stephen King novella. What novella is this?

12. Who suggests that Bobby invite Ted to the fair?

13. *Hearts in Atlantis* marked actor David Morse's third appearance in a King adaptation. What were the two previous King films featuring Morse?

14. What, according to Ted, "can be solid gold"?

15. What birthday gift does Bobby find inside the card from his mother?

MEDIUM DIFFICULTY

1. In what nearby town do Ted and Bobby go to the movie theater?

2. What, according to Elizabeth Garfield, did Bobby's father never meet that he didn't like?

3. After Sully's funeral, what refreshments are offered at the Veteran's Hall?

4. While reading the sports page to Ted, Bobby announces that a baseball player is poised to break Ty Cobb's stolen base record. Who is this?

5. What 1960 film does Ted describe as being about "evil little kids"?

6. What does Ted advise Bobby to do if he sees the "low men"?

7. We are first introduced to the adolescent Bobby on his birthday. How old is he?

8. What name is emblazoned on the side of the bicycle Bobby eyes in the shop window?

9. What western television series is Bobby watching when his mother informs him that she will be leaving for the weekend?

10. The three-card monte dealer uses the unusual phrase "easy-peasy Japanesy." A character from *The Shawshank Redemption* (1994) also uses this phrase. Who was the *Shawshank* character who said this?

11. What proclamation is scrawled inside the birthday card Bobby receives from Carol?

12. What is the name of the lost dog described on the first poster Bobby sees?

13.   What book does Ted explain "ends with a beheading"?

14.   In what city is the seminar Elizabeth Garfield is attending?

15.   How old was Bobby when his father died?

HARD AS HELL

1.   From what two Stephen King novellas was the film adapted?

2.   Near what city was the job Elizabeth Garfield found after being fired?

3.   What brand of cigarettes does Ted smoke?

4.   What was the working title of the Stephen King collection *Hearts in Atlantis*?

5.   Bobby reads the newspaper to Ted each day. In another King novella (and film adaptation), a boy visits an elderly man each day under the pretense that he is reading to him. What is the title of this novella?

6.   Bobby receives a newspaper clipping with Sully's baseball glove. What does the headline read?

7.   According to an article Bobby reads to Ted, who does J. Edgar Hoover deny recruiting to assist the Federal Bureau of Investigations?

8.   How much money does Ted win betting on Albini?

9.   What is the name of Bobby's wife?

10.   Who does Ted say was "brilliant, but foolish about money"?

11.   What is the name of Elizabeth Garfield's rapist boss?

12.   To whom is the film dedicated?

13. In what state does Elizabeth Garfield's boss joke about it being legal to shoot women?

14. What is the name of the bully who dresses in his mother's clothes?

15. What brand does Elizabeth Garfield say are "hardly even cigarettes"?

QUIZ #53: THE MANGLER 2 (2001)

Screenplay by: Michael Hamilton-Wright
Directed by: Michael Hamilton-Wright
Starring: Lance Henriksen, Chelse Swain, and Will Sanderson
Artisan Entertainment

Taking a page from the lamer-than-thou *Sometimes They Come Back* (1991) franchise, screenwriter/director Michael Hamilton-Wright brings us this unwanted sequel which has absolutely nothing to do with its predecessor. Simply put, *The Mangler 2* ranks among the worst of the bastardized B-movie schlock sequels "based" on King's work. The only aspect of this film which makes it even remotely watchable is actress Daniella Evangelista scantily-clad in a bikini top throughout most of the film. And while veteran actor Lance Henriksen is certainly no stranger to bad films, the poor guy deserves much better than this; one memorably bad scene finds Henriksen with electrodes attached to his head, quoting a Spice Girls song!

Watch this astoundingly poor film at your own risk.

EASY

1.   What is the name of the company Jo's father owns?

2.   What nickname does Jo give Chef Lecours?

3. What is the name of the virus Jo downloads into the computer system at her father's company?

4. Someone tampers with the school website, posting a picture of Headmaster Bradeen. What is he shown kissing in the picture?

5. Where does Emily say she's trying to "push" Jo?

6. What is the name of the website where Jo downloads the Mangler virus?

7. What piece of clothing does Corey say he hopes Emily will be wearing on the first day of school?

8. Who wrote the letter that Headmaster Bradeen accuses Jo of writing?

9. Who does Bradeen's computer call the "weakest link"?

10. What does Bradeen conclude that "hell hath no fury" like?

11. Who do the students refer to as "Mr. Porno"?

12. A mistake was made when printing the film title on the backs of the folding "director chairs" used on the set of *The Mangler 2*. What incorrect film title appeared on the chairs?

13. Corey believes the periodic table is actually an ancient language. Who does he believe created it?

14. When Will says, "Let's see what dirty little secrets this perv has been keeping from us," who is he referring to?

15. What does Dan ask if Corey and Emily can do while moving on their feet?

MEDIUM DIFFICULTY

1. A poster is visible in Jo's room for another film produced by Glen Tedham and starring actor Philippe Bergeron. What is this film?

2. When Emily complains that she cannot breathe, what does Chef Lecours offer her?

3. What condiment does Corey imagine eating on shredded lettuce?

4. What magazine is Mr. Vessey carrying when he is killed?

5. *The Mangler 2* is one of two 2001 horror sequels featuring actress Daniella Evangelista. What is the other film?

6. What does Jo's computer screen say just after she loads the Mangler virus?

7. What is the school motto?

8. Who are director Michael Hamilton-Wright and producer Glen Tedham collectively known as?

9. Who hacked into the school's website?

10. Who does Chef Lecours say the school's surveillance system reminds him of?

11. Michael Hamilton-Wright received his first screenwriting credit on a 1997 film directed by Louis Morneau. What is this film?

12. What do Bradeen's files say Will spends too much time doing?

13. What does Corey say may be Mr. Porno's favorite film?

14. How many copies of George Orwell's novel *1984* does Will say he owns?

15. Actress Chelse Swain made her screen debut in a 1999 film directed by Sofia Coppola. What is this film?

HARD AS HELL

1.   What is Emily's surname?

2.   What was significant regarding the first day of shooting for actress Chelsea Swain?

3.   What band performed all of the songs used in the film?

4.   What is the name of Jo's bodyguard?

5.   What does Emily say Chef Lecours is "wasting his life" doing?

6.   What is the name of the reporter writing the story about the school's security system?

7.   What is the name of the school janitor?

8.   Emily hits Bradeen in the face with a book. What is the title of this book?

9.   What is the name of the online magazine that profiles the school's security system?

10.   What is Will's surname?

11.   What term does William Newton prefer to 'artificial intelligence'?

12.   Who was the real-life owner of the automobile Corey drives in the film?

13.   The location where the outside shots of Jo's father's corporation was actually a school. What can be seen on the far left side of the screen, covered with black tarp intended to hide it?

14.   What does Bradeen's computer say "the black guy" doesn't always do first?

15.   Actress Chelse Swain, who plays Jo, is the sister of another film actress. Who is this?

QUIZ #54: CHILDREN OF THE CORN: REVELATION (2001)

Screenplay by: S.J. Smith
Directed by: Guy Magar
Starring: Claudette Mink, Kyle Cassie, and Michael Ironside
Dimension Films

Installment seven in the *Children of the Corn* series finds a young woman searching for her elderly grandmother. When she arrives at her grandmother's apartment building, which is surrounded by corn stalks (!?), she stumbles across a group of adolescent corn-worshipping cultists and a mysterious priest whose name is never given in the film. As in most bad horror films, the woman is repeatedly warned to leave or die, but remains anyway.

While *Revelation* is admittedly better than at least half of the *Children of the Corn* films, it is far from good. (This is a dubious distinction on par with being one of the best actors in a *Saw* movie.) Dimension Films once again uses the tried-and-true formula it's utilized with each of the *Children of the Corn* flicks: no-name actors, poor script, unknown director, et al. The end result is a straight-to-video product of low quality which is likely to make a profit anyway... Let us all say this prayer before we go to sleep tonight: "Please God, do not let there be any more *Children of the Corn* sequels. Please make them stop."

Amen.

EASY

1. When Jamie shows her grandmother's apartment to Det. Armbrister, she discovers that something is missing. What?

2. When Jerry bites into an ear of corn, what does he discover?

3. What "weapon" do the police find in the grocery store?

4. Who does the priest conclude "must have been a willful child"?

5. Where does Jerry hold the barbecue he invites Jamie to?

6. How many children survived the mass suicide Jamie and Armbrister read about?

7. When Armbrister invites Jamie to stay at his apartment, why does he say he won't be sleeping on the couch?

8. *Children of the Corn: Revelations* was one of five films released in 2001 which features actress Claudette Mink. One of the other films was directed by Henry Selick and features Stephen King as a character played by a "lookalike" who looks very little like King. What is this film?

9. Upon her arrival, what does Jamie find hanging on her grandmother's door?

10. Jamie finds a photograph in a cracked frame lying beside her grandmother's bed. Who is in the photograph?

11. What does Tiffany find hanging on her door which causes her to say, "Yuck"?

12. Jamie finds a door chained shut in the basement of the apartment building. What does the cardboard sign on the door say?

13. According to Tiffany, who are the worst tippers?

14. Why does Jamie find it difficult to believe her grandmother was reading the Bible?

15. How was Jamie's grandmother killed?

MEDIUM DIFFICULTY

1. In what state does Jamie reside?

2. In what city does the film take place?

3. Why does Jamie say she cannot meet Armbrister at seven o'clock?

4. What do the police find refrigerated inside the corner grocery store?

5. Armbrister finds something on the wall of Jamie's grandmother's apartment that he believes is blood. Upon closer inspection, what is the substance?

6. What prescription medicine does Jamie find on her grandmother's nightstand?

7. What were the working titles for *Children of the Corn: Revelation* used during filming?

8. Who informs Jamie that her grandmother is dead?

9. Actor Michael Ironside, who appears as the priest, was a cast member on the television series *V*. What was his character's name?

10. What message does Jamie find scrawled in chalk in the lobby of the apartment building?

11. What video game do the cultists play inside the grocery store?

12. What does Tiffany say she studied for ten years?

13. What team name is printed on the front of Tiffany's cheerleading uniform?

14. What does the priest conclude to be Jamie's "only chance for survival"?

15. How did Jamie's parents die?

HARD AS HELL

1. With what 1988 film did *Children of the Corn: Revelation* helmer Guy Magar make his directorial debut?

2. What is the name of the apartment building where Jamie's grandmother resides?

3. What is the street number on the front of the apartment building?

4. Who performs the song "Heartbreaker" which appears in the film?

5. What does Jamie call "a real fire hazard"?

6. What is the name of Jamie's editor?

7. Armbrister touches a corn stalk the first time he visits the apartment building. Whose dead hand is visible beneath the stalk?

8. What is Jerry's surname?

9. Actors Kyle Cassie and John Destry followed up their turns in *Children of the Corn: Revelation* with an appearance in another ridiculous horror sequel. What is the name of this 2002 film directed by Rick Bota?

10. What is the name of Jamie's grandmother?

11. What is the name of the grocery store across the street from the apartment building?

12. What was Jamie's grandmother's maiden name?

13.   What is the name of the club where Tiffany is employed?

14.   This *Children of the Corn: Revelation* executive producer served as assistant to Miramax Chief Bob Weinstein on the set of *Shakespeare in Love* (1998). Who is this?

15.   What is Jamie's surname?

QUIZ #55: ROSE RED (2002)

Screenplay by: Stephen King
Directed by: Craig R. Baxley
Starring: Nancy Travis, Matt Keeslar, and Kimberly J. Brown
Trimark Video

Following 1999's *Storm of the Century*, *Rose Red* became Stephen King's second original screenplay filmed as an ABC television miniseries. "I wanted to do another original and so did the network," King recalls. "*Rose Red* came naturally to mind. For one thing, I had first conceived of it as a novel—a big, fat, scary one. For another, it had always wanted to be longer than a film script. One of the things that kept it from being greenlighted as a feature was that it was just so damned heavy, and scary theatrical movies are generally short, relying more one shock than on character-driven stories that build their scares."

After the first installment of the miniseries aired, one King aficionado observed, "I am enjoying it, but it is, I'm afraid, overly derivative of King's own earlier works. In the first twelve minutes alone I identified references to 'Before the Play' (the turn of the century construction scenes); *Carrie* (telekinetic teen); *It* (bleeding refrigerator); *'Salem's Lot* (the house that is alive); "It Grows On You" (*Rose Red* growing by itself); *Firestarter* (telekinetic child); *The Shining* (the wasps—although I think they were bees in *Rose Red*); and *The Plant* (the spooky greenhouse)..." That same week the story broke that King was considering retirement. As if the author himself had the same realization as the aforementioned fan, King said he feared he was beginning to repeat himself.

EASY

1. Stephen King originally wrote this screenplay for a feature film-maker who later served as an uncredited executive producer on *The Haunting* (1999). Who is this?

2. Who does Nick Hardaway sarcastically label "a charmer"?

3. What is Rachel Wheaton's nickname?

4. What actor collapsed and died on October 9, 2000, while filming *Rose Red*?

5. What does Joyce Reardon believe to be the "key which will unlock Rose Red"?

6. One of Joyce's students is named Kathy Spruce. What is the significance of this name?

7. In what room of Rose Red does the team discover the reporter's camera?

8. Rachel says she cannot sleep when the closet door is open because it makes her afraid. This is similar to a short story by Stephen King which appeared in *Cavalier* magazine in March 1973 about a man who believes a monster lives inside the closet. What is the title of this short story?

9. Who appears in an uncredited role as a pizza delivery guy?

10. Joyce refers to the other members of the Rose Red team as "candles." What does she say Annie is?

11. What is Joyce's "first, last, and only" monetary offer to Emery Waterman?

12. King has stated that *Rose Red* was inspired by Shirley Jackson's novel *The Haunting of Hill House*. Which of King's novels is dedicated to Jackson?

13. What does Joyce believe to be a "noble pursuit"?

14. Annie listens to a Glenn Miller tune as she showers a neighboring home with stones. What is this song?

15. On Friday afternoon at 3:17 p.m. the Rose Red team observes the first supernatural occurrence. What is this?

MEDIUM DIFFICULTY

1. Joyce's Rose Red expedition takes place on a holiday weekend. What is this holiday?

2. Hyperion Books released a companion to *Rose Red* which credits character Joyce Reardon as its editor. What is the title of this book?

3. Another character is credited with penning the afterword of the aforementioned Joyce Reardon book. Who is this?

4. What does Steve Rimbauer find lying on the floor in the solarium?

5. *Rose Red* was the third King television project produced by Mark Carliner. What were the two previous King/Carliner collaborations?

6. What does Kay Waterman call "one of the only sensible things" Emery's father ever said?

7. What does Nick suggest the reporter be given if he's discovered inside Rose Red?

8. What beverage does Nick drink with his breakfast?

9.   Although some scenes were shot in Canada, most of *Rose Red* was filmed in one U.S. state. What state is this?

10. What was Ellen Rimbauer's age at the time of her disappearance?

11. What does Emery say he's not being paid for?

12. A team of scientists studying Rose Red in the Sixties heard the house "scream" a number of times. What did they conclude the sound to be?

13. *Rose Red* director Craig R. Baxley served as assistant director on a 1981 film nominated for twelve Oscars. What is this film?

14. What item does Joyce advise each of the expedition members to carry with them at all times?

15. When the actress disappeared in 1946, what item did she leave behind?

HARD AS HELL

1.   What is Victor's surname?

2.   Rachel describes a school for "people who are just like Annie." Where is this school located?

3.   What was the name of the dog that bit Annie?

4.   What was the name of John Rimbauer's business partner who hanged himself inside Rose Red?

5.   What is the name of the reporter who inquires about Joyce's "latest spook hunt"?

6.   Cinematographer David Connell had already worked on one King adaptation before joining forces with director Craig R. Baxley on *Storm of the Century* and *Rose Red*. What was this film?

7. What is the name of Annie's father?

8. What happened on January 15, 1909?

9. In what capacity did *Rose Red* director Craig R. Baxley serve on films such as *What's Up, Doc?* (1972), *Rollerball* (1975), and *Logan's Run* (1976)?

10. What is Pam's surname?

11. What is the name of the famous actress who disappeared at Rose Red in 1946?

12. What was the name of the Rimbauers' servant who was questioned and tortured by the police?

13. What was the name of the railroad man who died from a bee sting?

14. How old was April Rimbauer at the time of her disappearance?

15. *Rose Red* was the fifth collaboration between director Craig R. Baxley and cinematographer David Connell. What were the four films on which they had previously collaborated?

QUIZ #56: FIRESTARTER
REKINDLED (2002)

Screenplay by: Phillip Eisner
Directed by: Robert Iscove
Starring: Marguerite Moreau, Malcolm McDowell, and Dennis Hopper
USA Films

Although *Firestarter Rekindled* is little more than a film about a sexy young woman in tight clothes who destroys things, the telefilm earns a few points because of the decision to make this film a sequel to King's novel rather than the 1984 Mark Lester-helmed film which starred Drew Barrymore, David Keith, and George C. Scott.

Unfortunately, despite a few fun moments, the film ultimately fails. *On Screen* critic Kathie Huddleston explains, "After the breathtaking *Dune* miniseries, the Sci-Fi Channel had a lot of live up to. *Firestarter Rekindled* could never have matched *Dune* for depth of storytelling, but it certainly has depth in the cast and could have been a whole lot of fun to watch. It's disappointing that a miniseries with these kinds of resources couldn't even manage to strike a spark."

EASY

1. What does John Rainbird say "has always been the test"?

2. What year was Charlie born?

3. What does Vincent joke as being "very Andy Warhol"?

4. *Firestarter Rekindled* marked Skye McCole Bartusiak's second appearance in a Stephen King miniseries. What is the other King film featuring Bartusiak?

5. Rainbird tells Vincent that he will say two words, and then Vincent will tell him everything he knows about those words. What are the two words?

6. Under what alias is Charlie living at the beginning of the film?

7. "[The film is] ultimately a girl in tight pants blowing stuff up," observed one person involved with the production. Who said this?

8. What does Vincent offer Charlie in exchange for her research on Dr. Wanless' studies?

9. Which of the children does Rainbird refer to as "my boy"?

10. Who does Charlie say her favorite superhero is?

11. What does Mary Conant manage to say while lying on the autopsy table?

12. Mary Conant's finding herself alive on an autopsy table is similar to a Stephen King short story collected in both *Robert Bloch's Psychos* and King's own *Everything's Eventual*. What is the title of this story?

13. Who does Richardson say Lot 6 "messed with" most?

14. How much were each of the Lot 6 subjects paid for their participation?

15. *Firestarter Rekindled* was the second film for which Philip Eisner received a screenwriting credit. What was the first?

MEDIUM DIFFICULTY

1. After Malcolm McDowell and Dennis Hopper were cast, screen-writer Philip Eisner returned to his computer to fashion a new scene. Why?

2. What are the names of the two Federal Bureau of Investigations special agents who visit Rainbird?

3. What does Rainbird advise Joel to do so that he may maintain plausible deniability?

4. What does Vincent conclude one might find in an "official" morgue?

5. What is "Triphencyclomide with genetic therapy No. 4" better known as?

6. What are the names of the Czierniewski brothers?

7. What does Rainbird tell Charlie everyone should have?

8. In 1986, actor Danny Nucci appeared in a telefilm with *Christine* (1983) actor Keith Gordon. What is the name of this film?

9. How many of the Lot 6 survivors developed severe mental illness?

10. In what sport did Vincent letter in high school?

11. What does Rainbird say Charlie does when she is nervous?

12. Skye McCole Bartusiak appears as the young Charlie McGee, a role which was originated by Drew Barrymore. What 2001 film features both Bartusiak and Barrymore?

13. How old is Mary Conant at the time of her "death"?

14. What is the name of the doctor who oversaw the Lot 6 testing?

15. How old was Vincent when his father left his mother?

HARD AS HELL

1. During filming, the producers' on-site office was thoroughly trashed. Who trashed it?

2. What is the name of Vincent's brother?

3. To promote the film, the Sci-Fi Channel developed an elaborate website which included dossiers on each character in the film. A humorous sticky-note was attached to John Rainbird's dossier. What did it read?

4. What is the name of the company where Vincent is employed?

5. The Lot 6 operation was reestablished in 1991 under a new title. What is this title?

6. How many kilograms did the block of wood the 10-year-old Charlie ignited weigh?

7. What is Cody's surname?

8. In a manifesto which appeared on the Sci Fi Channel's website, Rainbird insists he does not want to play God. What does he say he'd rather do?

9. What, according to Rainbird, does his job require an "absolute lack of"?

10. What is the name of the college where the Lot 6 protocol tests were held?

11. What is Mary Conant's weight?

12. In what city does Mary Conant reside?

13. What are the names of the five Lot 6 subjects Vincent located before searching for Charlie McGee and James Richardson?

14. What action does John Rainbird warn Vincent as being "grounds for immediate termination"?

15. *Firestarter Rekindled* was actor Ron Perkins' second appearance in a King telefilm. What was his first King-related telefilm?

QUIZ #57: CARRIE (2002)

Screenplay by: Bryan Fuller
Directed by: David Carson
Starring: Angela Bettis, Patricia Clarkson, and David Keith
MGM/UA Television

While this remake of the nearly-flawless 1976 Brian De Palma classic is
undeniably another sign that Hollywood has run out of ideas, it's hard
to find much fault in this retelling. Veteran TV director David Carson
does a superb job at the helm, and Bryan Fuller's screenplay is so tautly
written that its dialogue may just be better than that of the original. But
the true star of this film is the actress at its center, Angela Bettis, who
outshines every other aspect of this film. Rather than attempting to copy
Sissy Spacek's performance, she reinterprets the character and makes it
her own, breathing new life into the long-dead corpse of Carrie White.

The downside to the film is its horrendous television production values, which lend the proceedings a "Movie of the Week" feel that somehow
seems at odds with the film's dark story.

EASY

1.   Carrie is a nickname. What is her real name?

2.   Actor David Keith also appears in another Stephen King adapta-
     tion about telekinesis that was later remade. What is that film?

3. What does Tommy promise to do to anyone who laughs at them during the prom?

4. Two girls are said to be "ultras." Who are they?

5. Who mistakenly refers to Carrie White as "Cassie Wright"?

6. What, according to Margaret White, do "good girls" not develop?

7. What word does Carrie search on the Internet for when she learns about telekinesis?

8. What singular word is chanted by Carrie's classmates in the shower room?

9. Who, according to Miss Desjarden, "turn out just fine"?

10. Detective Mulchaey suggests that three people conspired against Carrie. Who were they?

11. Carrie references the George Bernard Shaw play that was later adapted as *My Fair Lady* (1964). What is this play?

12. What sport does Carrie's gym class play just before her shower room discovery?

13. *Carrie* marked actress Patricia Clarkson's second appearance in a Stephen King adaptation. In her first King film she played Melinda Moores. Can you name this film?

14. What does Sue believe everyone wants?

15. Patricia Clarkson won an Emmy the same year this telefilm aired. She received the Emmy for the recurring role of Sarah O'Connor. What television show was this?

MEDIUM DIFFICULTY

1. What does Detective Mulchaey believe to be as addictive as heroin?

2. What color does Carrie's mother mistakenly believe her prom dress to be?

3. Angela Bettis was cast in the lead role after the producers saw an early cut of another film in which she starred. What was this film?

4. Tommy says that Carrie is not "different." What does he instead suggest she is?

5. What food does Carrie say causes her to break out with acne?

6. Why, according to Margaret White, may Jesus be hesitant to assist Carrie?

7. What insult does the boy on the bicycle scream just before being hurled into a tree?

8. What is Donna Kellogg's nickname?

9. Whose life does Carrie say she doesn't want?

10. Tommy references a Freddy Prinze Jr. film about an ugly duckling girl who turns out to be the most beautiful girl at prom. (Don't they always?) What is this film?

11. With what does Miss Desjarden suggest the girls make their boutonnieres?

12. What three words are scrawled on the outside of Carrie's locker?

13. Actress Jasmine Guy, who appears in the film as Ruby Moore, collaborated with screenwriter Bryan Fuller again the following year. This second collaboration came on a Showtime original series created by Fuller. What is this series?

14. What, according to Margaret White, is a curse?

15. What is the occupation of John Hargenson?

HARD AS HELL

1. What was the name of Miss Desjarden's character (played by Betty Buckley) in the original 1976 Brian De Palma film?

2. What is Detective Mulchaey's first name?

3. What is the theme of the prom?

4. What is the name of the girl at the prom who tells Carrie she's glowing?

5. Who is Helen Shyres's prom date?

6. Director David Carson directed Paris Hilton in a straight-to-video horror film (horrifying enough just in that it stars Paris Hilton!) two years after *Carrie*. Can you name this film?

7. What Biblical figure does Margaret White say is weak?

8. What is the name of the girl who shows Chris the prom ballots?

9. Sue says she always thinks of a painting whenever anyone mentions religion. What is this?

10. Carrie asks her mother's opinion on a prom dress. What is Margaret White's response?

11. What case does Principal Morton offer as a precedent to Mr. Hargenson?

12. What does CAPP stand for?

13. *Carrie* received a 2003 Saturn Award nomination. In what category was the film nominated?

14. From whose farm was the pig blood obtained?

15. At what age does Miss Desjarden say she received her first menstruation cycle?

QUIZ #58: THE DEAD ZONE (2002)

Screenplay by: Michael Piller and Sean Piller
Directed by: Robert Leiderman
Starring: Anthony Michael Hall, Nicole de Boer, and Chris Bruno
Lions Gate Films

Try to put yourself in *Dead Zone* (1983) helmer David Cronenberg's shoes. Imagine how difficult it must be for such a truly gifted filmmaker such as Cronenberg to have crafted a brilliant film with Oscar-caliber talent only to be one-upped by a television pilot made on a meager budget with a mostly no-name cast.

Most viewers remembered actor Anthony Michael Hall as the lanky nerd from 1980s teen angst films such as *The Breakfast Club* (1985) and *Weird Science* (1985). Certainly the announcement that Hall would be playing the lead did little to generate enthusiasm amongst Stephen King fans. But we were wrong. Since we'd last seen Anthony Michael Hall, he'd developed into a confident, good-looking actor with genuine talent.

The Dead Zone gets much of its strength from the writers' willingness to create something new and fresh rather than sticking to the original story. All in all, *The Dead Zone* works as both a terrific pilot and a satisfying film unto itself.

EASY

1. What was the Dr. Tran character's name in the original King novel?

2. What piece of evidence did the police find at all three murder sites?

3 Who is the Castle Rock killer?

4. How many years does Johnny spend in a coma?

5. What is Sara's maiden name?

6. What, according to Johnny Smith, is random in nature?

7. One year before his appearance in *The Dead Zone*, Anthony Michael Hall portrayed Yankees pitcher Whitey Ford in a film directed by Billy Crystal. What is this film?

8. What does Gene Purdy call "strong evidence of a higher power"?

9. Who are said to have a mutual liking for sports and cheeseburgers?

10. What does the carny barker say is only a fluke?

11. Johnny predicts that Allison's grave will be located next to a structure. What is this?

12. What country singer does Sara say she's given up her dreams of being "the next" version of?

13. Actor David Ogden Stiers is best known for his playing a character named Major Charles Emerson Winchester III on a long-running television series. What is this series?

14. There is one bit of disturbing news that Dr. Tran says he doesn't want to inform Johnny of "right away." What is this news?

15. One year before *The Dead Zone*, David Ogden Stiers had appeared in a film directed by *The Shawshank Redemption* (1994) director Frank Darabont. The film stars Jim Carrey. Can you name it?

MEDIUM DIFFICULTY

1. What former pro football player does Johnny joke about being the ambassador to the United Nations?

2. Gene Purdy says, "I destroy my enemy when I make him my friend." Who is Purdy quoting here?

3. What are Johnny's last words to Sara before his life-changing accident?

4. Dana Bright says she doesn't hang around the sheriff's office for love. What does she say she does hang out for?

5. Chris Bruno, who plays Walt Bannerman, provides the voice of Jack Slate on a popular video game. What is this game?

6. What does Walt say is a "pretty good" alibi?

7. In what city does Dr. Tran believe his mother was killed?

8. A song by Santo & Johnny is played in the film. It is also featured prominently in *Sleepwalkers* (1992). What is this song?

9. Bruce gives Johnny a stylish homecoming gift. What is this?

10. Actress Kristen Dalton, who appears as Dana Bright, made her film debut in a 1989 actioner starring Sylvester Stallone and Kurt Russell. What is this film?

11. What does Walt say Johnny can provide for him if he wants to help track down the killer?

12. Who was Walt visiting when he met Sara at the hospital?

13. What type of carnival shows does Johnny promise to keep Gene away from?

14. What are Johnny's first words upon waking from his coma?

15. What subject does Sara teach?

HARD AS HELL

1.   What is Allison's surname?

2.   This film is comprised of the first two episodes of the *Dead Zone* television series. The first episode shares its name with the first section of King's original novel. What is this?

3.   What is the name of nurse Elaine MacGowen's daughter?

4.   In what year does the film open?

5.   What is the name of janitor at the high school where Johnny and Sara teach?

6.   Anthony Michael Hall also appears in *The Dark Knight* (2008). What is the name of his character in that film?

7.   For how many seasons did the series *The Dead Zone* air?

8.   How many episodes of *The Dead Zone* were directed by Anthony Michael Hall?

9.   Actress Nicole de Boer had appeared previously on another television series created by *Dead Zone* creator Michael Piller. What is this series?

10.   Who was the first actor cast in the role of Gene Purdy?

11.   What size boot does Johnny say the killer wears?

12.   For how many years does the carny barker say he's been working on the wheel of fortune?

13.   What is Bruce's surname?

14.   For what publication does Dana write?

15.   Sheriff Bannerman's name wasn't Walt in the original King novel. What was it?

QUIZ #59: DREAMCATCHER (2003)

Screenplay by: William Goldman and Lawrence Kasdan
Directed by: Lawrence Kasdan
Starring: Morgan Freeman, Thomas Jane, and Jason Lee
Castle Rock Entertainment

Say what you will about Lawrence Kasdan's film *Dreamcatcher*, and critics have had plenty to say about it, but there can be no denying that, if nothing else, it features one hell of an ensemble. Thomas Jane, Jason Lee, Timothy Olyphant, and the underrated Damian Lewis are positively exquisite here. Unfortunately, that's about the only positive observation one can make of this film, which otherwise fails on a great many levels. Morgan Freeman drops by midway through the film as Col. Curtis and delivers what is possibly the blandest performance of his career. Then there are those huge fake eyebrows he's wearing, which provide a genuine "WTF?" moment... Morgan Freeman may not be embarrassed by this film, but he should be. (I'm hoping he was at least well paid for this.)

The storyline is not one of King's best and his attempts at the gross-out work well in the novel, but just feel lame in the film. Credit Kasdan and the great William Goldman for staying loyal to the source material, but sometimes horror just doesn't adapt well.

EASY

1. Colonel Curtis's name in King's original novel was Colonel Kurtz. This was a reference to a character played by Marlon Brando in a 1979 Vietnam War film. Can you name this film?

2. What does S.S.D.D. stand for?

3. Curtis says his silver-plated .45 was a gift. Who gave it to him?

4. Curtis says the civilians never miss an episode of their favorite television series. What is this?

5. Curtis refers to an imaginary line which offending parties sometimes cross. What is this?

6. What is Pete doing when he is first attacked by the "shit weasel"?

7. Who does Pete say is the only perfect person he's ever met?

8. The names Jonesy and Ripley are references to a 1979 horror film. What is this film?

9. What cartoon character graces the front of Duddits's lunchbox?

10. For how many years has Curtis been fighting the aliens?

11. *Dreamcatcher* was screenwriter William Goldman's third Stephen King adaptation. Can you name the two previous adaptations?

12. Who does Jonesy see across the street just before he's struck down by an automobile?

13. The alien references a famous poem by Robert Frost. What is this poem?

14. Beaver has a habit that ultimately costs him his life. What is this?

15. Donnie Wahlberg, who appears as Duddits, was a member of a popular music group in the 1980s. What is this group?

MEDIUM DIFFICULTY

1.   Someone's last words were said to be "Sometimes we have to kill, but our real job is saving lives." Who was this?

2.   What does Pete say car salesmen love?

3.   What is Colonel Curtis's first name?

4.   Under what rules does Blue Unit operate?

5.   By what generic nickname does Curtis refer to virtually anyone he speaks to?

6.   Beaver suggests the lost man may have eaten something which has given him bad gas. What is this?

7.   By what name is the alien who takes over Jonesy's body referred?

8.   What does Beaver say a perfectly good fuckaree can turn into in a flash?

9.   What is the name of the soldier's dog who is encouraged to "eat the red stuff"?

10. The name of Colonel Curtis's commanding officer is a nod to Stephen King's favorite author. What is this officer's name?

11. Beaver sings a Roy Orbison tune to Duddits. What is this song?

12. Jonesy says he keeps something inside a small office in the back of his memory warehouse. What is this?

13. Jonesy says he's not worried about where the animals are running. What does he say he is worried about?

14. *Dreamcatcher* was the second film directed by Lawrence Kasdan featuring actor Tom Sizemore. Can you name the first?

15. The scene in which the boys are shown walking along the railroad tracks is an homage to a 1986 Stephen King adaptation. What is this film?

HARD AS HELL

1. What is the name of Henry's patient who eats himself to death?

2. What is the name of the lost man Jonesy finds wandering around in the woods?

3. What is Duddits's name?

4. What is the name of the lost girl Duddits helps the boys locate?

5. What is Beaver's real name?

6. What highway does the alien plan to take to get to Massachusetts?

7. Whose funeral is depicted in the film's alternate ending?

8. What is Mr. G's surname?

9. What is the surname of the corporal Curtis shoots for having lied to him?

10. What restaurant does Pete believe to have the finest fried clams in Maine?

11. What brand of candy bar did Trish purchase before losing her keys?

12. What is the name of Duddits's mother?

13. Actor Timothy Olyphant appears in a 2002 Victor Nunez film with *Carrie* (2002) actress Angela Bettis. Can you name this film?

14. What is the name of the student who is assigned the 3,000 word essay on the Norman conquest?

15. Beaver references a 1989 Meg Ryan film. What is this film?

QUIZ #60: THE DIARY OF ELLEN RIMBAUER (2003)

Screenplay by: Ridley Pearson
Directed by: Craig R. Baxley
Starring: Lisa Brenner, Steven Brand, and Connie Posey
Greengrass Productions

The Diary of Ellen Rimbauer has a bit of an odd provenance for a "Stephen King" movie, in that it is not based on an actual work of fiction by King. Except that it is, kind of.

The book of the same name was part of a marketing and publicity push for the King-scripted TV mini-series *Rose Red* (2002). It was conceived as a *Blair Witch*-style campaign, presenting the "diary" as real, edited by "Dr. Joyce Reardon," a character from *Rose Red*. Novelist Ridley Pearson was selected to write the book, although when it was published, many fans believed (reasonably enough) that King himself was the author.

Since the book is a direct tie-in to the King miniseries, most of the important story elements are drawn directly from King's script. The rest of the "diary" is taken up with detailing the rather icky marital minutia of Ellen and John Rimbauer's union.

The film itself leaves most of the more explicit elements of the "diary" out, so it winds up being largely a re-hash of events already detailed in *Rose Red*, with some minor connecting details added for the sake of continuity.

EASY

1. Brad Greenquist played Marlin Thomas in the bio-pic *Ali* (2001) starring what rapper turned actor?

2. How long does John give Sukeena to leave the house?

3. John tells Ellen that Rose Red was brought "brick-by-brick" from where?

4. Steven Brand made an appearance in 2009 in one episode of the revamped version of what 1990s Aaron Spelling TV drama?

5. The Rimbauer's first child was born in what year?

6. Tsai Chin, who plays Madam Lu, was cast as "Madam Wu" in what 2007 James Bond film?

7. What does Ellen promise Rose Red at the séance?

8. What does Ellen see through the peephole found by Gail?

9. What does Fanny tell Ellen that people say about the past?

10. What does the servant bring to John and Ellen's room the night of the inaugural ball?

11. What game does Doug propose to the children to get them to leave the room before he kills himself?

12. What is the name of John's contractor?

13. What is the name of John's driver?

14. Where do Ellen and Sukeena follow the secret passage to?

15. Where does Ellen believe her daughter April might be found?

MEDIUM DIFFICULTY

1. Along with a number of other writers, including Stephen King, Amy Tan and Dave Barry, screenwriter Ridley Pearson is part of what musical act?

2. Cinematographer João Fernandes has worked under a variety of names, including Harry Flecks, the name he used as director of photography for what groundbreaking 1972 adult film?

3. Courtney Burness played the role of Tiffany in an episode of what mother-daughter TV dramedy starring Lauren Graham?

4. Eric Keenleyside has appeared in updated versions of what two seminal 1960s anthology series?

5. How does Connie describe her union with Doug?

6. In addition to his work as a director, Craig R. Baxley has a long list of credits as a stuntman and stunt coordinator, including what classic 80s action series?

7. In what African country does the map show the newlyweds landing?

8. Kate Burton appeared as Margo in what 1987 action film directed by John Carpenter?

9. Making his feature film directorial debut, Craig R. Baxley helmed what 1998 action flick starring Carl Weathers?

10. Sukeena asks Ellen if she believes in what?

11. Sukeena tells Ellen she must do what after the electrical failure?

12. Thornewood Castle in Lakewood, Washington, served as the stand-in for Rose Red in both *The Diary of Ellen Rimbauer* and the miniseries *Rose Red* (2002). It was also seen in what Paul Thomas Anderson movie?

13. What does John call Ellen when she feigns interest in him to allow Sukeena to sneak out?

14. What does Sukeena say to John when he reaches the tower?

15. Who reports Gail's disappearance?

HARD AS HELL

1. Although Tsidii Leloka reprised her role as Sukeena from the *Rose Red* miniseries, Ellen and John Rimbauer were played by different people in that production. Who were they?

2. Ellen tells John he should "tread lightly." Why?

3. Ellen writes in her diary that she finds the sounds of construction what?

4. In addition to *The Diary of Ellen Rimbauer*, Thomas H. Brodek served as producer on what two other Stephen King television adaptations?

5. John is moved to fire Doug after Doug's dalliance with what company employee?

6. Lisa Brenner began her acting career in two soap operas in the mid-1990s. What were they?

7. On the NBC series *Heroes*, Dierdre Quinn played "Texas" Tina, a friend of what super-powered internet stripper?

8. Screenwriter Ridley Pearson has an uncredited cameo as what character?

9. The car that first carries John and Ellen to Rose Red is a classic "brass era" automobile. What is the name of the manufacturer?

10. Tsidii Leloka was nominated for a Tony Award in 1998 for her work in what musical?

11. What change does Ellen tell Madame Lu she has noticed since the hanging?

12. What is the name of the servant who disappears?

13. What time do Sukeena and Ellen visit the butcher's room?

14. Which cast member appeared in a skit with WWE (then WWF) superstar Booker T. in an Aug. 6, 2001 episode of *Monday Night Raw*?

15. Which cast member played Dorothy Frankin in Ang Lee's chilly drama *The Ice Storm* (1997)?

QUIZ #61: SECRET WINDOW (2004)

Screenplay by: David Koepp
Directed by: David Koepp
Starring: Johnny Depp, John Turturro, and Maria Bello
Columbia Pictures Corporation

Blessed with an A-list cast—led by Johnny Depp, who had blown every-one away with his recent turn as Jack Sparrow in *Pirates of the Carribbean* (2003)—and led by David Koepp, one of Hollywood's go-to screenwrit-ers and a seasoned director, *Secret Window* made barely a ripple upon its release, although it did more-than-double its $40 million budget on worldwide ticket sales of $92 million. Critical reaction was mixed, with *Empire Magazine's* Ian Nathan reflecting the general reception thusly: "The presence of the sublime Depp will be enough to get *Secret Window* noticed, but even his latest set of rattling eccentricities is not enough to energise this deadbeat parlour trick."

The movie may have suffered from a slight case of viewer deja vu, as *Secret Window* shares a great deal with the earlier King adaptation *The Dark Half* (1993), namely a writer beset by a menacing, murderous "other" who may just be a part of the writer himself.

Koepp also managed to mishandle the third-act reveal, leaving a too-obvious trail of breadcrumbs that surely left most viewers unsurprised by the "twist." He also decided to off a pair of characters who survived in the novella—a trick that worked great for Stanley Kubrick but just feels gratuitous here.

EASY

1. A book by what famous author, whose alter-ego Raoul Duke was portrayed by Johnny Depp in a 1998 movie, is seen next to Mort's phone?

2. How long does Shooter give Mort to find the magazine "Secret Window" was originally published in?

3. Maria Bello has appeared in movies with Sean Bean and Viggo Mortensen, both of whom were in what sprawling fantasy trilogy?

4. The Stephen King story "Secret Window, Secret Garden," originally appeared in what collection?

5. Timothy Hutton appeared in what other Stephen King adaptation about a writer with a murderous alter-ego?

6. What brand of cigarettes does Mort keep hidden in his desk?

7. What does Amy say Mort was influenced by when he was writing "Secret Window?"

8. What does Mort fetch as a weapon when he and Ken are searching the house?

9. What does Mort nearly sit on in Tom Greenleaf's truck?

10. What is Mort's housekeeper's name?

11. What is the name of Mort's dog?

12. What is the name of the book that Mort's story is collected in?

13. What magazine does Mort tell Shooter his story first appeared in?

14. What page number is Mort's story on in the magazine?

15. Which cast member died quite graphically in the original *Nightmare on Elm Street* (1984)?

MEDIUM DIFFICULTY

1. Composer Philip Glass was the musical guest on a 1986 episode of what comedy sketch show?

2. David Koepp directed what *Blue Velvet* (1986) star in the 1996 thriller *Trigger Effect?*

3. Herb Stemple, portrayed by John Turturro in *Quiz Show* (1994), was at the center of a scandal involving what television game show?

4. How long were Mort and Amy married?

5. In an episode of the HBO mob series *The Sopranos*, Charles Dutton plays a traffic cop who gives a ticket to which character?

6. In Mort's story, the protagonist is named Tommy Havelock. What is his name in John Shooter's version?

7. In the original Stephen King novella, which two characters, killed by Mort/Shooter in the movie, survived?

8. *Monday Night Mayhem* (2002) starred John Turturro as what sportscasting legend?

9. Mort finds an empty bag of what in his desk drawer?

10. Producers Gavin Palone and Ezra Swerdlow and director David Koepp also teamed together on what 2008 comedy starring Ricky Gervais?

11. What is the number of the fire truck outside Amy's house?

12. What is the title of the document seen on Mort's computer at the beginning of the movie

13. What Tom Robbins novel is seen on the shelf next to the clock?

14. When Mort first goes to pick up the magazine, what Talking Heads song does he think of when he sees Amy and Ted together?

15. Which cast member had a recurring role the NBC hospital drama *ER?*

HARD AS HELL

1. Director David Koepp used footage from what film (on which he worked with Stephen Spielberg) for the waterfall sequence in Mort's dream?

2. Ezra Swerdlow was an associate producer on what nostalgic Woody Allen comedy starring Dianne Wiest and a young Seth Green?

3. How much is a gallon of regular gasoline at the station where Mort meets Ted?

4. How much is Mort paying Ken Karsch per day?

5. In 2004, John Turturro starred in two movies with the word "Secret" in the title, *Secret Window* and what other film?

6. In an episode of *Star Trek Voyager*, Len Cairou appeared as the father of what Starfleet officer?

7. In Mort's kitchen, we can see that he keeps what on the stovetop?

8. John Turturro graduated from what prestigious university's drama school?

9. Two castmembers have portrayed the legendary barber/butcher Sweeney Todd, one on film and one on Broadway. Who are they?

10. What famous author did Timothy Hutton portray in a 1993 made-for-television movie?

11. What game board is seen on Mort's coffee table?

12. What is Mort's parting shot to Ted at the insurance office?

13. What is the fire chief's name?

14. What is the name of Mort and Amy's insurance company?

15. What motel is Ken staying at while he's investigating Shooter?

QUIZ #62: SALEM'S LOT (2004)

Screenplay by: Peter Filardi
Directed by: Mikael Salomon
Starring: Rob Lowe, Donald Sutherland and Andre Braugher
Warner Bros. Television and Turner Network Television

This 2004 remake scored big numbers for TNT, drawing nearly six million viewers on its opening night, besting all cable television competition for the week as well as topping ABC and FOX offerings airing at the same time.

Executive producer Mark Wolper told *USA Today* that he decided to do the remake after watching the 1979 miniseries again and finding it a bit lacking. "If you remember a movie being great and you look at it again today and it just doesn't quite hold up, that's a perfect movie to remake," Wolper said.

Although both series follow nearly the same overall plot arc, makers of the 2004 version aimed to more closely capture the spirit of King's novel, exploring in more depth the themes of small-town corruption and human failings in addition to the supernatural threat of rampaging hordes of the undead.

EASY

1. Ben tells Straker that he's a writer, but that his critics call him what?

2. How does Joyce Petrie die?

3. How old was Ben when he first entered the Marsden house?

4. Rob Lowe also appeared in an ABC miniseries adaptation of what massive King novel?

5. The karaoke song at the bar where Mears and Susan get together references what beloved Stephen King adaptation?

6. What city do Mears and Mark Petrie chase Father Callahan to?

7. What does Cody fashion into wooden stakes when he, Mears, Callahan and Mark Petrie venture into the Marsden house?

8. What does Cody give Royce MacDougal in exchange for taking the baby Royce, Jr. to the hospital?

9. What does Mark Petrie's mother, Joyce, do for a living?

10. What is the name of cemetery where Mears' aunt is buried?

11. What is the name of the tenants in Lawrence Crockett's trailer park whose rent is due?

12. In 2007, Andre Braugher appeared in a second Stephen King adaptation. What is this film?

13. What was the name of the kid's gang that dared Mears to enter the Marsden House?

14. What was the name of the little boy found in the bathtub at the Marsden house?

15. Who is the first vampire killed at the Marsden house?

MEDIUM DIFFICULTY

1. "No one pronounced Jerusalem's Lot dead" on what date, according to Ben Mears' voiceover?

2. According to the sign welcoming visitors to town, what is the population of Jerusalem's Lot?

3. How does Dr. James Cody fight the "winter malaise" in Jerusalem's Lot?

4. James Cromwell appeared with Donald Sutherland's son Keifer in the television series *24* as what character?

5. On what charge is Ben Mears held after his altercation with Floyd Tibbets?

6. Rutger Hauer and Donald Sutherland appeared together in what other vampire movie?

7. Screenwriter Peter Filardi penned a film starring Donald Sutherland's son, Keifer. What is that film?

8. What does Straker tell Crockett is in the special crate to be delivered to the Marsden House?

9. What is the name of Lawrence Crockett's trailer park?

10. What is the name of Mears' book held up in class by Matt Burke?

11. What is the name of Straker's store?

12. What kind of cigarettes does Mears leave at his Aunt Cynthia's grave?

13. What was Danny's red cell count after his death?

14. Where does "lifelong bachelor" Matt Burke pursue his "alternative life?"

15. Where does Floyd tell Crockett is the best spot for ice fishing?

HARD AS HELL

1. Director Mikael Salomon also helmed a 2000 TV mini-series adapted from the book *Sole Survivor* by another bestselling horror novelist. Who is this?

2. How many children went missing during the Marsdens' time of residence in Salem's Lot?

3. In addition to the 1979 television miniseries, King's novel was also adapted as a radio play by what world famous broadcaster?

4. In what country did principal filming take place?

5. Robert Mammone and Samantha Mathis appeared together in an adaptation of what Stephen King short story in the *Nightmares and Dreamscapes* miniseries?

6. What are Ben Mears' last words?

7. What book is Mears reading in Burke's hospital room?

8. What day is garbage day on Joyntner Avenue?

9. What do Father Callahan and Ed Craig drink to celebrate Ed's upcoming wedding, and, according to Callahan, "the death of Freud?"

10. What is Chief Parkins' grandson's name?

11. What is the name of the county coroner?

12. What room is Matt in at the hospital?

13. What sport is on the television when Callahan attacks Burke in the hospital?

14. What unusual feature does Dr. Cody note upon first examining Mike Ryerson's body?

15. Where do Cody and Mears go to examine the body of Marjorie Glick?

QUIZ #63: RIDING THE BULLET (2004)

Screenplay by: Mick Garris
Directed by: Mick Garris
Starring: Jonathan Jackson, Ericka Christensen, and David Arquette
Motion Picture Corporation of America

Riding the Bullet was the first Mick Garris adaptation of a Stephen King work that had no actual involvement from the author himself. "I had just asked him if I could adapt his story, and he gave me the opportunity... he gave me the rope with which to hang myself," Garris said in an interview with MTV News.

In greatly expanding King's longish short story (or shortish novella, if you wish) to motion picture length, Garris said he introduced personal elements to the tale. "My wife and I had gone through crises in our lives... so we started thinking about mortality a lot... (The story is) about life-and-death choices... and it was an opportunity to tell a story that became really personal," he said.

Garris' choice to move the story from 1999 to 1969 works especially well. Intentionally or not, it helps sell the central conceit—a college student decides on a whim to hitchhike home to be with his sick mother—a lot better. Hitching was relatively commonplace among young people in the 60s, but not so much by the turn of the century. The film's 60s setting also opened the door for Garris to use a lot of great period rock music on the soundtrack.

Some of the material Garris adds to flesh out the story falls flat; a particularly ludicrous chase scene involving two shotgun wielding rednecks should have been left on the cutting-room floor. On the whole, though, Garris' additions work, and in some ways make the movie's story stronger than the original.

The movie was produced and distributed independently, and as such attracted scant attention at the box office, and remains one of the lesser known King adaptations. Considering some of the horrible films that have been released under the King banner, that's really a shame.

EASY

1. David Arquette played what character in the *Scream* trilogy?

2. How did Alan's mother say his father died?

3. Since 1993, Jonathan Jackson has played Lucky Spencer on what venerable ABC daytime drama?

4. The Bullet rollercoaster is found at what amusement park?

5. The last line of the movie, "We all shine on," is from what John Lennon song?

6. What does the farmer urge Alan to make a wish on?

7. What highway do Ferris and Alan take out of town?

8. What hospital is Alan taken to?

9. What is hanging from Staub's rear-view mirror?

10. What is in the farmer's wagon that George Staub runs into?

11. What is the actual epitaph on George Staub's gravestone?

12. What was Alan's father's name?

13.   What year did Alan's father die?

14.   When Staub grabs Alan at the amusement park, he says "They're coming to get you, Barbara!" What famous George Romero film is he quoting?

15.   Who is performing at the "Rock and Roll Revival" Jessica gives Alan tickets for?

MEDIUM DIFFICULTY

1.   Besides his Mom and Jessica, who does Alan say loves him?

2.   Director Mick Garris has a brief cameo in the film as what character?

3.   How many times does Staub tell Alan he rode the Bullet?

4.   In 2003, Barbara Hershey appeared in the TV movie *The Stranger Beside Me* about what notorious serial killer?

5.   In addition to John Lennon, Hector names three rock legends he never wants to see get "old, bald and fat." Who are they?

6.   In *Traffic* (2000), Erika Christensen played Caroline Wakefield. What actor played her father?

7.   What building at the University of Maine are Alan and Jessica seen coming out of?

8.   What classic Richard Matheson horror novel is seen lying open in Alan's apartment?

9.   What does Alan say when his mother asks is he remembers his father?

10.   What does Alan say when Mr. Clarkson asks him about his obsession with death?

11.   What is the date when the movie opens?

12.   What is the headline over Alan's picture in the paper?

13.   What is the name of the cemetery Alan wanders into?

14.   Where does the farmer say he promised his brother Ralph he'd take him?

15.   Where is the Halloween party Hector wants to attend?

HARD AS HELL

1.   Alan remembers his mother saving him a slice of what kind of pie?

2.   How far does Ferris say he can take Alan?

3.   In his flashback, what did Alan get on the paper he wants to show his mother?

4.   What card game does Alan say he and his mother played?

5.   What is the first thing George Staub asks Alan?

6.   What is the name of the kid who wants to buy the $750 Cadillac in Staub's story?

7.   What is the name of the man from ADC who visits Alan's mother?

8.   What is the name of the orderly who drops Alan's lunch tray at the hospital?

9.   What is the name on the side of the bus that passes Alan on the highway?

10.   What room is Alan's mother in at the hospital?

11.   What song comes on the radio that Staub tells Alan he really likes?

12.   When Alan thinks of the line "The dead travel fast," he remembers reading it in Bram Stoker's Dracula, but it is originally found in what classic German poem?

13. When was Jean Parker born?

14. Which cast member has appeared in two episodes of the TV series *Supernatural* as the character Ronald Reznick?

15. Who calls Alan to tell him about his mother's stroke?

QUIZ #64: THE MANGLER REBORN (2005)

Screenplay by: Matt Cunningham and Eric Gardner
Directed by: Matt Cunningham and Eric Gardner
Starring: Aimee Brooks, Reggie Bannister, and Weston Blakesley
Lions Gate Films

Just when you thought the bar for Stephen King-like sequels couldn't be set any lower, along comes *The Mangler Reborn*. Riddled with continuity errors, dogged throughout by leaden dialogue, and plagued with stilted acting, this Mangler is a real chore to sit through.

And it's rather odd, really, because, watching the making of feature on the DVD, it's clear these people had a blast making the movie. Too bad none of their raw enthusiasm made it to the screen.

This movie does have at least one thing going for it that the previous "sequel" didn't: The Mangler itself. Hadley Watson (the inside joke here is that the name of the manufacturer in the first movie was Hadley-Watson) has purchased the Mangler at an auction. He then proceeds to rebuild this massive industrial laundry press in his spare bedroom upstairs. And there's plenty of room left over for a water heater, a work bench, and enough open space for a poorly choreographed fight scene.

At some unknown point before the movie begins, Hadley is possessed by the machine, and decides it's not quite lethal enough, adding a number of swinging metal arms at the front with various pointy kitchen utensils attached to the ends. Unlike the original Mangler, this version is quite passive; it just sits around in the bedroom waiting for Hadley to bring it victims. It also makes a kind of blood soup for Hadley to eat, for some reason.

It almost seems, in fact, as if the original idea for this movie was Mangler-free. The "action" is entirely confined to Hadley's weird house, where various characters are trapped by knobless doors and bricked-up windows and terrified and abused by the demonic Hadley. One might even suspect that someone took a generic "crazy killer" screenplay and jammed the Mangler in there for marketing purposes.

The movie's sole redeeming value is Hadley's habit of whacking his victims on the head with a rubber mallet, which becomes more and more hilarious as the movie goes on. I'm pretty sure the comedy is unintentional.

EASY

1. Aimee Brooks appeared in what long-running CBS daytime drama?

2. Executive producer Barry Barnholtz also produced what two other Stephen King adaptation sequels?

3. How long has it been since Hadley has worked?

4. In addition to her break up with Sean, what other bad news does Jamie have for her mother?

5. Reggie Bannister starred in what 1979 horror classic as well as both of its sequels?

6. What brand of dryer is seen at Jamie's house?

7. What does Hadley tell Jaime about his relationship to the Mangler?

8. What does Mike say his mother needed?

9. What does Mike steal from the sleeping Hadley?

10. What is Jaime's lawn-mowing neighbor wearing under his plaid shirt?

11. What is the name of the company on the shirt Rick dons as a disguise?

12. What is the name of the girl Rick finds trapped in the house?

13. When did Mike quit smoking?

14. Where does Hadley stash his victims' belongings?

15. Where does Mike hide from Hadley?

MEDIUM DIFFICULTY

1. Aimee Brooks in 1986 and Reggie Bannister in 2008 appeared in movies with "Massacre" in the title. What were these two movies?

2. How many cigarettes is Rick seen smoking during the stakeout?

3. How much does Beatrice say Hadley spent on "that thing upstairs?"

4. In addition to his acting career, Reggie Bannister pursues what other artistic endeavor?

5. Sarah Lilly's first credited role was as a waitress in an episode of what classic sit-com set in Milwaukee?

6. What does Jamie tell Hadley she thinks is wrong with her washer?

7. What does Rick say he is "getting too old" for?

8. What illness is listed on the MedicAlert bracelet Rick finds?

9. What is the address number of Jamie's home?

10. Which cast member appeared with Bruce Campbell and Ossie Davis in *Bubba Ho-Tep* (2002)?

11. Who calls when Sean is breaking up with Jamie?

12. Who does Rick tell Mike is "in here killing people?

13. Whose driver's license does Mike find in the dresser?

14. Writer/director Eric Gardner worked as a production assistant for what Shaun Cassidy produced creepy TV series?

15. Writer/director Matt Cunningham was a production assistant on what TV series starring *Stand By Me's* Jerry O'Connell?

HARD AS HELL

1. Co-directors/writers Matt Cunningham and Erik Gardner worked together on what short-lived MTV drama series?

2. Cole McKay, who did stuntwork in the movie, appeared as "Pastry Chef" in what 2009 Disney film?

3. In what midwestern city was Juliana Dever born?

4. Rhett Giles took on the role of noted vampire hunter Abraham van Helsing in what movie?

5. Sarah Lilly and Aimme Brooks appeared in separate episodes of what youth-oriented horror/sci-fi series on NBC?

6. Scott Speiser has appeared with what popular performance art group at the Venetian in Las Vegas?

7. The box Jamie carries into her house bears the name of what bottled water?

8. Weston Blakesley appeared as two different characters in what Fox family sitcom?

9. Weston Blakesley played Dr. Bannister in an episode of what Aaron Sorkin drama?

10. What does Jamie have pictures of under her bedroom window?

11. What does Louise's shirt say?

12. What kind of flower is seen on the mantle at the beginning of the film?

13. Which cast member played a prostitute in the spoof-tacular Amazon Women on the Moon?

14. Which castmember also performs as part of the comedy/variety group Dinghis Khan?

15. Which castmember was part of Northwestern University's improve and sketch comedy troupe The Mee-Ow Show?

QUIZ #65: CREEPSHOW III (2006)

Screenplay by: Ana Clavell, James Glenn Dudelson, Scott Frazell, Pablo
C. Pappano and Alex Ugelsow
Directed by: Ana Clavell and James Glenn Dudelson
Starring: Stephanie Pettee, Roy Abramsohn, and Susan Schramm
Taurus Entertainment Company

Given the rate at which films trading on any connection to previous King-related works continue to roll out of Hollywood, it's unclear how long this little gem will hold onto its spot as the absolute worst on the list. What is clear is that usurping this rotten flick's place at the bottom will not be easy.

Creepshow III is aggressively bad. It is painfully obvious that the film-makers here were trying to make a "so bad it's good" movie. They did not succeed. This film goes past "so bad it's good," plummets right by "so bad it made my brain hurt" and straight into "so bad that the very existence of humanity is called into question."

Five screenwriters herein tell five "stories" that range in quality from abysmal to incomprehensible. As an added bonus, they decided to tie all the stories together, so that characters from one tale pop up briefly in other stories. Such is the quality of work at hand, however, that by the end of the film they've screwed up the continuity so badly that they create an actual temporal paradox!

Too bad time travel is impossible. I'd give just about anything to go back in time and stop myself from watching this abomination.

EASY

1. At whose house does Alice see a "cute guy?"

2. Charles and John say that Professor Dayton was known by what nickname?

3. During the break-in, what does the talking radio tell Jerry to watch out for?

4. How much money does Jerry find in the box?

5. Rachael picks up a small statuette of what famous New York City landmark when she first enters the house?

6. What apartment does Jerry live in?

7. What does Rachael use to blindfold Victor?

8. What does the banner hanging at the Lyric Theater say?

9. What is Alice's brother's name?

10. What is Alice's grandmother's job?

11. What is the advertised price on the cart for two hot dogs?

12. What is the first thing Kathy brings for Charles and John to eat?

13. What is the professor's first name?

14. What's the name of the prostitute Jerry first encounters in the stairwell?

15. Which "voodoo kit" does the professor buy?

MEDIUM DIFFICULTY

1. Akil Wingate played a character named Forrest Pendell on what series?

2.   Bunny Gibson appeared in one episode of what popular CBS crime procedural?

3.   Dusty is in what year at high school?

4.   How old is free clinic patient Mrs. Lexington?

5.   In *Ronny Camaro and Seven Angry Women* (2003), Elwood Carlisle plays a character with the same name as what animated bad boy?

6.   Roy Abramsohn appeared as a doctor in an episode of what Dick Van Dyke TV series?

7.   Selma Pinkard appeared with what rapper in 2007's *Black Supaman*?

8.   The actor who plays Ben is named Ben Pronsky. How was his last name spelled in the credits?

9.   What animal name is seen on Victor's shirt when he's at the computer?

10. What does Alice call Professor Dayton?

11. What is the name of Dr. Farwell's "regular" security guy?

12. When did Charles and John graduate?

13. Where did Kathy go to school?

14. Where does Rachael's new client, Victor, say he lives?

15. Which castmember appeared in the CBS sitcoms *Everybody Loves Raymond* and *Yes Dear*?

HARD AS HELL

1.   A lamp made out of what piece of sports equipment is seen in Jerry's kitchen?

2.   According to Charles and John, what is Professor Dayton's specialty?

3. Although the label on Jerry's whiskey bottle is blacked out, bottles of what kind of ale can plainly be seen on his kitchen table and the shelf behind him?

4. Cara Cameron, who provides the voice of Jerry's radio, has appeared onscreen in one movie. What is it?

5. Co-directors James Dudelson and Ana Clavell previously worked together on what 1990s Showtime original series?

6. Eileen Dietz' first role (as Eileen Scott) was in what 1966 teen crime flick?

7. Of the five credited writers, only one does not appear in the film itself. Which one?

8. The man who pulls into the parking lot at Jerry's security guard job is talking to on the phone to whom?

9. What is the license plate number on Rachael's BMW?

10. What relative does grandma say was a "pansy?

11. What time is showing on Jerry's clock radio?

12. Where is Professor Dayton's wedding to be held, according to the invitation?

13. Which castmember appeared in both David Lynch's *Mulholland Drive* (2001), and in *The Erotic Misadventures of the Invisible Man* (2003)?

14. Which three castmembers appeared in episodes of *Untold Stories of the ER*?

15. Who does Jerry see passed out in the alley?

QUIZ #66: DESPERATION (2006)

Screenplay by: Stephen King
Directed by: Mick Garris
Starring: Tom Skerritt, Steven Weber, and Annabeth Gish
Touchstone Television

In 2006, director Mick Garris teamed up yet again with Stephen King for the ABC TV movie *Desperation*, with a screenplay by King based on his novel. With a strong cast headed up by Tom Skerritt, gorgeous scenery courtesy of the landscape in and around Bisbee, Arizona, and a genuinely creepy premise, *Desperation* delivered a generally satisfying final product before falling off a bit in the third act. King, in fact, said in a news item on his website that it was "probably the best TV movie to be made from my work."

Critical response was decidedly mixed. *The New York Times* and *New York Post* delivered measured praise, but the *Washington Post* and *Chicago Tribune* were quite harsh. In the *Washington Post*, Tom Shales wrote "*Desperation,* mercifully, is over and out after killing only three hours of prime time."

Originally planned as a two-part mini-series, the movie was actually aired as a single, three-hour event on ABC. Unfortunately, the network decided to program it against Fox's juggernaut *American Idol* finals, a fact which King bemoaned. "When I see this kind of scheduling, my heart is warmed by how well I have been treated by all my friends at ABC," he sarcastically remarked on his website.

EASY

1. As seen on the sign at the beginning of the movie, US Highway 50 in Nevada is known as what?

2. Collie has a bobblehead figure of what animal on his dashboard?

3. Cynthia tells Steve that if he doesn't call her "Cookie," she won't call him what?

4. Eight years after his breakout role as Elliot in E. T. (1982), Henry Thomas took on a darker role, playing a younger version of what infamous big-screen killer?

5. How long does Tom Billingsley say Collie has been on the force?

6. How long has the theater been closed?

7. How many people survived the cave-in at the mine?

8. In what year was the town of Desperation established?

9. Over the course of seven seasons, Tom Skerritt played five different roles on what popular TV western?

10. What author does Cynthia tell Steve she mostly sticks with?

11. What is the name of the grocery store seen in Desperation?

12. What is the name of the movie David sees in the projectionist's booth?

13. What kind of motorcycle is Johnny Marinville riding?

14. What shaft did workers uncover "about a month ago," according to Billingsley?

15. What two offices does David search in the Municipal Building?

MEDIUM DIFFICULTY

1.   After shooting the cougar, Johnny imagines seeing a bumper sticker for what US president?

2.   Annabeth Gish joined Robert Patrick as part of the "new" team on the Fox sci-fi series *The X-Files*. What was her character's name?

3.   Cynthia tells Steve she was in a "literary commune" in what city?

4.   In a 2004 music video for the band Fountains of Wayne, Shane Haboucha plays a young man in love with whom?

5.   Kelly Overton got her professional acting start on what ABC daytime serial?

6.   Matt Frewer played what recurring character on the Sci-Fi/Syfy Channel series *Eureka*?

7.   Sylvia Kelegian played an ATF agent in two episodes of what Showtime series about polygamy?

8.   The moving truck driven by Steve Ames comes from what company?

9.   What does Collie Entragian call Mary Jackson?

10.   What does Mary tell David she's hungry enough to eat?

11.   What famous 60s TV show's opening narration does Peter jokingly quote to Mary when they see the dead cat?

12.   Where did Peter and Mary stop for gas in Fallon?

13.   Where were the Carvers headed when their tires went flat?

14.   Which castmember had a recurring role on the ABC series *Pushing Daisies*?

15.   Who does Collie say killed Princess Diana?

HARD AS HELL

1. According to David, who did Tak possess before Collie Entragian?

2. Charles Durning played what religious leader in a 1987 television movie?

3. Collie names two books by Johnny Marinville. What are they?

4. Director Mick Garris suggested changing the name of the movie house to the Chinese Theater. What was it called in Stephen King's novel?

5. How many people does Billingsley say Collie killed while taking him to jail?

6. The distinctive voice of Ron Perlman is well known to video game aficionados as the narrator of what post-apocalyptic game series?

7. What college does Peter's sister attend?

8. What does the poster that Johnny sees for Viet Cong Lookout say the movie is produced by?

9. What film is seen on the marquee in the picture of the Chinese Theater?

10. What was the name of the network executive played by Steven Weber on the series *Studio 60 on the Sunset Strip*?

11. When does Steve tell Cynthia that he worked with Bob Dylan?

12. When Pie references John Ford in the theater, she is actually misquoting a line from what movie?

13. When we first see him, Steve Ames is listening to the song "Fall to Pieces" by what rock and roll supergroup?

14. Where does David tell Collie that he lives?

15. Which cast member appeared in one episode on the USA Network series version of *The Dead Zone*?

QUIZ #67: 1408 (2007)

Screenplay by: Matt Greenberg, Scott Alexander and Larry Karaszewski
Directed by: Mikael Hafstrom
Starring: John Cusack, Samuel L. Jackson, and Mary McCormick
Dimension Films

For the most part, successful theatrical adaptations of Stephen King's work have drawn on his more realistic material. *Stand By Me* (1986), *Misery* (1990), and *The Shawshank Redemption* (1994) have no supernatural elements whatsoever. The original *Carrie* (1976), *The Dead Zone* (1983) and *The Green Mile* (1999) portray characters with strange powers, but those powers take a back seat to the larger story elements.

There are exceptions, of course. Stanley Kubrick's *The Shining* (1979) is the best example, and *Pet Sematary* (1989) remains popular. But the list of atrocities is much longer, and much more notable.

The filmmakers who adapted King's creepy short story "1408" took much the same route as Kubrick, making wholesale changes to the original. In this case, of course, the changes were necessary to produce a feature-length product, but unlike so many before them, the trio of writers and director Mikael Hafstrom actually *improved* upon the original. It certainly didn't hurt that John Cusack nailed the role of Mike Enslin, convincingly selling the transformation of the character from a cocky know-it-all to a man driven beyond the edge of sanity by the things he sees in the titular hotel room.

King himself was well pleased with the result, saying on his website that *1408* was "a genuinely disquieting movie—the damn thing gets under your skin and just CRAWLS there." Critical reception was likewise enthusiastic, and a final world-wide box office tally of over $130,000,000 crowned the achievement.

EASY

1. "Paranoia is" what, according to the hat Mike wears in the bookstore?

2. Early on, Mike says he's finally found something to write about, a ghost that does what?

3. How many deaths does Mr. Olin say have happened under his watch?

4. How much is a can of Beer Nuts from the mini-bar?

5. In 2003, John Cusack starred in what thriller about mysterious deaths at a creepy motel?

6. Mike is asked to sign a copy of what novel?

7. Mike is seen tossing a cap featuring what baseball team on his bed at the inn?

8. Mike says the painting of a schooner is done in the "predictably dull fashion" of what American printmakers?

9. Sam complains about having to eat lunch with the "idiot" from where?

10. Screenwriters Scott Alexander and Larry Karaszewski also wrote what 1999 bio-pic directed by Milos Forman?

11. Stephen King's short story was originally conceived as an example of how a story evolves in an appendix to what book?

12. Tony Shalhoub starred with Steven Weber, who played Jack Torrence in the TV version of *Stephen King's The Shining* (1997), in what long-running NBC sitcom?

13.   What time does the clock show the second time the radio bursts to life?

14.   While Mike is surveying the view from the window, the song "We've Only Just Begun" by what brother and sister act begins playing on the radio?

15.   Who joins Mike and Sam on the call about the Dolphin hotel?

MEDIUM DIFFICULTY

1.   *1408* was director Mikael Hafstrom's second English-language feature. What 2005 romantic thriller starring Clive Owen was his first?

2.   How long does Lily say it will take her to reach the Dolphin Hotel?

3.   In October, 1912, room 1408 claimed its first victim. Who was it?

4.   Isiah Whitlock, Jr., played glad-handing State Senator R. Clayton "Clay" Davis on what critically-acclaimed HBO crime drama?

5.   Olin tells Mike that someone drowned "in his chicken soup." Who?

6.   Samuel L. Jackson plays what S.H.I.E.L.D. agent in a number of Marvel Comics film adaptations?

7.   What do Mike's readers expect, according to Olin?

8.   What is the name of the facility where Mike's father is living?

9.   What is the phone number of the insurance company advertised on the airplane banner?

10.   What program does Mike use on his computer to contact Lily?

11.   What were the names of the Enslin's goldfish?

12.   Where does Mike tell the bookstore clerk is the best place to see a ghost?

13. Which cast member also appeared in *Secret Window* (2004), adapted from the Stephen King short-story *Secret Window, Secret Garden?*

14. Which cast member has appeared in the TV series *ER*, *West Wing*, and *Law & Order: Criminal Intent?*

15. Who was the last person to die in room 1408?

HARD AS HELL

1. A man and woman are seen walking what kind of dog in the lobby of the Dolphin?

2. Mike first finds a story about the Dolphin Hotel in what newspaper?

3. Mike is wearing a t-shirt made by what American clothing company?

4. Mike's tape recorder is made by what company?

5. Mr. and Mrs. Clark at the Weeping Beech Inn tell Mike a maid hung herself there in what year?

6. On what corner is the Dolphin Hotel located?

7. On what level is the spa located, according to the message Mike hears while on hold with the front desk?

8. What brand of tequila does Mike order in his dream dinner with Lily?

9. What breakfast item does Mike recommend at the inn?

10. What classic rock song by The Band is playing in the diner where Mike opens his mail?

11. What is the name of the desk clerk who asks Mike how to spell "Enslin?"

12. What is the name of the first film listed on the pay-per-view menu on the television?

13. Where did Lily's grandmother bring the family Bible from?

14. While on the phone with Sam, what kind of beer is Mike drinking?

15. Who does Mike get a birthday card from?

QUIZ #68: THE MIST (2007)

Screenplay by: Frank Darabont
Directed by: Frank Darabont
Starring: Thomas Jane, Marcia Gay Harden, and Laurie Holden
Dimension Films

Frank Darabont wanted to turn Stephen King's novella *The Mist* into a movie from the first time he encountered it. "I have loved this story since 1980 when I had first read it," Darabont said. But *The Mist* would have to wait. First, Darabont famously took another King novella, *Rita Hayworth and Shawshank Redemption*, and in 1994 turned it into one of the most beloved movies of the late 20ᵗʰ century. He followed up with another King adaptation, *The Green Mile*, in 1999, also to great acclaim.

The Mist will always be known as the least of these adaptations, receiving a generally lukewarm reception. Unlike the previous films, *The Mist* is a straight-up horror movie, although much of the tension is driven by the darker engines of human behavior and not the nameless creatures outside.

Darabont mostly stayed faithful to the novella, but decided to give the movie a much darker ending, one which King applauded. "The ending is such a jolt—wham!—it's frightening," King told *USA Today*. "But people who go to see a horror movie don't necessarily want to be sent out with a Pollyanna ending."

EASY

1. Despite being set in Maine, *The Mist* was shot entirely in what southern state?

2. Frances Sternhagen appeared as Virginia in what 1990 film adapted from a Stephen King novel?

3. How many members of the pharmacy expedition are lost?

4. How many people does David say his LandCruiser can seat?

5. How many rounds of ammo does Amanda Dumfries have in her purse?

6. Jeffrey DeMunn and Laurie Holden both appeared in what other Frank Darabont film?

7. Laurie Holden appeared as Marita Covarrubias in several episodes of what popular Fox television series, which also featured an episode written by Stephen King?

8. Thomas Jane starred with Morgan Freeman in the 2003 big screen adaptation of what Stephen King book?

9. What are the "new" store hours at the Food House?

10. What does Amanda Dumfries teach?

11. What does Dan Miller suggest using to make torches?

12. What is Ollie's position at The Food House?

13. What is the name of the military project occurring on the mountain?

14. Who kills the first of the invading "bugs?"

15. William Sadler has appeared in what two other Stephen King adaptations?

MEDIUM DIFFICULTY

1. Ambrose Cornell's shotgun is in his vehicle. What kind of vehicle is it?

2. Events in the film take place in Stephen King's iconic town of Castle Rock, Maine, but what real-world town was King's original novella set in?

3. How long does Jim estimate the batteries will last if the lights are turned on?

4. In 2006, Laurie Holden appeared in a movie based on what video game that featured a small town overtaken by strange creatures and an all-enveloping fog?

5. Marcia Gay Harden won an Oscar for Best Supporting Actress in what movie?

6. Mrs. Carmody tells Brent Norton that there is no defense against what?

7. Ollie stashes five bags of food in what checkout aisle?

8. The camera crew from what gritty TV drama was hired to help with filming?

9. The Stephen King novella of the same name first appeared in what horror anthology?

10. What anatomical feature of the "bugs" that appear the first night especially impress Mrs. Carmody?

11. What are the names of the soldiers who commit suicide?

12. What cult leader does David compare Mrs. Carmody to?

13. What iconic Stephen King character is portrayed in the painting being worked on by David Drayton?

14.   Where does Brent Norton work as an "important attorney?"

15.   William Sadler played the Grim Reaper in what 1991 comedy?

HARD AS HELL

1.   Firetrucks passing by the store the day after the storm bear the name of what Louisiana parish?

2.   Frank Darabont was a production assistant on what 1981 horror flick starring Linda Blair?

3.   The Food House has been serving Castle Rock since when?

4.   What comic book does David grab for his son at the pharmacy?

5.   What does Ollie suggest David use to cover his son?

6.   What is the name of the first known victim of the mist?

7.   What is the name of the pharmacy next to the store?

8.   What Maine radio station, owned by Stephen King, appears on Norm's t-shirt?

9.   What medicine for burns does Ollie say can be found at the drug store?

10.   What newspaper is Mrs. Reppler reading?

11.   What night do the Drayton's have planned for a date night?

12.   Where are medical supplies located in the store?

13.   Where are Sally's parents when the storm hits?

14.   Where does Ambrose Cornell originally believe the mist came from?

15.   Who is planning to barbecue some chicken on a gas grill?

QUIZ #69: DOLAN'S CADILLAC (2009)

Screenplay by: Richard Dooling
Directed by: Jeff Beesley
Starring: Christian Slater, Emmanuelle Vaugier and Wes Bentley
Minds Eye Entertainment

Once upon a time, *Dolan's Cadillac* was something of a hot property in Hollywood. Tom Cruise's production company owned the rights, and a number of big names were attached to the project at various junctures. The adaptation languished in development hell for over a decade before finally landing as a direct-to-video release in 2009.

In the end, the project attracted Christian Slater to star as Dolan. "I've always been a huge fan of (Stephen King) and the types of things that he writes—very scary, very edgy, very dark, very twisted, very intense and that's what this really presented itself as," Slater told the *Regina Leader-Post* during filming.

Wes Bentley of *American Beauty* (1999) fame plays the man seeking revenge after his wife is killed to stop her from testifying against the gangster Dolan. Veteran actress Emmanuelle Vaugier plays Robinson's wife Elizabeth.

The rest of the cast, the screenwriter, and the director are all virtual unknowns, and *Dolan's Cadillac* is certainly not going to do anything to change that fact.

EASY

1. According to the foreman, how hot does it get west of Indian Springs in July?

2. Christian Slater played the interviewer to Brad Pitt's vampire in *Interview with the Vampire* (1994), adapted from the novel by what author?

3. How much C4 does Robinson say was used to blow up Elizabeth's car?

4. How much does Robinson say his great-grandfather's watch is worth?

5. On what highway does Robinson set his trap for Dolan?

6. Robinson says he has "one more very important question" for Dolan. What is it?

7. Robinson tells Dolan he called 911, and that what emergency equipment is on the way?

8. Robinson tells his students that his great-grandfather was how old in 1869?

9. What Chinese gangs does Agent Fletcher tell Robinson and Elizabeth Jimmy Dolan works with?

10. What does Dolan tell Roman he hates?

11. What does Elizabeth tell Robinson she is doing after work?

12. What is the TVPA, according to Agent Fletcher?

13. When does Dolan go to Los Angeles?

14. When Elizabeth asks Robinson if she snores, what is his answer?

15. Why can't Dolan open the sunroof?

MEDIUM DIFFICULTY

1. After the failed assassination, Robinson sees a vision of Elizabeth. What does she say?

2. Dolan tells Robinson that the meaning of life is what?

3. Emmanuelle Vaugier appeared as Dr. Helen Bryce on what "super" TV series?

4. Fletcher tells Robinson he has sworn affidavits from whom?

5. How much money does Tony Wu want from Dolan for "20 units?"

6. On HBO's *The Sopranos*, Al Sapienza played Mikey Palmice, right-hand-man to what aging mobster?

7. Originally, what two actors were slated to play Robinson and Dolan?

8. Robinson calls Dolan the king of what?

9. Screenwriter Richard Dooling also worked on a Stephen-King related TV series. What was it?

10. What does Dolan answer when asked if he is Chief's friend?

11. What grade does Robinson teach?

12. What is the last car to pass the detour after Robinson sabotages Dolan?

13. What is the name of Elizabeth's pregnancy test kit?

14. What is the name of the hotel Dolan is seen staying at?

15. What was Tink's job in West Africa?

HARD AS HELL

1. According to Chief's computer search, where does Robinson live?

2. Although some exteriors were shot in Las Vegas, principal filming took place in what Canadian province?

3. Dolan offers Robinson how much money at first?

4. How many barrels does Robinson manage to put back at the site of the detour?

5. In 1999, Wes Bentley scored a breakthrough role in the Academy Award-winning film *American Beauty*. That same year, he played the title character in a film that starred Bob Hoskins and Antonia Banderas. What is this film?

6. Karen LeBlanc played Robin Taylor on ESPN's first original drama series. What was the title of this series?

7. What IP address does Robinson have Dolan type into his browser?

8. What is Tinker eating in the construction office?

9. What level is Elizabeth's car parked on?

10. What mythical creature is seen on the table next to the couch in Dolan's suite?

11. What piece of equipment does Tink teach Robinson to use?

12. What toy does Elizabeth take from a student's desk?

13. What words are tattooed on the construction foreman's fingers?

14. Which cast member appeared in the 2001 TV remake of the classic sports flick *Brian's Song*?

15. Who sent Jimmy eight women from the Ukraine?

QUIZ #70: CHILDREN OF THE CORN (2009)

Screenplay by: Daniel P. Borchers and Stephen King
Directed by: Daniel P. Borchers
Starring: David Anders, Kandyse McClure, and Daniel Newman
Children of the Corn Productions

This made-for-television version of Stephen King's much abused short story proves that it is possible to make a competent version of the tale. The formula? Stick close to the original plot, and give your adult leads something to work with. Here, David Anders and Kandyse McClure handle the material ably, making the first two-thirds of the movie really work.

Starting with the screenplay King submitted way back in 1984 for the first *Children of the Corn* (which earns King a co-screenwriting credit here, although he actually had no participation in the movie), Daniel P. Borchers makes sure things hew close to the source material. A producer on the original film, Borchers admits in a DVD feature that he became more and more disenchanted with that version as the years went by. He says he felt it was important to bring King's original vision to the screen.

In the end, the film is undercut somewhat by the titular children. It's just not easy to make young kids seem menacing, and some of these kids are *very* young. An extended cornfield chase drags the final third of the movie down as well, but it's certainly a vast improvement over all the *Corn* that has come before.

EASY

1. According to the road sign Burt and Vicki pass, they are 13 miles from Gatlin and 87 miles from what real Nebraska town?

2. Daniel Newman plays Gavin in what Terry Gilliam movie that was Heath Ledger's final film?

3. In what year do the children of Gatlin turn on the adults?

4. Isaac's sermon refers to the "time of the Blue Man." Who or what is the Blue Man?

5. On ABC's *Alias*, David Anders played Julian Sark, a constant thorn in the side of super spy Sidney Bristow. What actress played Bristow?

6. The young preacher gives his sermon wearing what children's costume?

7. What are the two types of gas available at the station on the edge of Gatlin?

8. What does Burt say they probably use for a "holy wafer" in Nebraska?

9. What don't you go to after your throat's been cut, according to Burt?

10. What is the date on the sermon board?

11. What is the first sacrifice the children of Gatlin make?

12. What is the name of the first business Burt pulls up in front of in Gatlin?

13. Where does Burt suggest all the townspeople might be?

14. Where does Isaac instruct the boys to chase Burt to?

15. Who does Malachai believe may eventually take Isaac's place as the prophet?

MEDIUM DIFFICULTY

1. David Anders played what nearly immortal character on NBC's *Heroes*?

2. David P. Borchers served as producer on *Meatballs 4* (1992), starring what former child actor who also appeared in *Stand By Me* (1986)?

3. How did Lt. Anastasia Dualla, the character played by Kandyse McClure on the re-imagined sci-fi series *Battlestar Galactica*, die?

4. How many names for God does Burt say they must have in Nebraska?

5. How much does a Whopper cost at the deserted bar and grill?

6. In 2002, Kandyse McClure appeared in seven episodes of what post-apocalyptic TV series starring Luke Perry?

7. In the 2002 remake of Stephen King's *Carrie*, which character did Kandyse McClure portray?

8. In what Nebraska neighbor was the movie filmed?

9. Isaac says He Who Walks Behind The Rows is a god of favor, but a god of what else as well?

10. Preston Bailey had a recurring role as Cody Bennett, the stepson of what premium cable serial killer/crime lab tech?

11. Preston Bailey plays Nicholas in the 2010 remake of what 1973 George Romero splatterfest?

12. Stephen King's story originally appeared in what men's magazine?

13. What is the name of the 8-year-old preacher Vicki remembers from her youth?

14. What kind of car are Burt and Vicki driving in?

15. When Vicki notes they haven't seen a car or truck for over an hour, what does Burt say might be the reason?

HARD AS HELL

1. Born in Oregon, David Anders has portrayed characters from a wide variety of nationalities. Where does the character played by Anders in the eighth season of Fox's terrorism drama *24* hail from?

2. Donald P. Borchars has directed two other films. What are they?

3. How long has Malachai led the biggest boys?

4. How many patrols did Burt go out on in Vietnam?

5. The 1963 calendar on the wall is courtesy of what local business?

6. This is actually the third filmed adaptation of King's short story. The first was a short film from 1983 made under what title?

7. Vicki says she'll be all right as soon as she and Burt are what?

8. What are the first names of the first two children born in Gatlin after 1963?

9. What does Isaac call Burt after Burt has been sacrificed?

10. What does the sign say is the population of Gatlin?

11. What event is advertised on the community notices board at the church?

12. What is Vicki's middle name?

13. Which cast member had a brief appearance as a "rock star" in the HBO series *Sex and the City*?

14. Which cast member made a brief appearance on a 2007 episode of the sketch-comedy *MADtv*?

15. Which cast member appeared as Tiffany in two episodes of the Disney series *The Suite Life of Zack and Cody*?

THE ANSWERS

QUIZ #1: CARRIE

EASY: 1. Carrie's breasts. 2. Being at the Prom. 3. *Eight Is Enough*. 4. Sin. 5. *It* (1990). 6. Three days suspension and a refusal of Prom tickets. 7. "Carrie White burn in hell." 8. Morty. 9. That he escort Carrie White to the Prom. 10. Move things. 11. Volleyball. 12. "Carrie White eats shit." 13. "You suck." 14. Producer Paul Monash. 15. She assisted her future hubby Jack Fisk with set decoration.

MEDIUM DIFFICULTY: 1. Cassie Wright. 2. Ralph. 3. The Last Supper. 4. *Blow Out*. 5. Edie McClurg. 6. Walking into the Prom with Carrie White. 7. Sue Snell. 8. Margaret White. 9. *The Competition* (1980), *Honeysuckle Rose* (1980), *Micki & Maude* (1984), *Rumpelstiltskin* (1987), *A Show of Force* (1990), *Carried Away* (1996), and *The Rage: Carrie 2* (1999). 10. *Salem's Lot* (1979). 11. Norma. 12. *Jennifer*. 13. Chris Hargenson. 14. Director Brian De Palma's son, Cameron De Palma. 15. Karo syrup and food coloring.

HARD AS HELL: 1. *The Teenager's Path to Salvation Through the Cross of Jesus*. 2. Six-feet-seven-inches. 3. "Love Among the Stars." 4. Mary Lila Grace. 5. Bates High School. 6. "What the hell?" 7. *The Fury* (1978). 8. Seeber's Prescriptions. 9. Miss Collins and Billy Nolan. 10. *Home Movies* (1979), *Dressed to Kill* (1980), and *Blow Out*. 11. Ernest. 12. *The Secret Science Behind Miracles*. 13. Best Actress (Sissy Spacek) and Best Supporting Actress (Piper Laurie). 14. *Greetings* (1968). 15. *Nichols*.

QUIZ #2: SALEM'S LOT

EASY: 1. Ferndale, California. 2. On the basement table. 3. Bangor. 4. *The Deer Hunter* (1978). 5. Plumbing contractor. 6. Baptist. 7. *Air Dancer*. 8. Eva Miller. 9. Barlow. 10. An evil house. 11. *The Killing* (1956). 12. *The Mangler* (1995). 13. *Christine*. 14. Jason Berk. 15. Doctor.

MEDIUM DIFFICULTY: 1. Werner Herzog. 2. "Watch for Grand Opening." 3. *Dracula Sucks* (1979). 4. Railroad Street. 5. *Sleepwalkers* (1992). 6. Kort. 7. "Boom Boom" Bonnie. 8. *Someone Is Watching* (1978). 9. The bulkhead door, the backdoor, the front door, and the door to the shed. 10. Richard Matheson. 11. The Edgar Allan Poe Awards. 12. *Heaven Can Wait* (1978). 13. *Needful Things* (1993). 14. Harmony Hill. 15. Elisha Cook, Jr.

HARD AS HELL: 1. *All Quiet on the Western Front*. 2. Stirling Silliphant, Lawrence Cohen, and Robert Getchell. 3. James Mason. 4. *Blood Thirst*. 5. Parkins. 6. Accountant. 7. *The Making of The Shining* (1980). 8. 2,013. 9. $100,000. (The producers paid an additional $20,000 to the owners of the already-existing cottage which served as the core of the house.) 10. Holly Elementary School. 11. *Carrie* (1976) and *The Rage: Carrie 2* (1999). 12. Whiskey. 13. Six. 14. *A Star Is Born* (1954), *Georgy Girl* (1966), and *The Verdict* (1982). 15. 112 minutes.

QUIZ #3: THE SHINING

EASY: 1. Delbert Grady. 2. Naked women sporting afros. 3. Carole Lombard. 4. Doc. 5. "He did it to himself." 6. Management at The Timberline Hotel where the film was shot requested this as they were afraid no one would ever stay in the room again. Therefore, the room number was changed to one which does not exist in that hotel. 7. French fries with catsup. 8. The line was improvised on set by Jack Nicholson. Kubrick liked it, and decided to keep it. 9. Danny. 10. Vermont. 11. "He who wakes up early meets a golden day." 12. Three. 13. Susie. 14. Lloyd. 15. At a carnival.

MEDIUM DIFFICULTY: 1. "How'd you like some ice cream, Doc?" 2. The Boiler Room. 3. The Stanley Hotel in Estes Park, Colorado, which served as the setting for Mick Garris' 1997 remake. 4. Daniel B. Ullman. 5. Apollo 11. 6. Chicago, Illinois. 7. A short story penned by Jack Torrance. 8. That he hacks Wendy and Danny to pieces. 9. 300. 10. Barry Nelson appeared as "Jimmy Bond" on the CBS television adaptation of *Casino Royale* which aired in 1954 as an episode of *Climax*. 11. Thirteen feet high. 12. A fire truck. 13. "[K]eep America clean." 14. A closing scene in which Mr. Ullman visits Wendy in the hospital. 15. Three-and-a-half hours.

HARD AS HELL: 1. Larry Durkin. 2. KDK-12. 3. Susan Robertson. 4. *It.* 5. *The King of Marvin Gardens* (1972), *One Flew Over the Cuckoo's Nest* (1975), and *The Fortune* (1975). 6. May 15 through October 20. 7. Room 237. 8. Mt. Hood, Oregon. 9. Twenty. 10. Continental Airlines. 11. 1970. 12. *Napoleon.* 13. Bourbon on the rocks. 14. Construction began in 1907, and the hotel was completed in 1909. 15. Carl Yazstremski.

QUIZ #4: CREEPSHOW

EASY: 1. *Baseball.* 2. In the bottom of his underwear drawer. 3. "Weeds." 4. Ryder's Quarry. 5. *Swamp Thing.* 6. A meat cleaver. 7. "I keep what is mine." 8. "The Crate." 9. *Carrie* (1976). 10. Jack Kamen. 11. Seattle, Washington. 12. *The Thing.* 13. To call her Billie. 14. Legendary makeup wizard Tom Savini. 15. *Creepshow 2* (1987).

MEDIUM DIFFICULTY: 1. Norman Castonmeyer. 2. Dexter Stanley's tobacco. 3. 25,000. 4. "The Lonesome Death of Jordy Verrill." 5. *The Fog* (1980). 6. Orlando, Florida. 7. The Department of Meteors. 8. Amberson Hall. 9. They are all played by the same actor, Bingo O'Malley. 10. "[A]t least one sex scene." 11. Sixty. 12. Stephen King's son, Joe King. 13. Horlicks University. 14. Julia Carpenter. 15. Five.

HARD AS HELL: 1. *Blaberus Blaberus* and *Blaberus Giganticus.* 2. Tom Atkins. 3. Greedo. 4. $3,200. 5. Mike. 6. Baked ham. 7. Comfort Station. 8. Rice Crispies. 9. 1834. 10. At the Cannes Film Festival. 11. Professor Terrell. 12. Granger Farm Supplies. 13. Mrs. Danvers. 14. Bob Backlund. 15. 129 minutes.

QUIZ #5: CUJO

EASY: 1. *Hardcastle and McCormick.* 2. Jan De Bont. 3. *Cat's Eye.* 4. *Impulse* (1984). 5. Stephen King. 6. The Audience Jury Award. 7. Roger Breakstone. 8. Frank Dodd, the Castle Rock deputy who doubled as a serial killer in *The Dead Zone.* 9. Barbara Turner. 10. *Who's the Boss?* 11. Peter Medale. 12. In the book, Tad dies. 13. Christopher Stone. 14. He fell from a swing. 15. *The Boogeyman* (1985) (A similar theme also appears in *Cat's Eye.*)

MEDIUM DIFFICULTY: 1. Scott Schwartz for *The Toy* (1982). 2. Tadpole. 3. Red Raspberry Zingers. 4. *Terror in the Aisles.* 5. Gary Pevier. 6. $5,000. 7. A thermos. 8. *Dances with Wolves* (1990). 9. Brett. 10. Danny Pintauro. 11. Sharp Cereal. 12. Five. 13. *The Stepford Wives.* 14. Charity. 15. *Alligator* (1980).

HARD AS HELL: 1. Harry. 2. *Rage.* 3. Maple Sugar Road. 4. Producer Daniel H. Blatt. 5. Kellogg's Corn Flakes. 6. 8585. 7. *Annie Get Your Gun.* 8. Tom Skerritt appears as Sheriff Bannerman in *The Dead Zone.* 9. *The American Success Company.* 10. Six miles, although Vic later says seven. 11. *Cockfighter,* which was retitled *Born to Kill.* 12. Connecticut. 13. Pac Man. 14. *Dirty O'Neil.* 15. Billy Jacobi, who appears as Brett Camber.

QUIZ #6: THE DEAD ZONE

EASY: 1. *The West Wing.* 2. The Weizak Clinic. 3. His talents as a "fortune teller." 4. Stewart's money. 5. His mother. 6. *Sleepy Hollow* (1999). 7. Producer. 8. George. 9. A high-chair. 10. "It wasn't meant to be." 11. Adolf Hitler. 12. A bullet. 13. Sarah. 14. The coma diet. 15. Herb Smith.

MEDIUM DIFFICULTY: 1. Denny. 2. Brenner. 3. Bill Murray. 4. Frank Dodd. 5. Marlboro. 6. Sonny. 7. Hal Holbrook. 8. A pair of surgical scissors. 9. Fifteen-years-old. 10. His father, Roger Stewart. 11. Five. 12. *The Brood* (1979). 13. Producer Debra Hill and director David Cronenberg. 14. Horses. 15. Andre Konchalvsky.

HARD AS HELL: 1. Charlene McKinzie. 2. Alma Frechette. 3. She knew her son was the murderer all along. 4. "No Future for Stillson." 5. Cronenberg was afraid that an *E.T.* doll visible in the girl's room would distract viewers. 6. Stanley Donen. 7. Sandy Ward. 8. He fired a handgun loaded with blanks. 9. Brian. 10. Walt. 11. Martin Sheen's son, Ramon Estevez. 12. God. 13. Cloverview Milk Company. 14. Johanna. 15. Amy.

QUIZ #7: CHRISTINE

EASY: 1. 1957. 2. "Shitter." 3. Keith Gordon. 4. Kirby McCauley. 5. Drop out of school. 6. *Firestarter* (1984). (Although the film would not be released until after *Christine*, both Phillips and director John Carpenter had worked on *Firestarter* in early stages of production.) 7. $250. 8. *5,000 Dirty Limericks*. 9. Human feces. 10. Love. 11. "Darnell's tonight." 12. *The Car* (1977). 13. Stephen King's *Christine*. 14. Buddy Repperton. 15. *The Green Mile* (1999).

MEDIUM DIFFICULTY: 1. Rockbridge, California. 2. A rust bucket. 3. Harry Dean Stanton. 4. Guilder. 5. *Cujo* and *The Dead Zone*. 6. Moochie. 7. "Keep A-Knockin'." 8. Darnell's Auto Wrecking. 9. Dennis and Leigh. 10. His wallet. 11. *The Last Temptation of Christ* (1988). 12. Kelly Preston. 13. *American Nightmare*. 14. The Chess Club. 15. Fellatio.

HARD AS HELL: 1. Roberts Blossom. 2. *Home Movies* (1979) and *Dressed to Kill* (1980). 3. Two. 4. "Beast of Burden." 5. Zero. 6. *Someone's Watching Me!* (1978). 7. Six. 8. 93,475. 9. Baker Auto. 10. "In God we trust, everyone else pays cash." 11. Twenty-six. 12. Sally Hayes. 13. Sgt. Stan Jablonski. 14. "[K]illing your kids." 15. CQB 241.

QUIZ #8: FIRESTARTER

EASY: 1. Frank Capra, Jr. 2. Dodi Fayed, best known as the man killed with Princess Diana. 3. Chimney Rock Lake. 4. John Rainbird. 5. *The Dead Zone.* 6. John Carpenter. 7. *T.J. Hooker* and *Dynasty.* 8. *Cat's Eye* (1985). 9. Lot Six. 10. *Cinefantastique.* 11. $500. 12. Charlie became angry at her mother and accidentally started her hands on fire. 13. Moses Gunn. 14. Screenwriter Stanley Mann. 15. *The Yellow Rolls-Royce* (1965) and *Movie Movie* (1978).

MEDIUM DIFFICULTY: 1. Herman. 2. Vicky's hair. 3. *The Collector* (1965). 4. Because Rainbird intercepts the letters. 5. Emilio Estevez appears in *Maximum Overdrive* (1986) and Ramon Estevez appears in *The Dead Zone.* 6. The dead body of his wife. 7. He blinds them. 8. *Conan the Destroyer.* 9. *The West Wing.* 10. Knoxville, Tennessee. 11. Because the electricity is off. 12. By flushing it down the toilet. 13. *Take This Job and Shove It* (1981). 14. Necromancer. 15. Frank Burton.

HARD AS HELL: 1. *Back to School.* 2. *Class of 1984* (1982). 3. Eight. 4. Longmont, Virginia. 5. Tomlinson. 6. Bill Phillips and Bill Lancaster. 7. Norma. 8. Joan. 9. Department of Scientific Intelligence. 10. *Shaft* (1971) and *Cornbread, Earl and Me* (1975). 11. Mike. 12. Joe. 13. Roberta. 14. Maui. 15. Cherokee.

QUIZ #9: CHILDREN OF THE CORN

EASY: 1. Stephen King. 2. A strawberry milkshake. 3. Everyone involved in the mutiny. 4. R.G. Armstrong. 5. Sarah. 6. Police officer. 7. Stephen King. 8. Malachai. 9. *Children of the Corn 666: Isaac's Return* (1999). 10. Stephen King's *Night Shift*, which contains the short story "Children of the Corn." 11. In the cornfield. 12. Ceremony. 13. A ghost. 14. Coffee. 15. Three.

MEDIUM DIFFICULTY: 1. "[T]o live happily ever after." 2. Lance Kerwin. 3. Michelle Pfeiffer. 4. James Cameron. 5. A crucifix fashioned from corn. 6. "Runaway" performed by Del Shannon. 7. Vicky's abduction. 8. Stanton. 9. Number six. 10. Sarah. 11. Baxter. 12. Four years. 13. Larry Borchers, who was the production executive at New World when *Children of the Corn* was made. 14. Joseph. 15. Sarge.

HARD AS HELL: 1. A blanket and a crow bar. 2. Hemingford. 3. Twenty-seven days. 4. Varied Directions Productions. 5. The top hat. 6. Amos'. 7. "The Raft." 8. Communists. 9. $500. 10. $1.25. 11. Four minutes. 12. Wells' Blue Bunny. 13. Peace. 14. The Vietnam war. 15. Community State Bank.

QUIZ #10: CAT'S EYE

EASY: 1. "I am Christine." 2. *Firestarter* (1984). 3. New York, New York. 4. *The Dead Zone* (1983). 5. *Salem's Lot* (1979). 6. $10. 7. *The Jewel of the Nile*. 8. A 1970 Ford Mustang. 9. That cats can steal children's breath. 10. *Cujo* (1983). 11. *Best Seller* (1987). 12. "96 Tears" performed by The North Orchestra. 13. *Riding in Cars With Boys*. 14. *Pet Sematary*. 15. *Armed and Dangerous*.

MEDIUM DIFFICULTY: 1. Ten-years-old. 2. Producer Dino De Laurentiis. 3. Victor. 4. The character was a boy. 5. Saint Stephen's School for the Exceptional. 6. When Norris loses his footing and waves his arms in the air, nearly falling, a cord attaching him to the building is clearly visible. 7. "Every Breath You Take" by The Police. 8. Marcia. 9. Alvin. 10. General. 11. "Twist and Shout." 12. Polly. 13. Where his daughter attends school. 14. Ducky. 15. Sebastian.

HARD AS HELL: 1. Norma Jean. 2. Sixteen. 3. Drew Barrymore's character, Amanda (billed as "Our Girl.") 4. $2,000. 5. Carlo Rimbaldi. 6. Marquis Ultra-Lights. 7. Seventy-three percent. 8. The bed on which the troll and General fight it out. According to Ann Lloyd's *The Films of Stephen King*, the bed was forty-one-feet long, and twenty-one-feet wide. The bed was sixteen-feet high and the headboard was twenty-one-feet high. 9. *Rambo: First Blood Part II*. 10. *The Girl, the Gold Watch, & Everything* (1980), which also starred Robert Hays. 11. *Firestarter*. 12.

The ledge was seven-feet tall. 13. The Los Angeles Dodgers. 14. Dick Morrison's love for his family. 15. Wilmington, North Carolina.

QUIZ #11: SILVER BULLET

EASY: 1. *Secret Admirer.* 2. Marty is 11 years old. 3. The Medcu Drive. 4. *Miami Vice.* 5. A smiley face. 6. Harmony Hill. 7. Kill himself. 8. Like most Dino De Laurentiis productions, *Silver Bullet* was filmed in Wilmington, North Carolina. (This is the location of De Laurentiis' production company.) 9. On welfare. 10. *Creepshow* (1982). 11. Five p.m. 12. Zero. 13. "The Peacemaker." 14. Two. Although Red has filed for his third divorce, it has not yet been finalized. 15. Don Coscarelli.

MEDIUM DIFFICULTY: 1. Private justice. 2. Lawrence Tierney. 3. "Amazing Grace." 4. *Maximum Overdrive* (1986). 5. Three. 6. *Insignificance.* 7. Kincaid. 8. Marty. 9. October first. 10. *Heartbreak Ridge* (1986). 11. Joseph Haller. 12. When there's a full moon. 13. Terry O'Quinn. 14. Owen Knopfler's bat. 15. Blue paint from the Reverend's car.

HARD AS HELL: 1. Rheingold beer. 2. *Prizzi's Honor* (1985). 3. Saturday. 4. Best Film. (Must have been a slow year for fantasy and horror films, huh?) 5. Reggie Jackson. 6. *Barbarella* (1968). (Coincidentally, *Apt Pupil*, 1998, star Ian McKellen tested for this film, but did not land the role.) 7. He will be singing soprano in the Vienna Boys Choir. 8. *Invasion U.S.A.* 9. A specialty publisher named Christopher Zavisa. 10. $1.49. 11. Ridge Road. 12. *Firestarter* (1984). 13. *The Sopranos.* 14. Nan Coslaw. 15. *The Last Flight* (1982), *Home Free All* (1984), and *Invasion U.S.A.*

QUIZ #12: THE WOMAN IN THE ROOM

1. Donna Elliott. 2. Brian Libby. 3. "You lose count." 4. Abdominal cancer. 5. Tissue paper. 6. Kevin. 7. One. 8. Aspirin. 9. Nothing; only static. 10. Cheryl. 11. His dick. 12. Five years old. 13. Eight a.m. 14. Sixty-five milligrams. 15. *Stephen King's The Shining* (1997).

QUIZ #13: THE BOOGEYMAN

1. *Tales from the Darkside*. 2. One o'clock. 3. John. 4. "The Boogyman."
5. Dr. Harper. 6. Miller Genuine Draft. 7. Dry cleaning bags. 8. "Be
back shortly." 9. 1982. 10. Gerald Ravel. 11. Rita. 12. Denny, Cheryl,
and Andy. 13. To the beach. 14. "Boogeyman." 15. The closet door was
open, but he knew he had shut it earlier.

QUIZ #14: MAXIMUM OVERDRIVE

Easy: 1. AC/DC. 2. Sewage. 3. *Silver Bullet* (1985). 4. Bubba. 5.
Giancarlo Esposito. 6. *The Dead Zone* (1983) and *Firestarter* (1984).
7. Worst Director (Stephen King) and Worst Actor (Emilio Estevez).
8. Happy Toyz. 9. Florida. 10. Wanda June. 11. Connie. 12. A genius.
13. Twelve. 14. More gasoline. 15. Because cinematographer Armando
Nannuzzi spoke only Italian.

MEDIUM DIFFICULTY: 1. She slaps him. 2. Marla Maples. 3. *Wisdom* (1986). 4. Tom Savini. 5. $7.43 million. 6. Make love. 7. A hand
grenade. 8. *High Society*. 9. My-T Tas-T. 10. "Who Made Who?" by
AC/DC. 11. Watermelons. 12. *The Exorcist* (1973). 13. The Dixie Boy
Truck Stop. 14. Pat Hingle. 15. That he's on parole.

HARD AS HELL: 1. Robinson. 2. "Humans here!" 3. Ten days. 4. Because locals and truck drivers kept stopping at the Dixie Boy to buy coffee,
the filmmakers took out an ad explaining that it was not a real truck stop.
5. George Romero. 6. June 19, 1987. 7. "King of the Road." 8. Conant's
Truck Stop & Diner. 9. $9.95. 10. Here comes another load of joy. 11.
The Langoliers (1995). 12. *Freejack*. 13. "Trucks," "The Mangler," and "The
Lawnmower Man." 14. Lisa Simpson on *The Tracey Ullman Show* and later
on *The Simpsons*. 15. Cinematographer Armando Nannuzzi.

QUIZ #15: STAND BY ME

EASY: 1. Twenty three years old. 2. Royal River. 3. Lachance. 4. *Misery*
(1990). 5. The Cobras. 6. Quarterback. 7. Oregon. 8. *Have Gun Will*

Travel. 9. A penny. 10. John Cusack. 11. Best Adapted Screenplay (Bruce A. Evans and Raynold Gideon). 12. Annette Funicello. 13. 12 years old. 14. Corey Feldman, Jerry O'Connell, River Phoenix, and Will Wheaton. 15. First assistant director Irby Smith.

MEDIUM DIFFICULTY: 1. *Starman* (1984). 2. Thirty-six. 3. Chopper. 4. *The Breathing Method.* 5. His comb. 6. Davey. 7. Darabont. 8. Mighty Mouse. 9. *The Running Man* (1987). 10. Attorney. 11. Ray Brower. 12. Eyeball. 13. Poor eyesight. 14. Dennis. 15. *Little Big League.*

HARD AS HELL: 1. 1959. 2. "Busboys in a restaurant." 3. Winston. 4. *Highway Patrol.* 5. *Lost in America.* 6. Vince Desjardins. 7. *True Police Cases.* 8. Connie Palermo. 9. Adrian Lyne. 10. 1,281. 11. $2.37. 12. Old Lady Simons. 13. *Kuffs.* 14. *Dark Blood*, which was never completed. 15. Samantha Mathis.

QUIZ #16: CREEPSHOW 2

EASY: 1. Special effects makeup expert Tom Savini. 2. Gornick Realty Company, named after director Michael Gornick. 3. Herself. 4. Stephen King. 5. Because it's full. 6. Dover. 7. "Thanks for the ride, lady." 8. David Holbrook is the son of actor Hal Holbrook. 9. A handgun. 10. Nine years. 11. Andy Cavanaugh. 12. Dorothy Lamour. 13. Four. 14. His class ring. 15. George Kennedy.

MEDIUM DIFFICULTY: 1. *Colliers* magazine. 2. $23,000. 3. Cinematographer. 4. *Pinfall.* 5. Classical. 6. $4,000. 7. Six. 8. Attorney. 9. Benjamin White Moon. 10. Spruce. 11. *The Cisco Kid.* 12. "You killed me!" 13. The hitchhiker's sign. 14. $10,000. 15. Lansing.

HARD AS HELL: 1. Dead River. 2. Bangor, Brewer, and Dexter. 3. Prince Domino. 4. George. 5. 11:15 pm. 6. "The Hitchhiker." 7. Trudy and Jim. 8. $1,743.92. 9. Highway 395. 10. Good intentions. 11. Prosperity. 12. $9.95. 13. "May your spirit rest, old one." 14. Hollywood. 15. "Lansing 2."

QUIZ #17: THE RUNNING MAN

EASY: 1. "I don't do requests." 2. Amber Mendez. 3. Talent, charisma, and balls. 4. "The Butcher of Bakersfield." 5. Ben. 6. "Only in a rerun." 7. Barbed wire. 8. *Predator* (1987) and *Batman & Robin* (1997). 9. Mick Fleetwood. 10. Edward. 11. Buzzsaw. 12. Bicarbonate soda. 13. Captain Freedom. 14. Fireball. 15. Jim Brown.

MEDIUM DIFFICULTY: 1. Sven. 2. *Gilligan's Island.* 3. Sixty. 4. *Climbing for Dollars.* 5. Dweezil Zappa. 6. Cadre Cola. 7. Chico. 8. Five years. 9. 400. 10. Damon. 11. Dynamo. 12. The Patriots Fund. 13. Professor Subzero. 14. "Right and Might." 15. Honolulu, Hawaii.

HARD AS HELL: 1. Nine. 2. 1,500. 3. Best Supporting Actor (Richard Dawson). 4. Whitman, Price, and Hadad. 5. Harold. 6. A217. 7. One hundred to one. 8. Edward Bunker. 9. 653-9X. 10. *Commando II.* 11. $6.00. 12. William. 13. Daniel and Mario Celario. 14. Dan. 15. The Wilshire Detention Zone.

QUIZ #18: A RETURN TO SALEM'S LOT

EASY: 1. Lawrence D. Cohen. 2. Samuel Fuller. 3. Inside the church. 4. *Creepshow* (1982). 5. Twenty-nine-years-old. 6. Three years. 7. Sally. 8. Rains. 9. Martha. 10. Reverend Gene Purdy. 11. Steven Weber, who appears in *The Shining* (1997). 12. Tobe Hooper. 13. *The Running Man* (1987) and *Creepshow 2* (1987). 14. Being dead. 15. A Nazi killer.

MEDIUM DIFFICULTY: 1. Tara Reid. 2. Peru. 3. Skepticism. 4. Pain. 5. *Creepshow 2.* 6. Rains. 7. By shooting him in the head. 8. Fourteen-years-old. 9. Evelyn Keyes. 10. Anthropologist. 11. $800. 12. He will "send his soul straight to hell." 13. *Hell Up in Harlem* and *Black Caesar.* 14. Vermont. 15. They want Joe to chronicle the history of the vampire race.

HARD AS HELL: 1. Janelle Cohen. 2. Miller's Pond. 3. "Dracula." 4. *It's Alive III: Island of the Alive, Deadly Illusion,* and *Best Seller.* 5. He throws holy water on her. 6. *Dante's Inferno.* 7. Because she prefers human blood. 8. 96 minutes. 9. Kesserling. 10. 1901. 11. *Q: The Winged Serpent* (1982), *The Stuff* (1985), and *It's Alive III: Island of the Alive.* 12. TWA gate 10. 13. *Hell Up in Harlem, Black Caesar, It's Alive* (1974), *God Told Me To* (1977), *It Lives Again* (1978), *Full Moon High* (1981), *Q: The Winged Serpent, The Stuff, It's Alive III: Island of the Alive, Wicked Stepmother* (1989), and *Maniac Cop II* (1990). 14. Peter Pan Bus Lines. 15. A Mercedes.

QUIZ #19: PET SEMATARY

EASY: 1. George Romero. 2. Doc. 3. He goes to sleep. 4. "Paxcow." 5. Goldman. 6. "[R]est and speaking." 7. Having Church shampooed. 8. Stephen King. 9. 666. 10. At death. 11. God's. 12. The film was quite justifiably nominated in the category of Worst Original Song for Dee Dee Ramone and Daniel Rey's "(I Don't Wanna Be Buried in a) Pet Sematary." 13. Winston Churchill. 14. A clam. 15. Seven.

MEDIUM DIFFICULTY: 1. Elvis Presley. 2. Eight-years-old. 3. Midnight. 4. Irwin. 5. His knife. 6. *Graveyard Shift* (1990). 7. Dory. 8. Thanksgiving. 9. Stonier. 10. "Have you hugged your M.D. today?" 11. To get a "hamburger or a chicken dinner." 12. Missy. 13. Smoke a cigarette. 14. Miko Hughes. 15. *The X-Files.*

HARD AS HELL: 1. 1971. 2. Zelda. 3. *Grand Isle* (1991). 4. "God sees the truth, but waits." 5. The ragman. 6. Cancer. 7. *Frank Herbert's Dune.* 8. Timmy. 9. One in 1,000. 10. 1924. 11. *Golden Years* (1991). 12. Orinco. 13. Margie Washburn. 14. Chicago, Illinois. 15. Mrs. Rogers.

QUIZ #20: TALES FROM THE DARKSIDE: THE MOVIE

EASY: 1. Amanda Drogan. 2. Jerry. 3. *Creepshow 2* (1987). 4. Andy's father. 5. *Creepshow* (1982) and *Creepshow 2.* 6. Love stories. 7. *Commando.* 8. *Wings.* 9. Brandy. 10. $100,000. 11. Chrysanthemums. 12. Inside Halston's body. 13. *Cat's Eye.* 14. A tennis racket. 15. The Penrose Scholarship.

MEDIUM DIFFICULTY: 1. A silver trust fund in his mouth. 2. A hummingbird. 3. Gage. 4. In the school newspaper. 5. $100. 6. His self image. 7. Buster Poindexter. 8. The cat's tail. 9. *Very Bad Things.* 10. His mother. 11. Just credentials. 12. Two of the mummy's fingers. 13. Dead flowers. 14. *Knightriders.* 15. *Night of the Living Dead.*

HARD AS HELL: 1. Dr. Carey. 2. $23,000. 3. Twenty-one. 4. *Knightriders.* 5. Preston's artistic vision. 6. Saul Loggia. 7. "The Doctor's Case." 8. Five thousand. 9. *Blowback* and *The Base II.* 10. Houston Street. 11. Eight. 12. Three months. 13. *Creepshow* and *Day of the Dead* (1985). 14. *New York Stories* (1989). 15. Emphysema.

QUIZ #21: IT

EASY: 1. *I Was a Teenage Werewolf.* 2. In Derry. 3. Beverly. 4. George "Georgie" Denbrough. 5. *Halloween III: Season of the Witch.* 6. Ben's father. 7. Tim Curry. 8. Architect. 9. Librarian. 10. Cancer. 11. Tozier. 12. Oz. 13. Time. 14. Mike. 15. *The Tonight Show.*

MEDIUM DIFFICULTY: 1. *The Glowing.* 2. Atlanta, Georgia. 3. Velma Daniels. 4. Reverend Mathew Fordwick. 5. The Korean War. 6. Harry Anderson. 7. The number of members in the Losers Club. 8. Ben. 9. Houston, Texas. 10. Mike Hanlon. 11. *Ghost Story.* 12. Audra. 13. "Eddie spaghetti." 14. Great Neck, New York. 15. Richie.

HARD AS HELL: 1. The Paramount Theater. 2. Sonia Kaspbrak. 3. *Fright Night Part II.* 4. Grecco. 5. Arlene. 6. 1930. 7. Outstanding Achievement in Music Composition for a Miniseries or a Special (Richard Bellis). 8. Patti. 9. 11:30 p.m. 10. Elmer. 11. Stephen Dorff for *Always Remember I Love You* (1990). 12. Alvin "Al" Marsh. 13. Hampstead Heath, England. 14. 253. 15. *77 Sunset Strip.*

QUIZ #22: MISERY

EASY: 1. Misery Chastain. 2. Annie's meat loaf. 3. Hot cocoa. 4. "Smudge." 5. *Dolores Claiborne* (1995) (uncredited rewrites), *Hearts in Atlantis* (2001), and *Dreamcatcher* (2003). 6. Profanity. 7. *Misery's Return.* (In the novel, however, Sheldon saves the novel and publishes it.) 8. *Stand By Me.* 9. *The Princess Bride* (1987). 10. Gravedigger Wilkes. 11. A 1965 Ford Mustang. 12. *The Shining.* 13. Misery. 14. Because of her temper. 15. Lauren Bacall.

MEDIUM DIFFICULTY: 1. Barry Sonnenfeld. 2. Two. 3. Director Rob Reiner. 4. The rain. 5. *Dick Tracy* (1990). (Ironically, James Caan appears in this film, as well.) 6. *Needful Things* (1993). 7. A cigarette, a match, and a glass of champagne. 8. She chops off his leg with an axe, and then cauterizes Paul's stump with a blowtorch. 9. *The Higher Education of J. Phillip Stone.* 10. He was twenty-four-years-old. 11. "There is a justice higher than that of man. I will be judged by Him." 12. *Lady in a Cage* (1964). 13. Liberace. 14. "Fuck." 15. *Misery's Child.*

HARD AS HELL: 1. *When Harry Met Sally* (1989). 2. In the Kimberly Diamond Mines. 3. He was an investment banker. 4. *'Night Mother* (1986). 5. "N." 6. Sibling Rivalry. 7. "Misery's Hobby." 8. Rocket Man. 9. Jim Taylor. 10. Denver, Colorado. 11. The Silver Creek Lodge. 12. Sherman Douglas. 13. He had just been diagnosed as having terminal cancer. 14. The Sistine Chapel and Misery's Child. 15. *Little Big League.*

QUIZ #23: GRAVEYARD SHIFT

EASY: 1. Independence Day. 2. "You're not the first." 3. Doris. 4. Nordello. 5. Charlie Carmichael. 6. Bachman Textile Mills. (A reference to Stephen King's pseudonym, Richard Bachman.) 7. West Virginia. 8. Moxie. 9. Larry and Bonnie Sugar. 10. *Star Search.* 11. *Wishmaster.* 12. Warwick. 13. Eleven p.m. to seven a.m. 14. Cy Ippeston. 15. *Pet Sematary* (1989) and *Pet Sematary 2* (1992).

MEDIUM DIFFICULTY: 1. $200. 2. Wisconsky. 3. *From Dusk Till*

Dawn (1996). 4. Marshall Extermination. 5. Zero. 6. Soda pop. 7. Castle Rock. 8. Stevenson. 9. Brogan. 10. This was the first attempt by an actor to speak with a Maine accent in a King adaptation. 11. Diet Pepsi. 12. Moving machinery. 13. Tucker Cleveland. 14. A drifter. 15. $2,500.

HARD AS HELL: 1. Warwick's. 2. Harry Wisconsky. 3. Chucky from the *Child's Play* (1988) films. 4. The story appeared in *Cavalier* magazine in October, 1970. 5. *Creepshow* (1982) and *Pet Sematary*. 6. Office manager. 7. "Surfin' Safari." 8. *Flatliners*. 9. Four weeks. 10. Short-order cook. 11. When "Christ was a kid." 12. He punches out both Jane's and his time cards. 13. Mondays and Wednesdays. 14. Munson Textile. 15. Jason Reed.

QUIZ #24: SOMETIMES THEY COME BACK

EASY: 1. Phelps. 2. *Cat's Eye* (1985) and *Maximum Overdrive* (1986). 3. Class of 1991. 4. Harold Davis High School. 5. Stratford, Connecticut. 6. *King Kong* (1976). 7. A rabbit's foot. 8. Mobsters. 9. A nickel. 10. Twenty-seven years. 11. "[A] piece of dust in someone's eye." 12. *The Dead Zone* (1983). 13. A locomotive. 14. Chicago, Illinois. 15. "Now he's going to scare you back to life."

MEDIUM DIFFICULTY: 1. *Fletch* (1985). 2. *Psycho IV: The Beginning* (1991). 3. Bob. 4. Jim named his son after his father, Scott Norman. 5. Milford. 6. *Star Trek VI: The Undiscovered Country* (1991). 7. In the King story, Jim Norman had no children. 8. Richard Lawson. 9. *The Outsiders*. 10. The story appeared in *Cavalier* magazine in March, 1974. 11. In the short story, she is killed. 12. Twelve cents. 13. He died. 14. Carl Mueller. 15. The name of a cemetery.

HARD AS HELL: 1. 1957. 2. *Critters 2: The Main Course* (1988). 3. Adams was to have appeared in *The Stuff*, but all of her scenes were cut from the film. As a result, her only affiliation with the film was a brief appearance in the trailer. 4. Terence Kelly. 5. Leaves. 6. October 22, 1963. 7. A blue jay. 8. *The Dead Zone*. 9. Nine. 10. Liberty, Missouri, Rocheport, Missouri, and Kansas City, Kansas. 11. Kansas City.

12. *Breach of Conduct* (1994). 13. Ten. These are: *Friday the 13th Part VI: Jason Lives* (1986), *Date With an Angel* (1987), *In a Child's Name* (1991), *Sometimes They Come Back, Something to Live For* (1992), *The Fire Next Time* (1993), *Murder of Innocence* (1993), *The Yarn Princess* (1994), *Take Me Home Again* (1994), and *Anya's Bell* (1999). 14. *The Rain Killer* and *Uncaged.* 15. Havana Sweets.

QUIZ #25: GOLDEN YEARS

EASY: 1. Seventy-years-old. 2. "The Gold Series." 3. David Bowie. 4. Captain Knauer. 5. *Thinner* (1997). 6. Dr. Ackerman. 7. Gina. 8. Stephen King. 9. *Misery* (1990). 10. Cap'n Trips. 11. John Rainbird. 12. Five. 13. Watches. 14. *Creepshow 2* (1987). 15. Keith Szarabajka.

MEDIUM DIFFICULTY: 1. Falco Plains. 2. Mrs. Rogers. 3. Five hours. 4. Richard. 5. Stanford. 6. Ethan. 7. Screenwriter Josef Anderson. 8. Good taste. 9. Inconspicuous. 10. Lieutenant. 11. Dr. Eakins. 12. "Just like old times." 13. Felicity Huffman. 14. Francie. 15. A landfill.

HARD AS HELL: 1. November 28. 2. Rick. 3. 10884. 4. Xavier P. Todhunter. 5. Cecil. 6. Louis. 7. KR3. 8. Dr. Craig Redding. 9. Highway 29. 10. Jude Andrews. 11. 1943. 12. Whitney. 13. *Gone With the Wind* (1939) and *Citizen Kane* (1942). 14. Staring at the freshly-painted hearse. 15. North Gate Mall.

QUIZ #26: SLEEPWALKERS

EASY: 1. Ron Perlman. 2. *Poltergeist.* 3. Robbie. 4. Cats. 5. Three: *Sleepwalkers, The Stand* (1994), and *Stephen King's The Shining* (1997). 6. "Be my Valentine." 7. Laurie. 8. Venice/Venice. 9. A rose. 10. Andy. 11. "Sleepwalk" performed by Santo & Johnny. 12. Bodega Bay. 13. Travis. 14. *The Stand* and *Quicksilver Highway* (1997), both directed by Mick Garris. 15. Stephen King.

MEDIUM DIFFICULTY: 1. Don Robertson. 2. *Twin Peaks*. 3. Castle County Elementary School. 4. Clive Barker and Tobe Hooper. 5. *Ghost Story*. 6. A pencil. 7. Paradise Falls. 8. Best Film (Garris), Best Direction (Garris), Best Screenplay (King), and Best Actress (Krige). 9. Mr. Fallows. 10. John Landis. 11. Joe Dante. 12. *Quicksilver Highway*. 13. *They Bite*. 14. *Marked for Death* (1990). 15. Tanya Robertson.

HARD AS HELL: 1. Sleepstalkers. 2. *The Chilicoathe Encyclopedia of Arcane Knowledge*. 3. Sixty-six Wicker Street. 4. *The Waltons*. 5. The Aero Theater. 6. Homeland Cemetery. 7. Lt. Jennings. 8. (What he presumes to be) Charles' generation. 9. Editor O. Nicholas Brown. 10. Popcorn and a medium Mr. Pibb. 11. Eight. 12. Clovis. 13. Sparks. 14. Pumpkin pie. 15. His son, Joe, who had fallen for the popcorn girl at the local theater.

QUIZ #27: PET SEMATARY 2

EASY: 1. Tiger. 2. Ten o'clock. 3. "Because I wanted to fuck her." 4. *The Sure Thing*. 5. Veterinarian. 6. Creed. 7. Kennebago. 8. Georgia. 9. *Terminator 2: Judgment Day* (1991). 10. Jason Voorhees of *Friday the 13th* fame. 11. Hallow. (As an actress, she goes by Renee Hallow Mathews.) 12. *Graveyard Shift* (1990). 13. A vampire. 14. He believes it's simply so weak it's not registering. 15. *The Shawshank Redemption*.

MEDIUM DIFFICULTY: 1. Marjorie. 2. Character creator. 3. "Maybe it takes a while." 4. His nose. 5. *Bonnie and Clyde*. 6. Potatoes. 7. "Pet sematary." 8. *Leap of Faith*. 9. Because he'll be dead. 10. Pets, fur, and meat. 11. *The Lawnmower Man*. (After the film was released as *Stephen King's The Lawnmower Man*, King successfully sued to have his name removed as the film bore no resemblance to his story.) 12. Six. 13. Gilbert. 14. That if the Indian burial ground doesn't resurrect Zowie, Jeff can't tell anyone that Drew buried the dog there. 15. Amanda.

HARD AS HELL: 1. 1955. 2. Lessons. 3. $10. 4. Dr. Quentin Yolander. 5. Elliot Rudman. 6. *Cagney & Lacey.* 7. Makeup artist Jeanine Lobell. 8. *Little Nemo: Adventures in Slumberland.* 9. "Shitlist." 10. Blanche Lambert Lincoln. 11. The Grand Prize. 12. *Needful Things* (1993). 13. A cross marker from one of the graves. 14. *Network* and *Taxi Driver.* 15. Gus.

QUIZ #28: THE DARK HALF

EASY: 1. Three. 2. This was the title of an early short story by Stephen King. Interestingly, this scene takes place in the same year that King wrote his story. 3. *Howards End* (1992) and *A Room With a View* (1986). 4. Psychopomp. 5. Actor Timothy Hutton used separate trailers on "Stark days" and "Beaumont days." 6. *The Donner Party* (1992). 7. His penis. 8. "Are You Lonesome Tonight" performed by Elvis Presley. 9. *Martin* (1977) and *Dawn of the Dead* (1978). 10. Because of financial difficulties at Orion Pictures. 11. "Not a very nice guy." 12. "High toned son of a bitch." 13. *The Dream Catcher.* 14. 1968. 15. *The Shawshank Redemption* (1994).

MEDIUM DIFFICULTY: 1. William. 2. Elizabeth. 3. In the book, the character was named Rawley DeLesseps, and was a man. 4. Director George Romero's wife and producer Christine Romero. 5. *Remains of the Day.* 6. Oxford. 7. *Digging to China.* 8. Their inner and outer beings. 9. 1985. 10. A red carnation. 11. "The sparrows are flying again." 12. Steve Brown. However, at least two people (Robert Weinberg and L.W. Curry) had already discovered that the copyright form for *Rage* listed Stephen King as the author. 13. Wendy and William Beaumont. 14. "Have a nice day." 15. Tom Hanks.

HARD AS HELL: 1. "Grandpa's Ghost." 2. Alexis Machine. 3. Richard Manuel. 4. Best Film (Romero), Best Screenplay (Romero), and Best Actor (Hutton). 5. Sarah and Elizabeth Parker. 6. "Cats." 7. *Steel Machine.* 8. Rosalie. 9. 109 W. 84th Street. 10. 129 E. 68th Street (apartment

23D). 11. Hillary. 12. Tom Savini's *Night of the Living Dead* (1990) remake. 13. Homer Gamache. 14. Mike Donaldson. 15. Four o' clock.

QUIZ #29: THE TOMMYKNOCKERS

EASY: 1. *Creepshow* (1982). 2. That Becka should "kill him." 3. Body Bags. 4. Pete. 5. "Buffalo Bill." 6. Gard. 7. *Final Surprise.* 8. Harry Houdini. 9. New Zealand. 10. Traci Lords. 11. *Ghost Story.* 12. *The Green Mile* (1999). 13. *NYPD Blue.* 14. *Maximum Overdrive* (1986). 15. "Rainy Season."

MEDIUM DIFFICULTY: 1. "Shoot a pickle." 2. "The Revelations of 'Becka Paulson." 3. Cola Cool. 4. Magic and his grandfather, Ev Hillman. 5. David Eggby. 6. Her hat. 7. Burning Woods. 8. *Father* (1989), *Sky Trackers* (1990), and *All the Rivers Run 2* (1990). 9. John Ashton. 10. He says he's coming down with the flu. 11. A book by Jim Gardner. 12. His collection of G.I. Joes. 13. Actress Marg Helgenberger's mother, Kay. 14. "Too late, Ruth." 15. E.G. Marshall.

HARD AS HELL: 1. Haven, Maine. 2. To the Twilight Zone. 3. Chuck Henry, who was co-anchor on Los Angeles' *Channel 4 News.* 4. 1953. 5. Preparedness. 6. 168 minutes. 7. "One voice." 8. A word accordion. 9. *Sunshine* (1973). 10. Bobbi Anderson. 11. *L.A. Law* and *NYPD Blue.* 12. The Buffalo Hunters. 13. *Mortal Kombat* and *Virtuosity.* 14. Larry Sanitsky. 15. He is a postal worker.

QUIZ #30: NEEDFUL THINGS

EASY: 1. Because he's "got a cold." 2. His uncle. 3. What's inside the locket. 4. Buster. 5. *The Greatest Story Ever Told.* 6. Cobb. 7. *Misery* (1990). 8. *Salem's Lot* (1979). 9. Brian Rusk. 10. Raider. 11. Nettie. 12. "Mickey Mantle sucks!" 13. She has arthritis. 14. Mel Allen. 15. "The young carpenter from Nazareth."

MEDIUM DIFFICULTY: 1. Moose Skowron. 2. Keeton Marine.

3. Hugh Priest. 4. Her pride. 5. Eleven-years-old. 6. Henry. 7. Best Supporting Actress (Amanda Plummer). 8. Michael Rooker. 9. Egypt. 10. "Crip space is all yours now." 11. George. 12. Trevor Denman. 13. 1956. 14. Her microwave oven. 15. "Say no to the devil!"

HARD AS HELL: 1. "A nice place to live and grow." 2. 1955. 3. *Between Friends*. 4. *Psalms* 9:17: "The wicked shall be turned into Hell." 5. Our Lady of the Serene Waters. 6. *Nixon* (1995). 7. Polly's engagement ring. 8. $20,000. 9. Alaska. 10. Akron, Ohio. 11. 95 cents. 12. Charlie Campion. 13. Pittsburgh, Pennsylvania. 14. *The Castle Rock Call*. 15. *The Adventures of Buckaroo Banzai Across the 8th Dimension*.

QUIZ #31: CHILDREN OF THE CORN II: THE FINAL SACRIFICE

EASY: 1. In an automobile accident. 2. A motor scooter. 3. Reverend Hollings. 4. Because he found his wallet. 5. Fornication. 6. Mary Simpson. 7. Long Island, New York. 8. Ruby. 9. A child. 10. Mordecai. 11. Bea. 12. A human hand. 13. Come and Sleep With Me Bed and Breakfast. 14. His father. 15. Richard.

MEDIUM DIFFICULTY: 1. "We are one." 2. A lollipop. 3. *Children of the Corn: Deadly Harvest*. 4. David. 5. *Used Cars*. 6. Rock Hudson. 7. "[Y]ou don't give a damn what happened here so long as it makes a good story." 8. *The Van Dyke Show*. 9. Her husband walked into a cornfield, and never returned. 10. $100,000. 11. A beating. 12. The Statue of Liberty. 13. Seventeen-years-old. 14. Nineteen. 15. Bobby.

HARD AS HELL: 1. Aflotoxin. 2. Sheriff Blaine. 3. Elmira. 4. Thirty-five-years-old. 5. Omaha, Nebraska. 6. $135. 7. Sherman. 8. $30. 9. *The World Enquirer*. 10. Tuesday. 11. The Department of Anthropology. 12. 185 pounds. 13. Best Film (David Price). 14. "Six Feet Under." 15. *Newsweek*.

QUIZ #32: THE STAND

EASY: 1. Jeff Goldblum. 2. "Amazing Grace." 3. Bub the Zombie. 4. Janie. 5. Portland, Maine. 6. Highway Fifteen. 7. Dumb. 8. Rospo Pallenberg. 9. Dr. Sam Weizak appears in *The Dead Zone* (1983). 10. Kareem Abdul-Jabbar. 11. Spies. 12. Arnette, Texas. 13. Ed Harris. 14. In the book, Rae Flowers was "Ray" Flowers, a man. 15. *Roots* (1977).

MEDIUM DIFFICULTY: 1. Glen Bateman. 2. Baseball (1994). 3. "Guilty." 4. Boulder, Colorado. 5. Joe Bob Briggs. 6. When the moon is full. 7. Director Mick Garris. 8. Donald Elbert. 9. "(Don't Fear) The Reaper." 10. Flu Buddy. 11. Nadine. 12. January. 13. That they forced him to leave because they were afraid he would impregnate someone with a retarded child. 14. Baja, California. 15. *No Way Out* (1950).

HARD AS HELL: 1. Russ Dorr. 2. Guy Davis. 3. Alice. 4. Al Kooper. 5. Cleveland, Ohio. 6. Outstanding Individual Achievement in Art Direction for a Miniseries or Special (Susan Benjamin, Nelson Coates, Michael Perry, Burton Rencher), Outstanding Individual Achievement in Makeup for a Miniseries or Special (Camille Calvin-Suftin, Bill Corso, David Dupuis, John Harlow, Steve Johnson, Ashlee Petersen), and Outstanding Sound Mixing for a Miniseries or Special (Grant Maxwell, Michael Ruschak, Richard Schexnayder, and Don Summer), and Outstanding Sound Editing for a Miniseries or Special (Maxwell, Ruschak, Schexnayder, and Summer). 7. Orunquit. 8. Perrier and a valium. 9. "The Crushed Rose." 10. Billy. 11. "The old way..." 12. *Proverbs*11:3: "When pride cometh, then cometh shame. For with the lowly is wisdom." 13. Ridley, Pennsylvania. 14. Director Mick Garris' wife, Cynthia Garris. 15. Sam Raimi.

QUIZ #33: THE SHAWSHANK REDEMPTION

EASY: 1. A rock hammer. 2. "Mr. Mozart." 3. Fraternity Vacation. 4. Mark 13:35: "Watch Ye therefore for Ye know not when the master of house cometh." 5. Stephen King's UMO professor, Burton Hatlen, who assisted King in getting his work published. 6. He was named prison librarian. 7. William ("Billy") Thomas. 8. Four. 9. "His judgment cometh and that right soon." 10. Six years. 11. Samuel. 12. A rock blanket. 13. Discipline and the Bible. 14. The Foodway. 15. Ten.

MEDIUM DIFFICULTY: 1. *Archie's Pal, Jughead.* 2. Floyd. 3. Haywood. 4. Twenty percent. 5. "No charge. Welcome back." 6. *The Seven Year Itch* (1955). 7. $35,000. 8. Alabaster and soap stone. 9. Bogs Diamond. 10. Jake. 11. "Salvation lies within." 12. Blasphemy. 13. 1947. 14. Portland, Maine. 15. *One Million Years B.C.*

HARD AS HELL: 1. Alfonso Freeman, son of Morgan Freeman. 2. Peter and Benny. 3. Six. 4. Dekins. 5. $60,000. 6. Mansfield Reformatory. 7. Rooster. 8. 1949. 9. David Proval. 10. Tyrell. 11. Ellis Boyd Redding. 12. "The sisters never bothered Andy again, and Bogs never walked again." 13. 600. 14. *Gilda* (1946). 15. "The Marriage of Figaro."

QUIZ #34: CHILDREN OF THE CORN III: URBAN HARVEST
EASY: 1. Family. 2. His Bible. 3. Modest dress. 4. *Demonic Toys* (1992). 5. T-Loc. 6. *Thinner.* 7. Charles Brady. 8. They disappeared. 9. Benjamin Guggenheim. 10. Her parents. 11. At the foot of the scarecrow. 12. Pizza. 13. Zero. 14. Stephen King's *Night Shift.* 15. *Friday* (1995).

MEDIUM DIFFICULTY: 1. *Leprechaun* (1993). 2. Germany. 3. Mr. Esau. 4. Frank. 5. *The Unborn II.* 6. Elkman. 7. Eli's Bible. 8. Jim Metzler. 9. Samantha Gordon. 10. "Belly of the Beast." 11. Johnny Legend (a.k.a. Martin Marguiles). 12. Porter. 13. Ears of Corn. 14. *Children of the Corn III: Urban Nightmare.* 15. "Repent: The hour of judgment is close at hand."

HARD AS HELL: 1. *The Oswego News.* 2. *The Bentley Times.* 3. 123 people (and apparently dwindling daily!). 4. Anne V. Coates. 5. Director James D.R. Hickox's father, Douglas Hickox. 6. "Let the harvest begin." 7. *Angel 4: Undercover.* 8. Chapter thirty-seven. 9. At the Chicago Board of Trade. 10. Fourteen-years-old. 11. *The Gatlin Gossip.* 12. October 17th. 13. Dee. 14. *The Hired Gun.* 15. Forty-seven people.

QUIZ #35: THE MANGLER

EASY: 1. Time. 2. Gartley's money and powerful friends. 3. *Salem's Lot* (1979). 4. Sherry Oulette. 5. They're both played by the same actor, Jeremy Crutchley. 6. George. 7. John. 8. A bird. 9. The blood of a virgin. 10. Hutton's vow to close his business. 11. Her pills. 12. A demon. 13. Willie. 14. Three. 15. *Eaten Alive* (1976) and Tobe Hooper's *Night Terrors* (1993). (The two also worked together on *Freddy's Nightmares*.)

MEDIUM DIFFICULTY: 1. Ezy-Gel. 2. "[B]ullshit." 3. *Sleepwalkers* (1992). 4. Blue Ribbon Laundry. 5. "The industrial heart of Maine." 6. Cherry tomatoes. 7. The rites of exorcism. 8. Barry Earnshaw. 9. A bloody hand print. 10. Labor. 11. Uncle Billy. 12. Sherry. 13. Annette Gillian. 14. Ted Levine. 15. Daniel Matmor.

HARD AS HELL: 1. Hadley-Watson. 2. The New Franklin Laundry. 3. Second unit director and visual effects supervisor. 4. Fourteen years. 5. July 10, 1983. 6. Berkley. 7. 15,667. 8. Jackson. 9. 1216 Lake. 10. Judge Bishop. 11. Six miles. 12. Best Actor (Robert Englund). 13. Molly. 14. Gates. 15. Sandy.

QUIZ #36: DOLORES CLAIBORNE

EASY: 1. $1,600,000. 2. Peter. 3. *Buried Alive* (1990). 4. Twelve dollars per week. 5. William Goldman. 6. According to Vera Donovan, Dolores has never been more than fifty miles away from the island. 7. *The Devil's Advocate* (1997). 8. *Misery* and *The Stand* (1994). 9. Fifteen. 10. Eric Bogosian. 11. What Selena thinks. 12. His mother. 13. Half a page. 14. Five hundred dollars. 15. Husbands die.

MEDIUM DIFFICULTY: 1. Vassar. 2. Five. 3. The guys he works with on the boat. 4. Being a bitch. 5. Vinegar and baking soda. 6. *The Shawshank Redemption*. 7. At least two hours. 8. The seventh grade. 9. One hour. 10. Shawshank Prison. 11. Thirteen-years-old. 12. Eighteen years. 13. Richard M. Nixon. 14. David Strathairn. 15. Six-and-a-half minutes.

HARD AS HELL: 1. $3,006.56. 2. Baltimore, Maryland. 3. Jack. 4. Phoenix, Arizona. 5. The Devereaux Hotel. 6. Forty dollars. 7. Eleven years. 8. Eighty-five. 9. The Joshua Slocum. 10. His mistress' home. 11. Eight years. 12. *The Bangor Daily News.* 13. Six. 14. All of his mother's china. 15. Twenty-two years.

QUIZ #37: THE LANGOLIERS

EASY: 1. Boston, Massachusetts. 2. Deduction. 3. Shawna. 4. *Maximum Overdrive* (1986). 5. Brian. 6. Screenwriter/director Tom Holland. 7. Eight. 8. Twenty-nine. 9. Darren Crosby. 10. His father, Roger Toomy. 11. "The Vulcan Sleeper Hold." 12. *Thirtysomething*. 13. Sleeping. 14. The violin.15. *Revenge of the Living Zombies* (1994).

MEDIUM DIFFICULTY: 1. *The Stand* (1994). 2. Annie. 3. Baxter Harris, who appears as Rudy Warwick. 4. Bangor International Airport. 5. Bum. 6. Human Highway. 7. *Dolores Claiborne* and *The Mangler*. 8. Ludwig van Beethoven. 9. Mystery novelist. 10. Outstanding Individual Achievement in Sound Mixing for a Drama Miniseries or Special (Grant Maxwell and Jay Meagher). 11. Seventy percent. 12. Miss Lee. 13. *Thinner*. 14. Fifth grade. 15. The Mojave Desert.

HARD AS HELL: 1. Mr. O'Banion. 2. Michael Russo, Frank Soares, and Douglas Damon. 3. One hundred and fifty miles-per-hour. 4. Junior Attaché to the British Embassy. 5. Vicky. 6. There are no remnants (watches, pace-makers, wigs) left behind. 7. 4:07. 8. American Pride. 9. Tom Holby. 10. "[A] woman pressing her hand over a crack in the wall of a commercial jetliner." 11. At Boston's Prudential Center. 12. $43 million. 13. The Berklee School of Music. (In King's novella the school is referred to as the Berklee College of Music.) 14. *The Crossing Guard* (1995). 15. $30 million.

QUIZ #38: THINNER

EASY: 1. Mr. Bangor. 2. $5.00. 3. A judge. 4. He is Tom Holland's son. 5. Mike Houston. 6. 297 pounds. 7. *Tales from the Darkside: The Movie* (1990). However, it should be noted that George Romero adapted the King story, "The Cat from Hell," with McDowell writing the rest of the film. 8. Strychnine. 9. Justice. 10. "Lizard." 11. Frank Spurton. 12. Kill him and say it's from Duncan Hopley. 13. The curse of the white man from town. 14. "[S]oda pop and baking soda." 15. One hundred and fifty-nine pounds.

MEDIUM DIFFICULTY: 1. His wife. 2. Bar Harbor. 3. What friends tell him and what he can see. 4. In his mouth. 5. *The Langoliers* (1995). 6. A gunshot. 7. Cancer. 8. Biff. 9. "White Man from Town Says Take It Off." 10. Richie the Hammer. 11. $5,000. 12. Special Agent Stoner. 13. "[W]ithout faith, good deeds are dead." 14. Two weeks. 15. *Knightriders* (1981).

HARD AS HELL: 1. Gypsy Pie. 2. Disease, crime, and prostitution. 3. Susanna Lempke. 4. *The Stand* (1994) and *The Langoliers*. 5. Duncan. 6. Seven a.m. 7. His wife, Inez. 8. 106-years-old. 9. The Glassman Clinic. 10. Leda. 11. Henry. 12. "Dr. Mikey." 13. Lars Arncaster's farm. 14. At the Mayo Clinic. 15. 1917.

QUIZ #39: SOMETIMES THEY COME BACK...AGAIN

EASY: 1. Subotsky had died five years before the film's release. 2. Speed Racer. 3. The victim's still-beating heart. 4. *Children of the Corn V: Fields of Terror*. 5. *Sometimes They Come Back 2*. 6. Marcia's ears. 7. Human teeth. 8. It belonged to Lisa Porter, her aunt. 9. Father Archer. 10. "[A] lot of people." 11. "Shut" and "up." 12. Pagel. 13. Psychoanalyst. 14. Vinnie Ritacco. 15. *Boys Don't Cry*.

MEDIUM DIFFICULTY: 1. A pig. 2. Moore. 3. The Devil. 4. Steve. 5. "When do we eat?" 6. Eighteen-years-old. 7. Newt. 8. *Needful Things* (1993). 9. "Mind giving me a hand?" 10. *The Dark Tower II: The Draw-*

ing of the Three. 11. His blood-soaked hat and human teeth. 12. Once a week. 13. Glenrock. 14. Best Friend Priority. 15. Patrick Renna.

HARD AS HELL: 1. 7:32 a.m. 2. Eighteen. 3. J.J. 4. "A poorly extinguished fire." 5. Norma Jean & Marilyn. 6. Jim Norman. 7. At the Glenrock Recycling Center. 8. One million. 9. *The Glenrock Gazette.* 10. She was killed in an automobile accident. 11. Page Porter. 12. A heart attack. 13. Henry's. 14. Newt the pig. 15. Kounterfeit.

QUIZ #40: CHILDREN OF THE CORN IV: THE GATHERING

EASY: 1. Pistachio. 2. Grand Island Junior High School. 3. That she's not Catholic. 4. Scott and Charles McLellan. 5. Bad news. 6. The Cold Equations. 7. *The Exorcist.* 8. The Grand Island Community Clinic. 9. Grace. 10. Syringes. 11. Inside a well on the Spelling farm. 12. *Soul of the Game.* 13. By bathing them in ice water. 14. The way they begin. 15. Sentinel County.

MEDIUM DIFFICULTY: 1. Thirty. 2. A voodoo doctor. 3. *The Astronaut's Wife* (1999). 4. He never aged. 5. *Movies Money Murder* (1996). 6. Margaret. 7. Ezekiel and Caleb. 8. *Border Radio* (1987). 9. Eight a.m. to five p.m. 10. She won't step beyond the walkway. 11. *Persons Unknown* (1996). 12. Josiah. 13. At Rosa and Jane Nock's house. 14. That they're always changing. 15. Midnight Blue.

HARD AS HELL: 1. *Gods and Monsters* (1998). 2. *The Prophecy II* (1998). 3. Mercury. 4. Jake. 5. Jonathan and Joshua Patterson. 6. A cricket. 7. *That Thing You Do!* and *2 Days in the Valley.* 8. "He will have the child." 9. Scorpio. 10. *No Way Back.* 11. A human head. 12. William Windom. 13. January 8, 1955. 14. Denver, Colorado. 15. *The Oprah Winfrey Show.*

QUIZ #41: STEPHEN KING'S THE SHINING

EASY: 1. Sam Raimi. 2. Horace Derwent. 3. Hughes played Gage

Creed in *Pet Sematary* (1989). 4. This is the Torrances last day at the Overlook Hotel. 5. Miguel Ferrer. 6. *The Big Happy Taxi.* 7. You're sober. 8. "In the Midnight Hour." 9. On the elevator. 10. *The Fly II.* 11. "TV dinners." 12. Creole shrimp. 13. Danny accidentally caused the backboard to shatter just as a basketball player went for a lay-up. 14. Cynthia Garris, the wife of director Mick Garris. 15. Happy thoughts.

MEDIUM DIFFICULTY: 1. George Hatfield. 2. To take "one day at a time." 3. In Stuart Ullman's office. 4. *Maximum Overdrive* (1986). 5. The Colorado Lounge. 6. *Sweet Sweetback's Baadasss Song.* 7. *City of Industry* (1997). 8. "Boo!" 9. A tube of lipstick. 10. Preston Sturges, Jr. 11. *Quicksilver Highway*, which featured King's "The Chattery Teeth." 12. Outstanding Miniseries. 13. A wasp's nest. 14. "Okay, Doc, you gonna gimme a hand or ya just gonna stand there?" 15. Drinking whiskey from the bottle.

HARD AS HELL: 1. Mighty Fine American. 2. 303. 3. Michigan. 4. "If you can, motherfucker." 5. *The Outer Limits.* 6. December 29th. 7. Colorado Phoenix Inc. 8. Blonde, beautiful, and full of bull. 9. This hotel served as the inspiration for King's original novel. 10. Mark Torrance. 11. Poplar Apartments. 12. On the seat of the snowmobile. 13. October 20th. 14. Woodrow Wilson, James Harding, Franklin Delano Roosevelt, and Richard Nixon. 15. Sixteen.

QUIZ #42: QUICKSILVER HIGHWAY
EASY: 1. *Stephen King's The Shining.* 2. *A Tale of Two Cities* by Charles Dickens. 3. Hogan. 4. His son's birthday. 5. The Hand of Glory. 6. The top of the wedding cake. 7. Clive Barker. 8. They are both played by the same actor, Matt Frewer. 9. $3.00. 10. Mark Mothersbaugh. 11. School. 12. John Landis. 13. Los Angeles, California. 14. Six weeks. 15. John McTiernan.

MEDIUM DIFFICULTY: 1. *Evil Dead 2: Dead By Dawn.* 2. "Man," "Dude," and "Dudemar." 3. Scooter's Grocery and Roadside Zoo. 4.

"Cookie Face." 5. Myra. 6. Sammy's. 7. The black heart of America. 8. Bill Nunn. 9. UPC labels. 10. Best Film (Mick Garris). 11. Cynthia Garris is the wife of director Mick Garris. 12. "The Others." 13. Parker. 14. Aaron. 15. Network.

HARD AS HELL: 1. Instinct. 2. Jack. 3. Ellen. 4. Pacific Park. 5. Targetto. 6. 416. 7. King James 100s. 8. $15.95. 9. Lita. 10. Glenn. 11. Thirty-nine-years-old. 12. The right. 13. "Viva la revolution." 14. Four. 15. J.T.

QUIZ #43: THE NIGHT FLIER

EASY: 1. *Inside View.* 2. The short story "Strawberry Spring." 3. The novel *Thinner*, which King penned under the pseudonym Richard Bachman. 4. A pile of dirt. 5. *Stephen King's The Shining.* 6. Superman's pal, Jimmy Olsen. 7. Jack the Ripper, the Cleveland Torso Murderer, and the Black Dahlia. 8. The novella *The Breathing Method.* 9. The Alderton Funeral Home. 10. Two-years-old. 11. The short story "The Lawnmower Man." 12. The short story "Children of the Corn." 13. Derry. 14. "Stay away." 15. The novel, *Needful Things.*

MEDIUM DIFFICULTY: 1. A crucifix. 2. An FBI agent. 3. The novel *The Dead Zone.* 4. Slice. 5. *Stitches* (2000). 6. "Stop now." 7. Selida McCammon. 8. Sixty-eight-years-old. 9. "Never believe what you publish, and never publish what you believe." 10. Cessna Skymaster 337. 11. "Psychic Dogs of the Stars." 12. Buck Kendall. 13. *Prime Evil: New Stories by the Masters of Horror.* 14. Best Home Video Release. 15. At Washington National Airport.

HARD AS HELL: 1. "Night Flier Defanged!" 2. N101BL. 3. Dwight Frye was the name of the actor who played Renfield in *Dracula* (1931). 4. 5,500. 5. Blair. 6. *Pet Sematary* (1989), *Tales from the Darkside: The Movie* (1990), *Golden Years* (1991), *The Stand* (1994), *The Langoliers* (1995), and *Thinner* (1996). 7. The Falling Star Motel. 8. Merton Morrison. 9. *Knightriders* (1981). 10. Dottie Walsh. 11. Ellis. 12. His camera, his plane, and his stories. 13. *Wishmaster* (1997). 14. Martha. 15. His appetite for blood.

QUIZ #44: TRUCKS

EASY: 1. *Stephen King's The Shining.* 2. Two years. 3. "[T]rucks or pump jockeys." 4. His father. 5. Two. 6. Navy Blend coffee. 7. The Michigan Avenue riot in Chicago, Illinois. 8. Jack. 9. Seven years. 10. Detroit, Michigan. 11. Chicago, Illinois. 12. Jack. 13. She was a registered nurse. 14. "[I]n places of great emptiness." 15. Canada.

MEDIUM DIFFICULTY: 1. *Kulli Foot* (2000). 2. Cabin One. 3. He was a member of the Chicago Police Department. 4. *Dr. Jeckyll and Ms. Hyde* (1995). 5. Two weeks. 6. Phil's Salvage. 7. *Air Bud.* 8. Zero. 9. He's a car salesman. 10. A meteor crashed. 11. To die. 12. *L.A. Confidential* (1997). 13. Search for Extraterrestrial Intelligence. 14. Meditate. 15. Banned.

HARD AS HELL: 1. Lunar Expeditions. 2. *V.* 3. Eighteen months. 4. "Guaranteed cool." 5. Hearst. 6. This is the name of the chemical spilled in a nearby military tanker truck accident. 7. *Meteorites!* (1998). 8. Project Phoenix. 9. He owns and operates a bookshop. 10. $1.25. 11. *Omen IV: The Awakening.* 12. The Air Force. 13. Las Vegas, Nevada. 14. Sacramento, California. 15. "Someone must pump fuel. Someone will not be harmed. All fuel must be pumped. This shall be done now. Now someone will pump fuel."

QUIZ #45: CHILDREN OF THE CORN V: FIELDS OF TERROR

EASY: 1. *Pulp Fiction.* 2. Kir. 3. Love, family, and purpose. 4. *The Running Man* (1986). 5. *House II: The Second Story* (1987). 6. Eighteen-years-old. 7. His father. 8. Threatening an officer. 9. Cut his throat. 10. Kir. 11. Allison. 12. "[T]hen you could eat me." 13. Scaring away the birds. 14. The Pittsburgh Steelers, the Oakland Raiders, and the Kansas

City Chiefs. (Although Williamson was originally drafted by the San Francisco 49ers, he was traded before the season began and hence never played for the franchise.) 15. *Return of the Jedi* and *Gremlins*.

MEDIUM DIFFICULTY: 1. *Black Caesar* (1973), *Hell Up in Harlem* (1973), and *Original Gangstas* (1996). 2. Cyanide fruit punch. 3. Jerry. 4. *L.A. Confidential*. 5. Her right shoulder. 6. "[A] few skeletons in our closets." 7. *Bride of Chucky*. 8. A 7-11 store. 9. Luke Enright. 10. Americana. 11. Smeat. 12. Fourteen-years-old. 13. *Urban Legends: Final Cut*. 14. Zane. 15. "He Who Walks Beyond the Clouds."

HARD AS HELL: 1. Laszlo and Charlotte. 2. Stunt coordinator Kane Hodder, best known for playing Jason Voorhees in the *Friday the 13th* franchise. 3. Antelope. 4. *The Book of Divine Enlightenment*. 5. *Death Journey* (1975). 6. Divinity Falls. 7. Skaggs. 8. Lily. 9. Eight a.m. and eight p.m. 10. Kurt. 11. Fertilizer. 12. Diva Zappa, the sister of actor Ahmet Zappa. 13. Sota FX. 14. The Death Rays. 15. Lewis directed Bill Cosby in the special *Bill Cosby: 49*.

QUIZ #46: APT PUPIL
EASY: 1. *Gods and Monsters* (1998). 2. Edward French. 3. Elias Koteas. 4. Milk. 5. Editor/composer John Ottman's mother, Mary Ottman, who also served as medical advisor on the film. 6. *X-Men*. 7. A toilet. 8. 1984. 9. His mailbox. 10. Arthur Denker. 11. *Urban Legend: The Final Cut*. 12. Richard Bowden. 13. Todd's parents were born. 14. Joey. 15. Best Film and Best Supporting Actor (Ian McKellen).

MEDIUM DIFFICULTY: 1. Ricky Schroeder. 2. Honesty. 3. *Jaws*. 4. 1985. 5. Monica. 6. *Killer Instinct*. 7. Timmy. 8. A shovel. 9. Victor Bowden. 10. Becky Trask. 11. *Lion's Den* (1992), *Public Access* (1993), and *The Usual Suspects* (1995). 12. Alan Bridges. 13. *I Dream of Jeannie*. 14. Santo Donato High School. 15. *Lion's Den* and *Public Access*.

HARD AS HELL: 1. Dr. Isaac Weiskopf. 2. February 1946. 3. The Pirates.

4. A leader. 5. Benjamin Kramer. 6. Twenty-five. 7. 1965. 8. From June 1943 through June 1944. 9. E.F. Montgomery Costume and Clothing. 10. Donato Beverage. 11. Saturday. 12. *Hitler's Spies*. 13. Poor eyesight. 14. 1955. 15. Five.

QUIZ #47: SOMETIMES THEY COME BACK...FOR MORE

EASY: 1. Ice Station Erebus. 2. Max Perlich. 3. *The Lawnmower Man*, which was initially released as *Stephen King's The Lawnmower Man*. 4. Schilling. 5. Shebanski. 6. She was a nurse. 7. *Murphy Brown*. 8. Geologist. 9. Lieutenant. 10. *G vs E*. 11. Sam. 12. *Poltergeist* (1982). 13. A pentacle. 14. Leeta. 15. Callie.

MEDIUM DIFFICULTY: 1. *Kill You Twice* (1998). 2. The radio. 3. A pickax. 4. *Sometimes They Come Back...Again* (1996). 5. J.H. James Brodie. 6. Level six. 7. A diamond ring. 8. Is Robert Reynolds still alive, and where is Schilling? 9. Jennifer O'Dell. 10. Michael Stadvec. 11. Jennifer Wills. 12. *Sometimes They Come Back* (1991). 13. *Sometimes They Come Back...Again*. 14. Carl. 15. Cage will be going with him.

HARD AS HELL: 1. Special effects supervisor Frank Ceglia. 2. *Frozen and Ice Station Erebus*. 3. *Public Enemies*. 4. *Carnival of Souls* (1998). 5. 1916. 6. Defrosting. 7. To prepare for Satan's return. 8. Raising Demons. 9. To "spook" them into calling for a transport. 10. Captain. 11. Brian. 12. Twenty-four hours. 13. Deborah Ann Henderson. 14. The taking of a human life. 15. Love.

QUIZ #48: STORM OF THE CENTURY

EASY: 1. *Dolores Claiborne* (1995). 2. Roanoke Island. 3. Colm Feore. 4. Daly voices Superman on the animated series *Superman* and *The New Batman/Superman Adventures*. 5. Stephen King. 6. Peter Godsoe. 7. 1989. 8. *Transylvania 6-5000*. 9. *The Shining*. 10. The Boston Celtics. 11. *Wings*. 12. *The Green Mile*. 13. *Point of No Return*. 14. A wolf. 15. Wee Folks Daycare.

MEDIUM DIFFICULTY: 1. Martha Clarendon. 2. "Give me what I want and I'll go away." 3. "The Man That Corrupted Hadleyburg." 4. Robbie Beals. 5. A "storm alert warning" scrawl ran across the bottom of the screen, apparently leading some viewers to believe there was a real storm. 6. Repetition. 7. Pippa. 8. *The Night Flier* (1997). 9. Reds. 10. Island-Atlantic Realty. 11. Chemistry. 12. Billy Soames. 13. "[A] man sitting on the bunk in his cell, heels drawn up, arms resting on his knees, eyes unblinking." 14. *The Shawshank Redemption* (1994). 15. "Do the Dead Sing?"

HARD AS HELL: 1. At the Methodist church. 2. Jenna. 3. Buster. 4. Boston, Massachusetts. 5. Best Genre TV Supporting Actor (Colm Feore). 6. Nine. 7. Melinda. 8. Zero. 9. Lewiston. 10. "Punishments of God." 11. Mark Carliner. 12. Harry. 13. $6,000. 14. *The A-Team*. 15. 1-800-STICK-EM.

QUIZ #49: THE RAGE: CARRIE 2

EASY: 1. "The Devils Rule." 2. Daisies. 3. Robert Mandel. 4. Ralph White. 5. A snake. 6. Lou Stark. 7. Mrs. Porter. 8. *Carrie 2: Say You're Sorry*. 9. Used car salesman. 10. Walter. 11. Jason London. 12. Flashback scenes from the original *Carrie*. 13. Love. 14. *Home Improvement*. 15. Pigs; according to director Katt Shea, this is a subtle nod to the original film.

MEDIUM DIFFICULTY: 1. *Hackers* (1995). 2. $300. 3. King University. (A nod to Stephen King.) 4. Emily Bergl. 5. Tracy Campbell. 6. "Shiny Happy People." 7. "[B]ecause she's so skanky." 8. A hanging tampon string. 9. Barbara Lang. 10. The film was also titled *The Rage*. 11. The bucket that dumped pig blood on Carrie White. 12. Twenty dollars. 13. George Bellows. 14. Director Katt Shea. 15. Bill Kirk.

HARD AS HELL: 1. Preppies. 2. Best Performance by a Younger Actor/Actress (Emily Bergl). 3. One p.m. 4. Arkham Asylum. (For the uninitiated, this is a Batman reference.) 5. Kelton. 6. Shea incorrectly believed Morgan had served as Director of Photography on *Pink Floyd The Wall*

(1982). 7. Brad Winters. 8. Garbage. 9. 366 Broad Street. 10. Amy Kirk. 11. Lawyer. 12. Boyd. 13. A yarn factory. 14. Royal Photo Mat. 15. Thirty.

QUIZ #50: CHILDREN OF THE CORN 666: ISAAC'S RETURN

EASY: 1. Ten. 2. Rachel. 3. Isaac. 4. Cora. 5. Colby. 6. Martin. 7. Chris. 8. Coming to the harvest. 9. Gabriel. 10. Halloween. 11. Isaac. 12. Her birthright. 13. "[T]he power we give you." 14. Isaac. 15. Stacy Keach.

MEDIUM DIFFICULTY: 1. *Men With Guns*. 2. Samuel. 3. Pain. 4. Jake. 5. Sleep. 6. Stacy Keach. 7. "Bang!" 8. Jesse. 9. Sheila Hammond. 10. Prophecy. 11. "Why do you think I do it?" 12. John Franklin. 13. "Get out or die." 14. The truth. 15. Matt.

HARD AS HELL: 1. William Prael. 2. Jasper McQuade. 3. "It's Your Death." 4. "Daughters of Cult Members Unite." 5. Assistant to the Producer. 6. 1978. 7. Room 10. 8. Nineteen years. 9. Python. 10. East. 11. Buddha, Ghandi, and Jesus Christ. 12. Under the sink. 13. Brother-hood of Death. 14. Omaha, Nebraska. 15. An eight ball.

QUIZ #51: THE GREEN MILE

EASY: 1. "Old Sparky." 2. Two cents. 3. Earl. 4. Brutus Howell. 5. Bruce Willis. 6. Eighteen-years-old. 7. "Listen to him squishin' in his pants." 8. "Billy the Kid." 9. *Forrest Gump* (1994) and *Apollo 13* (1995). 10. "E" block. 11. Cold Mountain Penitentiary. 12. Melinda. 13. Barry Pepper appears as Dean Stanton and actor Harry Dean Stanton appears as Toot-Toot. 14. Kathe and Cora Detterick. 15. *Two-Fisted Tales*.

MEDIUM DIFFICULTY: 1. "No jobs here—Transients turn back." 2. Percy. 3. A nickel. 4. *The Langoliers*. 5. Near Tallahassee, Florida. 6. *Saving Private Ryan* (1998). 7. Jack Van Hay. 8. *Dancer in the Dark* (2000). 9. His work record. 10. Dean Stanton. 11. 1935. 12. *Top Hat* (1935). 13. Three. 14. *Black Cat Run* (1998). 15. Briar Ridge.

HARD AS HELL: 1. "I Have Too Many Lovers." 2. A lemon. 3. 1932. 4. Thomas Newman. 5. Dr. Bishop. 6. *In the Belly of the Beast: Letters from Prison.* 7. Mae West. 8. *Christine* (1982). 9. *Tales from the Crypt.* 10. Best Picture, Best Adapted Screenplay (Frank Darabont), Best Supporting Actor (Michael Clarke Duncan), and Best Sound (Willie D. Burton, Michael Herbick, Robert J. Litt, and Elliot Tyson). 11. July 10, 1935. 12. *Hell Night.* 13. He was working on the ABC miniseries, *The Shining* (1997), which was filming in Estes Park. 14. Louisiana. 15. King advised Darabont to trim the film, saying, "I think it's maybe 15 minutes too long."

QUIZ #52: HEARTS IN ATLANTIS

EASY: 1. Molly. 2. Federal Express. 3. Gerber. 4. Bobby's father. 5. Bobby's belt. 6. Because he carries his belongings in paper bags. 7. Root beer. 8. Home. 9. "Sleep Walk." 10. Bronko Nagurski. 11. *The Library Policeman.* 12. Carol. 13. *The Langoliers* (1995) and *The Green Mile* (1999). 14. Books. 15. A library card.

MEDIUM DIFFICULTY: 1. Bridgeport. 2. An inside straight. 3. Cake and coffee. 4. Maury Wills. 5. *Village of the Damned.* 6. "Run like hell." 7. Eleven. 8. Black Phantom. 9. *The Lone Ranger.* 10. Brooks Hatlen. 11. "Friends 4 ever!" 12. Spot. 13. *A Tale of Two Cities* by Charles Dickens. 14. Providence. 15. Five.

HARD AS HELL: 1. *Low Men in Yellow Coats* and *Heavenly Shades of Night Are Falling.* 2. Boston. 3. Pall Mall. 4. *Why We're in Vietnam.* 5. *Apt Pupil.* 6. "Local Silver Star Hero Dies in Fwy Car Tragedy." 7. Psychics. 8. $2000. 9. Jill. 10. Ben Johnson. 11. Don Biderman. 12. Cinematographer Piotr Sobocinski, who died before the film was completed. 13. Montana. 14. Harry Doolin. 15. Kool.

QUIZ #53: THE MANGLER 2

EASY: 1. Newton Corporation, Inc. 2. Chef Boyardee. 3. The Hunta virus. 4. A dog. 5. "The checkout aisle marked '10 stupid ideas or less.'" 6. The Hacker's Mall. 7. Knee-high socks. 8. Emily. 9. Will. 10. "[A] rebellious teenager... and a cook, too." 11. Mr. Vessey. 12. *Mangler 11.* (God help us all if this franchise ever gets that far...) 13. "[A]lien astronauts." 14. Bradeen. 15. Communicate.

MEDIUM DIFFICULTY: 1. *Rejected by Vultures* (1999). 2. A cigarette. 3. Mustard. 4. *Playpen* magazine. 5. *Wishmaster 3: Beyond the Gates of Hell.* 6. "You've been mangled." 7. "Not for ourselves alone." 8. The Banana Brothers. 9. Corey. 10. His ex-wife. 11. Retroactive. 12. "[A] sking stupid questions." 13. *Good Will Humping.* 14. Three. 15. *The Virgin Suicides.*

HARD AS HELL: 1. Stone. 2. It was her eighteenth birthday. 3. Ferocious Le Fonque. 4. Paul Cody. 5. "[C]ooking hamburgers and hotdogs." 6. Robert Walsh. 7. Bob. 8. 101 Ways to Deal with Anger. 9. Hightechdigest.com. 10. Walsh. 11. High modular interface. 12. Producer Glen Tedham. 13. A yellow school bus. 14. Die. 15. Dominique Swain.

QUIZ #54: CHILDREN OF THE CORN: REVELATION

EASY: 1. Her grandmother's hat. 2. It's filled with blood. 3. A toy tomahawk. 4. Jamie's grandmother. 5. On the roof of the apartment building. 6. One. (Jamie's grandmother.) 7. Because he doesn't own one. 8. *Monkeybone.* 9. A notice of eviction. 10. Jamie and her grandmother. 11. A wreath made of corn. 12. "Do not enter." 13. Cops. 14. Because she was "a lifelong atheist." 15. She was struck by a train.

MEDIUM DIFFICULTY: 1. California. 2. Omaha, Nebraska. 3. Because she has a story deadline. 4. The severed head of the grocer. 5. Chocolate. 6. Lorazepam. 7. *Children of the Corn 2001* and *Children of the Corn VII.* 8. The priest. 9. Ham Tyler. 10. "Jamie go home." 11. *The*

House of the Dead. 12. Classical ballet. 13. Wildcats. 14. Leaving immediately. 15. They burned to death in a house fire.

HARD AS HELL: 1. Retribution. 2. Hampton Arms. 3. 696. 4. Diondre Hall. 5. The corn wreaths. 6. Evan. 7. Tiffany's. 8. Ulrich. 9. *Hellraiser VI: Hellseeker.* 10. Hattie Soames. 11. Long Grocery. 12. Markham. 13. The Fun Club. 14. Louis Spiegler. 15. Lowell.

QUIZ #55: ROSE RED

EASY: 1. Steven Spielberg. 2. Emery Waterman. 3. Sister. 4. David Dukes. 5. Annie Wheaton. 6. This is a nod to King's wife, Tabitha, whose maiden name was Spruce. 7. "The Mirror Library." 8. "The Boogeyman." 9. Stephen King. 10. A searchlight. 11. $5,000. 12. *Firestarter.* 13. The investigation of psychic phenomenon. 14. "In the Mood." 15. "[A] phantom draft."

MEDIUM DIFFICULTY: 1. Memorial Day. 2. *The Diary of Ellen Rimbauer: My Life at Rose Red.* 3. Steven Rimbauer. 4. A cell phone. 5. *Stephen King's The Shining* (1997) and *Storm of the Century.* 6. That "a deal's a deal." 7. "[A] cup of tea and a good spanking." 8. Champagne. 9. Washington. 10. Seventy-years-old. 11. His services as a porter. 12. Water running beneath the ground. 13. *Reds.* 14. A flashlight. 15. An earring.

HARD AS HELL: 1. Kandinsky. 2. "[J]ust outside of Tacoma." 3. Buddy. 4. Douglas Posey. 5. Kevin Bolinger. 6. *The Night Flier* (1997). 7. George Wheaton. 8. The Rimbauers moved into Rose Red. 9. Stunt man. 10. Asbury. 11. Deanna Petrie. 12. Sukeena. 13. George Meter. 14. Six-years-old. 15. *Twilight Man* (1996), *Bad Day on the Block* (1997), *Chameleon II: Death Match* (1999), and *Storm of the Century.*

QUIZ #56: FIRESTARTER REKINDLED

EASY: 1. Charlie. 2. 1980. 3. The fire extinguishers in Charlie's apartment. 4. *Storm of the Century* (1999). 5. "Charlene McGee." 6. Tommy

Andrews. 7. Screenwriter Philip Eisner. 8. A cheeseburger. 9. Cody. 10. Batman. 11. "Help me." 12. "Autopsy Room Four." 13. John Rainbird. 14. $100. 15. Event Horizon (1997).

MEDIUM DIFFICULTY: 1. Because the script contained no scenes which would feature both actors. 2. Pruitt and Garcia. 3. "Don't ask too many questions." 4. Dead bodies. 5. Lot 23. 6. Jack and Max. 7. "[A]t least one good friend." 8. *Combat High.* 9. Six. 10. Track. 11. Chews on her bottom lip. 12. *Riding in Cars with Boys.* 13. 48-years-old. 14. Dr. Joseph Wanless. 15. Nine.

HARD AS HELL: 1. Raccoons. 2. Henry. 3. "Note to self: Have whoever compiled these notes killed." 4. Systems Operations Incorporated. 5. Radiant Thunder. 6. Five. 7. Weinberg. 8. "I want to make him." 9. Imagination. 10. Millington College. 11. 125 lbs. 12. Reno, Nevada. 13. Smithers, Pierce, Johnson, Goldman, and Mary Conant. 14. Aiming a handgun at his employer. 15. *Storm of the Century.*

QUIZ #57: CARRIE
EASY: 1. Carrietta. 2. *Firestarter* (1984). 3. "I'll kick their ass." 4. Chris Hargenson and Sue Snell. 5. Principal Morton. 6. Breasts. 7. Miracles. 8. "Period." 9. The miserable students. 10. Tommy, Chris, and Sue. 11. *Pygmalion.* 12. Softball. 13. *The Green Mile* (1999). 14. To belong. 15. *Six Feet Under.*

MEDIUM DIFFICULTY: 1. Glazed doughnuts. 2. Red. 3. *May* (2002). 4. Mysterious. 5. Cake. 6. Because he no longer loves her. 7. "Creepy Carrie." 8. "Dirty Donna." 9. Her mother's. 10. She's All That (1999). 11. Tampons. 12. "Plug it up." 13. *Dead Like Me.* 14. Menstruation. 15. He's a lawyer.

HARD AS HELL: 1. Miss Collins. 2. John. 3. "Springtime in Venice." 4. Norma Watson. 5. Roy Evarts. 6. Nine Lives (2004). 7. Eve. 8. Tina Blake. 9. Leonardo Da Vinci's *The Last Supper.* 10. "It's Godless." 11. Clarkson County School District vs. Crane. 12. Consciousness Affected

Physical Phenomenon. 13. Best Single Television Presentation. 14. Irwin Hinty. 15. Ten.

QUIZ #58: THE DEAD ZONE

EASY: 1. Dr. Sam Weizak. 2. Cigarettes. 3. Frank Dodd. 4. Six. 5. Bracknell. 6. Nothing. 7. *61* (2001). 8. Johnny's recovery. 9. Johnny and Walt. 10. Winning once. 11. A windmill. 12. Shania Twain. 13. *M*A*S*H*. 14. That his mother is dead. 15. *The Majestic* (2001).

MEDIUM DIFFICULTY: 1. O.J. Simpson. 2. Abraham Lincoln. 3. "Love you." 4. "The doughnuts." 5. *Dead to Rights*. 6. Johnny's being in a coma during the first murders. 7. Saigon. 8. "Sleepwalker." 9. A pair of leather gloves. 10. *Tango & Cash*. 11. The killer's name and address. 12. His dying grandmother. 13. "The hoochie-coochie shows." 14. "Something's wrong." 15. Music.

HARD AS HELL: 1. Conover. 2. "The Wheel of Fortune." 3. Maggie. 4. 1976. 5. Lars. 6. Mike Engel. 7. Six. 8. Zero. 9. *Star Trek: Deep Space Nine*. 10. Michael Moriarty. 11. Eleven-and-a-half narrow. 12. Nine. 13. Lewis. 14. *The Bangor Daily News*. 15. George.

QUIZ #59: DREAMCATCHER

EASY: 1. *Apocalypse Now*. 2. Same shit different day. 3. John Wayne. 4. *Friends*. 5. The Curtis line. 6. Urinating. 7. Duddits. 8. Alien. 9. Scooby Doo. 10. 25. 11. *Misery* (1990) and *Hearts in Atlantis* (2001). 12. Duddits. 13. "Stopping by Woods on a Snowy Evening." 14. Chewing on toothpicks. 15. New Kids on the Block.

MEDIUM DIFFICULTY: 1. Lt. Owen's father. 2. A challenge. 3. Abram. 4. "The rules of combat." 5. Bucko. 6. Woodchuck turds. 7. Mr. Gray. 8. A fuckero. 9. Ike. 10. General Matheson. 11. "Blue Bayou." 12. Secret stuff. 13. What they're running from. 14. *Wyatt Earp* (1994). 15. Music.

HARD AS HELL: 1. Barry Nieman. 2. Rick McCarthy. 3. Douglas

Cavell. 4. Josie Rickenhauer. 5. Joe Clarendon. 6. I-95. 7. Duddits's. 8. Goselin. 9. Maples. 10. The West Wharf. 11. Mars bar. 12. Roberta. 13. Coastlines. 14. David. 15. Promised Land.

QUIZ #60: THE DIARY OF ELLEN RIMBAUER

EASY: 1. Will Smith. 2. One week. 3. England. 4. *Beverly Hills 90210.* 5. 1911. 6. *Casino Royale.* 7. "I will never stop building you." 8. John's study. 9. "It does have a habit of repeating itself." 10. A bowl of ice. 11. Hide and seek. 12. Jack Finney. 13. Daniel. 14. Garage. 15. Rose Tower.

MEDIUM DIFFICULTY: 1. The Rock Bottom Remainders. 2. *Deep Throat.* 3. *Gilmore Girls.* 4. *The Twilight Zone* and *The Outer Limits.* 5. A marriage of convenience. 6. *The A Team.* 7. Kenya. 8. *Big Trouble in Little China.* 9. *Action Jackson.* 10. The power. 11. Thank Rose Red. 12. *There Will Be Blood* (2007). 13. Little Miss Prim and Proper. 14. "Remember Africa, sir?" 15. Mrs. Abernathy.

HARD AS HELL: 1. Julia Campbell and John Procaccino. 2. One never knows who's next. 3. Soothing. 4. *Rose Red* (2002) and *Storm of the Century* (1999). 5. A clerk. 6. *All My Children* and *Another World.* 7. Niki Sanders. 8. Head butler. 9. Mitchell. 10. *The Lion King.* 11. The house is colder. 12. Laura. 13. 10 p.m. 14. Lisa Brenner. 15. Kate Burton.

QUIZ #61: SECRET WINDOW

EASY: 1. Hunter S. Thompson. 2. Three days. 3. *Lord of the Rings.* 4. *Four Past Midnight.* 5. *The Dark Half* (1993). 6. L&M. 7. Jack Daniels. 8. An oar. 9. Hatchet. 10. Mrs. Garvey. 11. Chico. 12. *Everybody Drops the Dime.* 13. *Ellery Queen's Mystery Magazine.* 14. 83. 15. Johnny Depp.

MEDIUM DIFFICULTY: 1. *Saturday Night Live.* 2. Kyle MacLachlen. 3. Twenty-One. 4. 10 years. 5. Tony Soprano. 6. Todd Downey. 7. Amy and Ted. 8. Howard Cosell. 9. Doritos. 10. *Ghost Town.* 11. 57. 12. "Four days." 13. Villa Incognito. 14. *Once In A Lifetime.* 15. Maria Bello.

HARD AS HELL: 1. *The Lost World: Jurassic Park.* 2. *Radio Days* (1987). 3. $1.55 4. $500. 5. *Secret Passage.* 6. Captain Kathryne Janeway. 7. Tea Kettle. 8. Yale University. 9. Johnny Depp and Len Cairou. 10. F. Scott Fitzgerald. 11. Chess. 12. Rubbernecker. 13. Wickersham. 14. General Mutual. 15. Irv's Lakesider.

QUIZ #62: SALEM'S LOT

EASY: 1. A typist. 2. Broken neck. 3. Nine. 4. *The Stand* (1994). 5. *Stand By Me* (1986). 6. Detroit. 7. Baseball bats. 8. His BMW. 9. Waitress. 10. Harmony Hill. 11. The McDougals. 12. *The Mist* (2007). 13. Bloody Pirates. 14. Ronnie Barnes. 15. Mike Ryerson.

MEDIUM DIFFICULTY: 1. February 6. 2. 1, 319. 3. Fine dining and new clothes. 4. Jack Bauer's father Phillip. 5. Drunk and disorderly. 6. *Buffy the Vampire Slayer* (1992). 7. *Flatliners* (1990). 8. A valuable sideboard. 9. Four Point Mobile Haven. 10. Damage Control. 11. Village Antiques. 12. Special Filters. 13. Forty-five percent. 14. Portland. 15. Bishop's Lake.

HARD AS HELL: 1. Dean Koontz. 2. Five. 3. The BBC. 4. Australia. 5. "The Fifth Quarter." 6. "Hunting season's over." 7. *Vampires: The Occult Truth.* 8. Monday. 9. Jameson whiskey. 10. Connor. 11. Carl Foreman. 12. 3A. 13. Hockey. 14. Atypical lividity. 15. Graziano's Funeral Home.

QUIZ #63: RIDING THE BULLET

EASY: 1. Dewey Riley. 2. A car accident. 3. *General Hospital.* 4. Thrill Village. 5. "Instant Karma." 6. The harvest moon. 7. US 68. 8. Penobscott County Hospital. 9. Pine-scented air freshener. 10. Pumpkins. 11. Well begun, too soon done. 12. Julian. 13. 1954. 14. *Night of the Living Dead* (1968). 15. John Lennon and the Plastic Ono Band.

MEDIUM DIFFICULTY: 1. Baby Jesus. 2. Dr. Higgins. 3. Four. 4. Ted Bundy. 5. Jimi Hendrix, Janis Joplin, and Jim Morrison. 6. Michael Douglas. 7. Carnegie Hall. 8. *Hell House.* 9. "Not so much." 10. "Everyone does life." 11. 10/30/69. 12. "Caught in the Act." 13. Homeland. 14. The nursing home in Gates. 15. Kappa Gamma Nu.

HARD AS HELL: 1. Peach. 2. Hampton Center. 3. A gold star. 4. Gin rummy. 5. "Headed up the city?" 6. Nelson. 7. Mr. Darymple. 8. Ian. 9. Crossroads Bus. 10. 487. 11. "Time Has Come Today." 12. Lenore. 13. 08/07/21. 14. Chris Gauthier. 15. Mrs. McCurdy.

QUIZ #64: THE MANGLER REBORN

EASY: 1. *Days of Our Lives*. 2. *The Mangler 2* (2001) and *Sometimes They Come Back...Again* (1996). 3. A week. 4. She lost her job. 5. *Phantasm* (1979). 6. Whirlpool. 7. "I am the machine." 8. Stability. 9. His key ring. 10. Overalls. 11. UDS. 12. Gwen. 13. A month ago. 14. Dresser drawer. 15. The attic.

MEDIUM DIFFICULTY: 1. *Sorority House Massacre* and *Spring Break Massacre*. 2. Three. 3. All of their savings. 4. Music. 5. *Laverne & Shirley*. 6. A broken pipe. 7. Cameras and Dobermans. 8. High blood pressure. 9. 2435. 10. Reggie Banister. 11. Her mother. 12. "A freaking maniac." 13. Gwen's. 14. *American Gothic*. 15. *Sliders*.

HARD AS HELL: 1. *Live Through This*. 2. *Hannah Montana: The Movie* (2009). 3. St. Louis, Missouri. 4. *Way of the Vampire* (2005). 5. *Eerie, Indiana*. 6. Blue Man Group. 7. Aquafina. 8. *Malcolm in the Middle*. 9. *The West Wing*. 10. Flowers. 11. Rave Reggae Rock. 12. Rose. 13. Sarah Lilly. 14. Renee Dorian. 15. Scott Speiser.

QUIZ #65: CREEPSHOW III

EASY: 1. Fat Joe's. 2. Dr. Frankenstein. 3. More cats. 4. Over $300,000. 5. Statue of Liberty. 6. 2D. 7. Necktie. 8. "Jesus Saves." 9. Jesse. 10. Dean. 11. Two dollars. 12. Pierogies. 13. Emmett. 14. Eva. 15. The very advanced.

MEDIUM DIFFICULTY: 1. *Homicide: Life on the Street*. 2. *CSI*. 3. Junior. 4. Seventy-four. 5. Bart Simpson. 6. *Diagnosis Murder*. 7. Master P.

8. Pronsky. 9. Cougars. 10. The weirdo on 25. 11. Jerry. 12. Four years ago. 13. University of Moscow. 14. 26 Cabrillo Avenue. 15. Leigh Rose.

HARD AS HELL: 1. Bowling pin. 2. Quantum engineering 3. Arrogant Bastard. 4. *Pig Hunt* (2008). 5. *Hot Springs Hotel*. 6. *Teenage Gang Debs*. 7. Alex Ugelow. 8. Eddie. 9. 2SAM564 10. Uncle Brett. 11. 12:03 PM. 12. First Church of Creeps (Bonus answer: The church's address is 4321 Creepy Lane). 13. Elina Madison. 14. Nathan Kirkland, Selma Pinkard, and Elina Madison. 15. Mandy.

QUIZ #66: DESPERATION

EASY: 1. The Loneliest Road in America. 2. A bear. 3. Cake. 4. Norman Bates. 5. Twelve years. 6. Twenty years. 7. Two. 8. 1849. 9. *Gunsmoke*. 10. Dean Koontz. 11. Worrel's Food Co-Op. 12. *TAK!* or *The Unformed Heart*. 13. Harley-Davidson SoftTail. 14. The Rattlesnake Shaft. 15. Town Services and Police Services.

MEDIUM DIFFICULTY: 1. Lyndon Baines Johnson (LBJ). 2. Monica Reyes. 3. Chicago. 4. Stacy's Mom. 5. *All My Children*. 6. Jim Taggert. 7. *Big Love*. 8. Cross State Rentals. 9. A New York deviant. 10. Woodchuck pate. 11. *The Twilight Zone*. 12. The Conoco. 13. Tahoe. 14. Sammi Hanratty. 15. Yuppies.

HARD AS HELL: 1. Carey Ripton. 2. Pope John XXIII 3. *Delight* and *Song of the Hammer*. 4. The American West Theater. 5. Half a dozen. 6. Fallout. 7. Rand College. 8. Guilt. 9. *All This and Heaven Too*. 10. Jack Rudolph. 11. 2005. 12. *The Man Who Shot Liberty Valance*. 13. Velvet Revolver. 14. 248 Poplar St., Wentworth, Ohio. 15. Tom Skerritt.

QUIZ #67: 1408

EASY: 1. Total awareness. 2. Offers turn-down service. 3. Four. 4. $8. 5. Identity. 6. *The Long Road Home*. 7. Chicago White Sox. 8. Currier and Ives. 9. Random House. 10. *Man on the Moon*. 11. *On Writing*. 12. *Wings*. 13. 8:07. 14. The Carpenters. 15. Clay.

MEDIUM DIFFICULTY: 1. *Derailed.* 2. Fifteen minutes. 3. Kevin O'Malley. 4. *The Wire.* 5. Mr. Grady. 6. Nick Fury. 7. Grotesqueries and cheap thrills. 8. Mount Louise Nursing Home. 9. 1-LOW-FEE-1408. 10. Yahoo Messenger. 11. Boris and Doris. 12. Haunted Mansion in Orlando. 13. Len Cariou. 14. Mary McCormack. 15. David Hyde.

HARD AS HELL: 1. Poodle. 2. *New York Bulletin Tribune.* 3. Wicked Quick. 4. Sanyo. 5. 1860. 6. 45th and Lexington. 7. The Coral Level. 8. Patron. 9. Eggs Benedict. 10. "The Weight." 11. Marie. 12. Spring Break. 13. Hungary. 14. Dos Equis. 15. David.

QUIZ #68: THE MIST
EASY: 1. Louisiana. 2. Misery. 3. Two. 4. Eight. 5. Twelve. 6. *The Majestic* (2001). 7. *The X-Files.* 8. *Dreamcatcher* (2003). 9. Seven a.m. to eight p.m. everyday. 10. Third grade and special education. 11. Charcoal fluid and mops. 12. Assistant manager. 13. The Arrowhead Project. 14. Amanda Dumfries. 15. *The Shawshank Redemption* (1994) and *The Green Mile* (1999).

MEDIUM DIFFICULTY: 1. A red pickup. 2. Bridgton, Maine. 3. Five minutes. 4. *Silent Hill.* 5. Pollock. 6. The will of God. 7. Two. 8. *The Shield.* 9. Dark forces. 10. The stingers. 11. Morales and Donaldson. 12. Jim Jones. 13. Roland Deschain, The Gunslinger. 14. New York. 15. *Bill & Ted's Bogus Journey* (1991).

HARD AS HELL: 1. Caddo Parish. 2. *Hell Night* (1981). 3. 1967. 4. *Hellboy.* 5. Furniture Pads. 6. John Lee. 7. King Pharmacy. 8. WKIT. 9. Silvadene. 10. *The Castle Rock Times.* 11. Thursday. 12. Aisle three. 13. At her aunt's in Boston. 14. The mills down at Rumsford. 15. Mr. Mackey.

QUIZ #69: DOLAN'S CADILLAC
EASY: 1. 117 degrees. 2. Anne Rice. 3. Two kilograms. 4. Two grand. 5. US 71. 6. "Do you believe in God?" 7. Jaws of life. 8. 24. 9. The Snakeheads and Triads. 10. Mysteries. 11. Going riding. 12. Trafficking

Victims Protection Act. 13. The first Sunday of every month. 14. "Like a walrus." 15. No power.

MEDIUM DIFFICULTY: 1. "You're gonna be a daddy." 2. That it stops. 3. *Smallville.* 4. Three unindicted conspirators. 5. $800,000. 6. Corrado "Junior" Soprano. 7. Kevin Bacon and Sylvester Stallone. 8. Nowhere. 9. *Kingdom Hospital.* 10. "To a certain point." 11. Sixth. 12. Highway patrol. 13. First and true. 14. The Montressor. 15. Diamond digger.

HARD AS HELL: 1. Red City, Nevada. 2. Saskatchewan. 3. $1.2 million. 4. One. 5. *The White River Kid.* 6. *Playmakers.* 7. 192.168.0.666. 8. Onion rings. 9. Level 5. 10. Dragon. 11. Wheel loader. 12. Bulldozer. 13. Deep and Kaka. 14. Aidan Divine. 15. Vadim.

QUIZ #70: CHILDREN OF THE CORN

EASY: 1. North Platte. 2. *The Imaginarium of Doctor Parnassus* (2009). 3. 1963. 4. A policeman. 5. Jennifer Garner. 6. Cowboy outfit. 7. Hi-Test and Regular. 8. Cornbread. 9. Any more Kiwanis meetings. 10. Sept. 7, 1965. 11. A pig. 12. Dad's Place Bar and Grill. 13. Town square. 14. The clearing of the blue man. 15. Nahum.

MEDIUM DIFFICULTY: 1. Adam Monroe. 2. Corey Feldman. 3. Suicide. 4. 9000. 5. 55 cents. 6. Jeremiah. 7. Sue Snell. 8. Iowa. 9. Sacrifice. 10. Dexter Morgan. 11. *The Crazies.* 12. *Penthouse.* 13. Baby Hortense. 14. Ford Thunderbird. 15. Nebraska has a home game.

HARD AS HELL: 1. Russia. 2. *Perfect Fit* (1999) and *Grave Secrets* (1989). 3. Three years. 4. 61. 5. Gatlin Lumber and Hardware. 6. Disciples of the Crow. 7. A thousand miles away from here. 8. Adam and Eve. 9. Scarecrow. 10. 542. 11. Church Bazaar and Rummage Sale. 12. Jean. 13. Daniel Newman. 14. Robert Gerdisch. 15. Alexa Nikolas.

www.ingramcontent.com/pod-product-compliance
Lightning Source LLC
Chambersburg PA
CBHW070544270326
41926CB00013B/2195